Minding the Church

Minding the Church

Scholarship in the Anabaptist Tradition

Essays in honor of E. Morris Sider

Edited by David L. Weaver-Zercher

Foreword by Richard T. Hughes

Pandora Press U.S.
Tne original name of Cascadia Publishing House
Telford, Pennsylvania

copublished with
Herald Press
Scottdale, Pennsylvania

Pandora Press U.S. orders, information, reprint permissions:
Use contact options for Cascadia Publishing House, the new name of Pandora Press U.S.:
contact@CascadiaPublishingHouse.com
1-215-723-9125
126 Klingerman Road, Telford PA 18969
www.CascadiaPublishingHouse.com

Minding the Church
Copyright © 2002 by Pandora Press U.S., Telford, PA 18969
All rights reserved.
Copublished with Herald Press, Scottdale, PA
Library of Congress Catalog Number: 2001058849
ISBN: 1-931038-05-8
Book design by Pandora Press U.S.
Cover design by Gwen M. Stamm

The paper used in this publication is recycled and meets the
minimum requirements of American National Standard for Information
Sciences—Permanence of Paper for Printed Library Materials, ANSI Z39.48-1984.

All Bible quotations are used by permission, all rights reserved and unless otherwise noted are from *The New Revised Standard Version of the Bible*, copyright 1989, by the Division of Christian Education of the National Council of the Churches of Christ in the USA; quotes marked KJV are from *The King James Version*.

Library of Congress Cataloguing-in-Publication Data
Minding the church : scholarship in the Anabaptist tradition : essays in honor of E. Morris Sider / edited by David L. Weaver-Zercher
  p. cm.
Includes bibliographical references and index.
ISBN 1-931038-05-8 (alk. paper)
  1. Anabaptists--United States--Biography. Christian college teachers--United States--Biography. I. Sider, E. Morris. II. Weaver-Zercher, David, 1960-

BX4940 .M56 2001
001.2'088'24-dc21

2001058849

10 09 08   10 9 8 7 6 5

For E. Morris Sider,
whose scholarship incarnates
his commitment to the church

Contents

Foreword by Richard T. Hughes   9
Preface and Acknowledgments   13
Introduction: Scholarship? In the Anabaptist Tradition? By David L. Weaver-Zercher   17

PART I: THE HUMANITIES

1. The Notebook in My Back Pocket • 31
   Jeff Gundy (Literature)
2. What Does Athens Have to Do with Zurich?
   Reflections on Life as an Anabaptist Philosopher • 46
   Caleb Miller (Philosophy)
3. Seeking the Rhetoric of Jesus • 59
   Susan Biesecker-Mast (Rhetoric)
4. Anabaptist Visions at the Library of Congress
   (and Other Tales from the Edge of Evangelicalism) • 72
   Perry Bush (History)
5. Professing the Question • 87
   David L. Mosley (Music)

PART II: THE SOCIAL SCIENCES

6. Select Your Mother Carefully:
   Reflections on a Sociological Journey • 99
   Donald B. Kraybill (Sociology)
7. Anabaptism and Psychology: From Above and Below • 111
   Alvin C. Dueck (Psychology)

8 The "Anabaptist School" of Economics:
   Problems and Proposals • 126
   James M. Harder (Economics)

9 Where's the Political Science Department? • 140
   Mark W. Charlton (Political Science)

10 Education as the Practice of Faith • 152
   Polly Ann Brown (Education)

PART III: BIBLICAL AND RELIGIOUS STUDIES

11 Anabaptists and the Old Testament:
   Two Peas in Different Pods • 168
   Terry L. Brensinger (Old Testament)

12 Keeping Faith:
   New Testament Scholarship and the Church • 181
   Mary H. Schertz (New Testament)

13 Naming Myself a Theological Scholar
   in the Anabaptist Tradition • 193
   Lydia Neufeld Harder (Theology)

14 The Academy Is No Friend of the Church
   (But Does the Church Really *Deserve* a Friend?) • 208
   J. E. McDermond (Christian Ministries)

PART IV: RESPONSES AND CONCLUSION

15 Minding the Scholars: A View from the Pew • 222
   Harriet Sider Bicksler

16 Contours of the Christian Mind,
   Anabaptist and Reformed • 235
   David A. Hoekema

17 Conclusion: The Life of the Mind as a Life of Service • 250
   Shirley Hershey Showalter

In Honor of E. Morris Sider   266
Index   268
Contributors   275

Foreword

"Is THERE, OR SHOULD THERE BE," EDITOR David Weaver-Zercher asks in the preface to this volume, "something distinctive about the scholarship produced by Anabaptist Christians?" The essays in this remarkable book provide a ringing affirmation of "Yes!" to both questions.

One of the most distinctive dimensions of Anabaptist scholarship is the way Anabaptist scholars remind one another—as the title of this book suggests—to "mind the church." *Mind the church?* Most scholars, even in church-related institutions of higher learning, would find this language jarring. Mind the church? Scholars are taught to cultivate the life of the mind and to do so for the sake of the discipline, perhaps for the academy, and more rarely still for the larger community. But mind the church? What could this language possibly mean?

It means, quite simply, that scholars in the Anabaptist tradition do their work on behalf of the church, even as the mission of the church inspires the direction their work will take. The church in this context is not a community of happenstance, but a story-formed community, one shaped by the collective memory of persecution and martyrdom, on the one hand, and by the shared commitment to an "upside-down kingdom," on the other. As Shirley Showalter points out in the book's final essay, "Scholarship that is committed to an 'upside-down kingdom' will be rigorously defiant, asking questions about ideas and systems that the comfortable and powerful may not think of (or conveniently ignore)." Such is the nature of scholarship that minds the church.

Because the Anabaptist community is story-formed, it is fitting that the essays in this book conform to the genre of personal narrative. In keeping with that genre, perhaps it is also fitting for me to share my story of how I discovered the Anabaptist tradition and have learned from it what it might mean to mind the church amid academic work.

In spring 1965, while a student at the Harding Graduate School of Religion in Memphis, Tennessee, I determined to become a college professor in the field of church history. At the time I had no sense whatsoever that the Anabaptist tradition would shape my sense of vocation in profound and far-reaching ways. Indeed in 1965 I don't think I knew what an Anabaptist was.

Then, in fall 1966, I enrolled in a master's program in church history at Abilene Christian University. During my first semester at ACU, one of my professors, Dr. Everett Ferguson, suggested I read Franklin H. Littell's *The Origins of Sectarian Protestantism*. Dr. Ferguson could not have known at the time how pivotal this book would become for my own spiritual and academic development.

As I read this text, I was fascinated, even dumbfounded. For I learned there about a church that sounded remarkably like my own. That may not seem like such a significant discovery, but it was significant for one important reason: We in the Churches of Christ believed the Christian church had, shortly after the days of the apostles, experienced a disastrous fall from its original purity. We believed that fall had infected all of Christian history and that the church in virtually all its manifestations was still badly corrupted. We, however, were part of a movement dedicated to recovering the purity of the Golden Age of the Christian faith. By definition, then, we stood separate and apart from other Christian traditions, and I was fairly confident that we stood alone in all of Christian history. Now, I found myself stunned and amazed to learn from Littell that "the dominant theme in the thinking of the mainline Anabaptists was the recovery of the life and virtue of the early church."

What struck me about these Anabaptists was not only their commitment to the task of restoration. I was also impressed that they invested the restoration vision with a depth of meaning and commitment I had not encountered in my own tradition. For example, we in the Churches of Christ had almost always defined the restoration vision in terms of forms, patterns, and polity concerns. We asked questions like, "How was the ancient church organized? How was it governed? How did it worship? What was the proper form of baptism? What was the proper form and frequency for the Lord's Supper?" While we didn't ignore the question of meaning undergirding all these issues, we seldom placed that question front and center.

On the other hand, the Anabaptists defined the restoration vision in terms of personal and corporate discipleship. These were their key questions: "What did it mean to be a disciple of Jesus in the earliest days of the church? According to the New Testament documents, what demands should discipleship make today? What would the community of the faithful look like in terms of lifestyle commitments? In terms of their relationship to the larger culture? In terms of their relationship to the state?" Despite my restorationist background, these were questions I had never been taught to ask.

The Anabaptist tradition had captured my imagination with a whole new way of understanding the Christian faith. Yet this "new way" was grounded in the "old way" with which I was completely familiar: the goal of restoring the ancient Christian faith.

I was so taken by the Anabaptist vision that I decided to focus my M.A. thesis on a comparison of the Anabaptist movement with my own tradition, with particular reference to the ideal of restoration. That thesis, in turn, eventually became the basis for my first published article, "A Comparison of the Restitution Motifs of the Campbells (1809-1830) and the Anabaptists (1524-1560)," which appeared in *Mennonite Quarterly Review* in October 1971.

More important, the Anabaptist vision slowly began to work its way into the deepest recesses of my heart, especially as I realized the extent to which this vision squared with Jesus' own teachings. Gradually, as I matured, I discovered that I had become an Anabaptist in a very real sense, though I have never abandoned my commitment to the Churches of Christ.

Once I completed my graduate studies and undertook my chosen career, I was forced to ask, "What difference do my Anabaptist commitments make for teaching, scholarship, and the life of the mind?" The answer seemed fairly obvious. If Anabaptism calls one to countercultural living, it calls the scholar to countercultural teaching and countercultural scholarship. That meant dedicating my life to inspiring my students to similar countercultural commitments. This I have sought to do in various ways over the course of more than thirty years of teaching.

Such teaching, though, can be terribly risky, especially in institutions where the majority of students hold an understanding of Jesus far removed from the Anabaptist vision. Several years ago, while teaching in Pepperdine's London program, I chose to use Donald Kraybill's *The Up-*

side-Down Kingdom as a text in an introductory course on the New Testament. One day a student angrily denounced both Kraybill's book and me. "If this is what Jesus is all about," he said, "then forget it."

It struck me then with enormous force—though I had known this all along—that many of our students are not terribly interested in lessons on countercultural living. Most, perhaps, see their baccalaureate degree as a ticket to the good life, not as a point of entry into the world of upside-down service and radical discipleship.

After that class, I took the elevator up to the faculty flat in Pepperdine's London facility. The student's comment had depressed me no end, and I shared my despondency with my wife, Jan. She responded, "Just consider yourself a missionary." I found her words enormously meaningful, and I quickly realized that I had always been a missionary of sorts—that I had always done my teaching and my scholarship while minding the gospel and minding the church. I realize today—especially after reading the essays in this book—that my commitment in this regard owes much to the Anabaptist vision I encountered at Abilene Christian University over thirty years ago.

I only wish I had read this book at that time, for here, between these pages, readers will be able to listen to a variety of Anabaptist scholars, representing a variety of academic disciplines, reflect on what it might look like to do one's teaching and scholarship while "minding the church," what it might mean to engage in countercultural teaching and thinking, and what, after all, is truly distinctive about scholarship done from the heart of the Anabaptist tradition. For all these reasons, this book stands as a sterling contribution to the growing body of literature that explores the meaning of higher education in the Christian genre.

—*Richard T. Hughes, Director*
  Center for Faith and Learning
  Pepperdine University

Preface and Acknowledgments

*I*N CERTAIN WAYS THE IMPETUS FOR THIS BOOK arose almost forty years ago, when historian E. Morris Sider joined the faculty of Messiah College in Grantham, Pennsylvania. Messiah was a vastly different place in 1963, concerned more with year-to-year survival than with securing a national reputation for academic excellence. Morris Sider not only contributed to the flourishing of this small, sometimes struggling college, he left behind a scholarly legacy—twenty books, scores of journal articles, hundreds of well-educated students, and a couple thousand lectures—that his remaining colleagues at Messiah would do well to emulate. It is only fitting that, upon his retirement from full-time college teaching in spring 2000, the college commissioned a *festschrift* in his honor.

As one of Morris's former students, I was pleased to be asked to edit the festschrift, which I hoped would somehow reflect his unique talents and contributions. As I discussed possible topics with several other former students, two themes quickly surfaced: Morris was a disciplined and productive scholar, and Morris was a deeply committed Anabaptist. The more we talked, the more we realized that these themes were not unrelated, but in subtle ways interacted with and informed one another. So emerged the topic of this book: scholarship in the Anabaptist tradition.

As I explain more fully in the volume's introduction, the notion of "Christian scholarship" is receiving close attention these days in many church-related colleges and universities. These particular institutions, which have almost always placed a greater emphasis on classroom teaching than on research and publishing, have nonetheless been fertile ground for creative thinking and scholarly activity. Increasingly, teacher-scholars at these institutions have determined that an important part of their task as professional educators is to provide their respective disciplines (philosophy, psychology, biology, etc.) with new findings, more refined arguments, and fresh, artistic expressions. Correspondingly, some of these same scholars have envisioned and gained audiences for their work that extend far beyond their campus classrooms, reaching readers, listeners, and viewers around the world.

In concert with this growing emphasis on Christian faculty members producing groundbreaking scholarship, questions have arisen about the very nature of Christian scholarship. These questions have taken many forms, though they might best be summarized as follows: Is there, or should there be, something distinctive about the scholarship produced by Christians? And if so, what is the nature of that distinctiveness?

As with many issues in the academy, these questions have evoked a range of answers, some radically opposed to one another, and it's unlikely a consensus on them will emerge anytime soon. Still, the questions are worth pursuing, especially as church-related institutions decide how to distribute limited resources to faculty members wishing to explore unknown realities or hoping to make fresh connections between things already known.

Of course, this volume pushes one step further these questions about Christian scholarship by acknowledging that there are, in fact, many Christian traditions, one of which is the Anabaptist tradition. The book therefore reframes the fundamental questions as follows: Is there, or should there be, something distinctive about the scholarship produced by Anabaptist Christians? And if so, what is the nature of that distinctiveness?

Even in this more circumscribed context of Anabaptist scholars, the answers to these questions vary, and readers of this volume will consequently be hard pressed to locate a party line. Still, while the answers given by the various contributors to this volume may vary and even diverge from one another, several common themes (e.g., the importance of community, the centrality of reconciliation, a commitment to lived discipleship, an incarnational epistemology, and concern for society's most vulnerable members) reveal these scholars to be thinking and writing from the Anabaptist tradition of the Christian faith. In that way and others, these essays underscore the importance of Anabaptist scholars reflecting upon their scholarly pursuits in light of their theological commitments, their ecclesiological connections, and their self-consciousness as Anabaptist Christians.

♣

Numerous people helped make this volume possible, none more so than the seventeen persons who contributed autobiographical essays or response chapters. These seventeen scholars were not looking for work when I solicited their involvement in this project, and none needed to publish one more article to pad their vitaes, but they graciously agreed to write. My greatest debt as volume editor is to them.

The lead administrators at Messiah College also have my gratitude for their ongoing support for this project. At Messiah we are fortunate to have a president—Rodney Sawatsky—who values the life of the mind in both word and deed, and who encourages scholarly pursuits by example. A vigorous thinker, he will agree with some assertions in this book and disagree with others, but he will mostly value the conversations it generates.

Former provost Donald B. Kraybill granted me release time to edit this volume. He contributed the essay on sociology, and he offered all kinds of good advice on how to do (and not do) a festschrift.

Finally, current provost Kim Phipps inspires all of us at Messiah College with her energy and enthusiasm, and I am no exception. Her support for my work has been generous, and her interest in this project in particular has been a gift.

In addition to their enthusiasm for good teaching and solid scholarship, these administrators have been strong supporters of the college's Anabaptist tradition and commitments. Messiah College has sometimes been criticized as not very Anabaptist by some of its constituencies, and as too Anabaptist by others. Indeed, the college has consciously chosen a middle way, underscoring in concrete ways its unique Brethren in Christ-rooted theological heritage and, at the same time, choosing to be inclusive of students and faculty from other Christian traditions. The result thereby parallels what we would wish for all Christians: rootedness in a particular tradition, yet (we hope) humble acknowledgment that no one theological tradition has the corner on truth.

Additionally, Messiah offers on one campus what many Christian faculty members find only at occasional conferences: an ecumenically zesty mix of Anabaptists, Wesleyans, Catholics, Evangelicals, Episcopalians, Pentecostals, and persons from the Reformed tradition who talk with one another daily about teaching, scholarship, and the purpose of Christian higher education. And in that regard, I would be remiss if I failed to thank Messiah College faculty members Rhonda and Doug (Jake) Jacobsen, who have worked very hard to make these sorts of intra-campus conversations happen over the past few years. In particular, I am grateful for the scholarship colloquy they co-led during the 1999-2000 school year, which raised some of the questions this volume seeks to address.

From the beginning of this project, I have worked closely with Michael A. King at Pandora Press U.S. Michael's wise counsel has benefited this project at many turns. More generally, I am grateful for his ability as a publisher to produce books that generate productive, thoughtful conversations. Michael and I are both thankful for the generous financial support of the Brethren in Christ Church, the Brethren in Christ Foundation, and the Brethren in Christ Historical Society, all of which helped to underwrite some of this project's costs. I would be remiss if I didn't acknowledge the constant support of my wife, Valerie, who provides for me in countless ways. Her good mind and kind heart combine to make her the best partner I could hope for. She and our son, Samuel, are the joy of my life.

Finally, let me again thank E. Morris Sider. His work as a teacher and scholar has nourished his students, inspired his colleagues, and served his church. We, the contributors to this volume, dedicate this book to him.

—*David L. Weaver-Zercher*
Grantham, Pennsylvania

Introduction: Scholarship? In the Anabaptist Tradition?

David L. Weaver-Zercher

*T*HE THREE BEST THINGS ABOUT BEING A TEACHER, so goes a familiar joke, are June, July, and August. As a college faculty member myself, I find some truth in that assessment, though not because I spend the summer months in happy escape from work. Rather, like many faculty colleagues, I find the period between commencement in the spring and the first day of classes in the fall the best time to engage in research, reading, and writing, the intellectual activities that exercise my mind, help me think new thoughts, and reinvigorate me as a teacher-scholar.

While classroom teaching continues to be the most recognizable (and publicly understood) role of college faculty members, many college and university professors have determined these more mysterious pursuits—research and writing—to be absolutely central to their educational vocations. That is not to suggest that these men and women have deemed teaching to be unimportant or even secondary; to the contrary, most would argue that sustained intellectual or creative work actually enhances their classroom performance. Some might press this point even further, asking how a professor of sociology can presume to help her students think sociologically unless she's wrestling with the most influential sociological theories of the day. More generally, how can a professor of any subject teach his students to do more than parrot other people's ideas if the professor is not doing original thinking himself?

The Scholarly Vocation

This book is about that activity, one that frequently goes by the name *scholarship*. According to Valparaiso University's David Morgan, scholarship is "the rigorous, professional study of human beings and the universe in which they exist, the creation of knowledge and the pursuit of wisdom."[1] In other words, scholarship is an intellectually rooted exercise that differs from both teaching and learning.

While it is dependent upon learning, scholarship goes beyond learning in two ways. First, scholarship entails a disciplined approach to learning, an approach that is usually honed by advanced training in a specific field. Second, scholarship goes beyond *learning information about something* to *fashioning something new* that can then be shared with others.

Similarly, scholarship is distinct from the activity of teaching. Most notably, scholarship demands a degree of originality that is often found in the best teaching, but is not essential to the teaching task. If a teacher refuses, after a time, to introduce creative teaching methods and new ideas into his classroom, he is still a teacher (though probably not a very good one). If a scholar refuses to set forth new ideas or produce creative works, she ceases to be scholar.

As most college professors can attest, institutions of higher education possess varying opinions about the importance of scholarship, opinions that are typically correlated with institutional reward systems. At so-called "research universities," scholarship often takes center stage. Faculty members at these institutions are expected to produce first-rate scholarship in the form of books, articles, or works of art. If they do, they receive promotions, pay raises, and other sorts of institution-based rewards; if they fail to produce such work, they may find themselves unemployed casualties of the university's "publish-or-perish" paradigm.

At the other end of the spectrum, scholarship counts for very little at some colleges and universities, many of which think of themselves as "teaching institutions." At these institutions, a faculty member's performance in the classroom, as judged by students, faculty colleagues, and administrators, takes preeminence in the reward system. In the most extreme cases, teaching institutions provide little or no incentive for faculty members to stay current in their academic disciplines by attending conferences or taking sabbaticals. In these (admittedly) extreme cases, the only thing that matters with respect to a faculty member's continuing employment is receiving positive teaching evaluations from students or peers.[2]

Historically speaking, church-related institutions of higher education have tended toward the teaching end of the teaching-research spectrum. And while generalizations about such institutions are sometimes overdrawn, it's nonetheless true that, compared to larger, state-funded institutions of higher learning, scholarly activity at church-related schools has tended to be less than robust.

Still, many faculty members who find themselves at church-related institutions—including Anabaptist-related institutions like Goshen College, Bluffton College, and Messiah—think of themselves not only as teachers but as scholars, and believe that their scholarly pursuits should be valued by their institutions and the churches that support them. From the perspective of these teacher-scholars, scholarly endeavor is not a luxurious add-on, something to be done only when the important work of lecturing and grading is done. To the contrary, they see scholarly activity as fundamental to their callings as academics.

Indeed, many Christian scholars, whether they work at church-related institutions or not, believe scholarly activity to be comparable to other callings (e.g., evangelism, justice work, and spiritual mentoring) in spiritual significance. For if the primary purpose of the church is to establish God's reign in the world, the primary purpose of colleges and universities is to pursue truth, formulate the best approximations of truth, and disseminate those approximations to their various constituencies.

At church-related colleges and universities, this truth dissemination often happens in theology classes or in other settings that use theological language. But truth can also be expressed via sociological findings, historical narratives, and mathematical theorems. In that sense, all scholars—not just theologians, and not just those who consider themselves Christians—participate in the process of exploring God's creation and articulating what they find.

Still, Christian scholars possess something that distinguishes them from many of their fellow scholars: the firmly held conviction that a loving God created the universe and the beings who inhabit it. Whether or how this theological conviction affects their scholarly endeavors is, as we shall see, a matter of debate. In any case, it is precisely this conviction that compels many Christian scholars—mathematicians as well as biblical scholars, economists as well as theologians—to perceive their scholarly endeavors as concrete expressions of Christian discipleship.

Perspectivalism and Christian Scholarship

During the last quarter of the twentieth century, scholars in many different academic disciplines came to a shared conclusion about the relationship between reality and those who studied it. Sometimes called "perspectivalism," this notion asserts that a student's research findings are often affected (and sometimes radically so) by the perspective the student assumes or the social location she occupies. Physicists were among the first to make this argument when, for example, they discovered that, depending upon the kind of observation method employed, electrons were either "like waves" or "like particles."[3]

As the twentieth century ran its course, scholars in other fields, especially those in the humanities and social sciences, likewise discovered that a student's perspective affected the way something looked and the student's interpretation of what she saw. This discovery, which was fueled by growing ethnic, racial, and gender diversity in the academy, sparked numerous debates over the nature of truth itself. While these debates continue, few scholars would deny that perspectivalism has largely superseded the notion of "objectivity," which asserted that, if an investigator was appropriately detached from her subject, she could be completely objective in her investigation.[4]

The implications of perspectivalism on scholarly inquiry are enormous, extending far beyond the scope of this book. What is relevant for us is the fact that some Christian scholars have employed the notion of perspectivalism to contend for the legitimacy of *Christian* perspectives within the realm of mainstream scholarship. Most vocal in this regard has been historian George Marsden, a Reformed scholar who teaches at the University of Notre Dame. In his widely discussed book, *The Outrageous Idea of Christian Scholarship*, Marsden asserted that "[k]eeping within our intellectual horizons a being who is great enough to create us and the universe . . . ought to change our perspectives on quite a number of things," including things that are discussed and debated at most academic institutions.[5]

More controversially, Marsden contended that it was patently unfair for the academic community to expect Christian scholars to divorce their faith commitments from their scholarly explorations and arguments. In response to critics who warned that Marsden's idea of linking faith and scholarly inquiry would subvert the possibility of meaningful scholarly conversation, Marsden responded that all scholars, believers or nonbelievers, should be bound by similar rules of discourse (e.g., Christian historians would not be allowed to invoke "God did it" into their explanations for why an event occurred). But this, said Marsden, would not pose a problem to Christian scholars:

> The fact is . . . Christian convictions do not very often have substantial impact on the techniques used in academic detective work. . . . Christians, just as other scholars, must employ the requisite degree of detachment to weigh evidence judiciously. And even though they may be passionately motivated to do the best job of truth-seeking, they must be duly dispassionate to think clearly and to present their results effectively.[6]

In other words, in most respects, scholars who are Christians do their work just like scholars who do not consider themselves Christians.

Which leads to the obvious question: What difference does it make? If a Christian psychologist performs his psychological inquiries in the same manner as a nonbelieving psychologist, why should anyone complain if the mainstream academy asks the Christian psychologist to keep his faith to himself while on the job? Won't the results of his scholarly work be the same?

Many Christian scholars ask a similar question, approaching the issue from a different direction. Isn't the calling of a Christian scholar, they ask, simply to be a good scholar, playing by the investigatory rules of one's discipline in a way that sheds light on one's subject matter? If so, shouldn't we expect good scholarship that's performed by Christians to be indistinguishable from good scholarship that's performed by non-Christians? More to the point, isn't it unrealistic to expect a Christian microbiologist to produce scholarship that's so *distinctively* Christian that, when we read her publications in a scientific journal, it's clear that the investigator is a Christian?

While such questions challenge the claim that "Christian scholarship" is anything more than scholarship done by Christian people, some Christian scholars contend that, in many cases, there *is* something distinctive about Christian scholarship. For even though the technical aspects of most scholarly endeavors are not substantially affected by the scholar's identity as a Christian (e.g., Christian historians will date historical events in the same way that other historians date events), a scholar's faith commitment has the potential to affect her scholarly work in a myriad of ways. For instance, a Christian scholar may pursue a different research agenda on account of her faith, asking different questions of her subject or teasing out different implications of her findings. Moreover, the Christian scholar may find herself challenging ideas about the nature of reality that make sense from a purely naturalistic perspective but do not make sense from a theistic point of view.

Again, in the more technical aspects of their scholarly work, most Christian scholars will likely adopt what sociologist Peter Berger once called "methodological atheism," a research approach in which God is not invoked as an explanatory device.[7] But this approach does not mean that the Christian scholar's faith commitment will never affect his or her scholarly work in any way.

The question, of course, is "*How* does a scholar's faith affect her scholarship?" In a paper entitled "Reflections on the Nature of Christian Scholarship," Douglas and Rhonda Jacobsen delineate a series of useful categories for thinking about this question.[8]

Recognizing that scholarly productions assume many different forms and are produced for many different audiences, the Jacobsens make a distinction between "faith-informed scholarship" and "scholarly faith," two different expressions of Christian scholarship. According to the Jacobsens, faith-informed scholarship is scholarship that "is undertaken in self-conscious awareness of the scholar's own religious faith." Such scholarship is sometimes explicit in nature, when a faith-related issue becomes an open and explicit concern within the scholarship one produces, whatever the subject might be. In many cases, however, faith-informed scholarship is implicit in nature, affecting the selection of scholarly projects and providing the motivation for pursuing them but not incorporating faith as an open concern.

In addition to these two types of faith-informed scholarship, Christian scholars might also contribute to the development of "scholarly faith." Scholarly faith is "faith [itself] subjected to the kind of disciplined reflection and creative thinking that characterizes all scholarship." In other words, scholarly faith is the product of critical and constructive reflection on faith, a process that takes place in light of the most up-to-date knowledge about reality. In this sort of scholarly activity, the audience for the scholar's work is primarily the Christian community which, if it's functioning responsibly, possesses a unique and abiding concern for articulating the Christian faith in a way that incorporates humanity's fullest understandings of truth and goodness. While other audiences may encounter this work and perhaps learn from it, the production of scholarly faith is the work scholars do specifically and self-consciously for the church.

In these ways and possibly others, Christian scholars can produce scholarship that is distinctly (if not uniquely) Christian. Of course, to talk about scholarship as "distinctively Christian" neglects the fact that Christianity possesses many theological traditions, among them the Anabaptist tradition. To this particular perspective we shall finally turn.

The Promise of Anabaptist Scholarship

With respect to perspectivalism, what is true of Christian scholars generally is true of Anabaptists specifically. Whether they realize it or not, all Christians participate in particular traditions, and while these various Christian traditions share many things in common, they also possess emphases and concerns that are distinct from one another. Perhaps more than most North American Christians, Christians in the Anabaptist tradition—which includes Amish and Mennonite churches, as well as Mennonite Brethren, Church of the Brethren, and Brethren in Christ churches—have long recognized that their understandings of the Christian faith sometimes clash with the understandings of other North American Christians, making the Anabaptist tradition a Christian tradition with a difference. While it would be incorrect to claim that these Anabaptist emphases are entirely unique to Anabaptists, they do constitute an identifiable mélange of distinct Anabaptist concerns. And in *some* instances, *some* Anabaptist scholars find *some* of their work *somehow* connected to these Anabaptist concerns.[9]

One example will suffice. In their reader, *The Missing Peace: The Search for Nonviolent Alternatives in United States History*, James C. Juhnke and Carol M. Hunter offer alternate interpretations of various events in U.S. history, highlighting the possibility of nonviolence to challenge more traditional, violence-sanctioning historical interpretations.[10] According to the authors, their nonviolent interpretive bias (which is rooted in their peace-church commitments) stands in sharp contrast to the prominent bias of "redemptive violence" that informs most historical writing about the United States. For example, when these two historians look at the American Revolution, they recognize that, in addition to having been unnecessary for Americans to gain greater measures of self-determination, the war was not at all revolutionary in bringing freedom to the people who needed it most, the African-American slaves. In other words, this war was not the redeeming event that historians so often portray it to be, a recognition that, while perhaps not unique to Anabaptist scholars, is nonetheless a distinctly Anabaptist perspective.[11]

Granted, not all scholarly work done by Anabaptist scholars will reveal such clear connections to the scholars' Anabaptist commitments. Still, this volume begins with the assumption that connections can and do exist, and it invites its readers to listen as fourteen Anabaptist scholars reflect on that possibility.

These scholars represent fourteen different academic disciplines, five in the humanities (literature, philosophy, rhetoric, history, and music), five in the social sciences (sociology, psychology, economics, political science, and education), and four in the realm of religious studies (Old Testament, New Testament, theology, and Christian ministries).[12] All fourteen writers consider themselves Anabaptist Christians who engage in scholarly work which, for the purposes of this volume, is defined as "the discovery, development, and transmission of original or creative ideas to scholarly and/or lay audiences."[13]

All but one of the contributors teach at church-related institutions of higher education, most of which have some connection to Anabaptist denominations. Even so, most also participate in professional societies that extend their scholarly work beyond Anabaptist audiences. Most of these writers therefore find themselves navigating the sometimes precarious but wonderfully invigorating terrain between the church and the world, finding language that communicates clearly to both.

In that sense, the title of this volume—*Minding the Church*—falls short of accurately representing reality, for most of the contributors to this volume do their scholarship with more than their fellow church members (or even "the church") in mind. Still, the title *Minding the Church* seemed appropriate, for it possesses three layers of meaning that epitomize the volume's fundamental concerns.

First, the phrase "minding the church" underscores the reality that the people contributing essays to this volume are intellectuals who, through both calling and training, have devoted their intellect and their creativity to the service of the church. Second, the phrase reminds us that Anabaptist scholars often feel a responsibility to attend to the church's concerns and, in some cases at least, do their work primarily for the church's sake. Third, "minding the church" acknowledges that Anabaptist scholars are sometimes frustrated by the theological, cultural, and political boundaries set by the institutional church.

Indeed, doing original work invariably runs the risk of challenging old orthodoxies and offending those who hold them, a reality that is often painful to scholars who, by virtue of their work, are often breaking new ground. In that sense (as well as the former two senses), Anabaptist scholars find themselves minding the church in the course of their scholarly work.

One final word about the formation and organization of this volume. In the essays that follow, fourteen writers describe their lives as Anabaptist scholars.[14] From the standpoint of both structure and content, these essays share certain commonalities, since each contributor was invited by me to write an "autobiographically oriented essay" that considered the following questions:

> What propelled you into academia and, more specifically, into your academic discipline? What questions have you asked (or what problems have you addressed) in your scholarly pursuits? Do these questions and problems connect to your Anabaptist faith and, if so, how? What contribution do you hope your scholarly work will make to the church and/or the world? In other words, how do you see your scholarly work as a Christian vocation? What frustrations have you encountered as you've sought to be both a scholar and an Anabaptist? Why should an Anabaptist person view your scholarly work as necessary, or at least important?

After the final discipline-specific essay, three additional writers reflect on what they observe in these fourteen autobiographies. Two of these respondents are "outsiders," one an Anabaptist church leader who works outside the walls of academia (Harriet Sider Bicksler, a writer and editor), the second an academic from outside the Anabaptist tradition

(David Hoekema, a philosopher at Calvin College). In the volume's conclusion, Goshen College president Shirley Hershey Showalter offers her perspective on being a scholar and doing scholarship in the Anabaptist tradition.

Notes

1. David Morgan, "Scholarship, Teaching, and Practices: Reflections on Lutheran Identity," in *The Lutheran Reader*, ed. Paul J. Contino and David Morgan (Valparaiso, Ind.: Valparaiso University, 1999), 99.

2. Of course, most North American colleges and universities claim to value both teaching and scholarship. Few and far between are college administrators who would say publicly that "we don't value teaching at our school," or, on the other hand, "we think scholarship is a waste of time." Nevertheless, a close look at the policies of a given college or university—policies ranging from the distribution of faculty development money to faculty promotion parameters—will reveal the degree to which an institution values its faculty members' scholarly endeavors.

3. This finding, set forth by Danish physicist Niels Bohr, was accompanied by other discoveries that undergirded the claims of perspectivalism, most notably Albert Einstein's theory of relativity and Werner Heisenberg's principle of indeterminancy.

4. For a consideration of perspectivalism in the discipline of history, see Peter Novick, *That Noble Dream: The "Objectivity Question" and the American Historical Profession* (Cambridge: Cambridge University Press, 1988).

5. George M. Marsden, *The Outrageous Idea of Christian Scholarship* (New York: Oxford University Press, 1997), 4.

6. Ibid., 47.

7. Peter L. Berger, *The Sacred Canopy: Elements of a Sociological Theory of Religion* (Garden City, N.Y.: Doubleday, 1969), 100, 179-85. Marsden prefers the term "methodological secularization" to Berger's term "methodological atheism," claiming that the word secularization "does not [like atheism] imply an absence of God" but rather means that, for the time being, God's relationship to the world is kept "in the background." Analogous to a scholar's resort to methodological secularization, most Christian pilots fly their planes according to aeronautical instruments, not according to the Holy Spirit's leading. It's not that these pilots disbelieve in God's presence and are therefore atheists. It's simply that they have chosen to glean vocationally relevant knowledge from instruments that, unless broken, deliver useful information about the world God created. For references to Berger and the pilot analogy, see Marsden, *Outrageous Idea*, 91, 132 n. 12.

8. Douglas and Rhonda Jacobsen, "Reflections on the Nature of Christian Scholarship," presented on February 8, 2000, at the Christian Scholars' Seminar at Messiah College, Grantham, Pennsylvania. All quotations in this paragraph are from the Jacobsens' paper.

9. That does not mean that scholarship produced by Anabaptists is (or should be) meant for Anabaptist audiences alone. For a compelling argument that the work of

Christian scholars should "give itself for the nations," see Derek Alan Woodard-Lehman, "Concluding Theological Postscript on *Scholarship Reconsidered*: An Apocalyptic Identity and Scholarship of Possibility for the Ancient-Future," *Christian Scholar's Review* 30 (2001): 419-33. Woodard-Lehman's argument is indebted to the work of John Howard Yoder, whom he cites frequently and generously.

10. James C. Juhnke and Carol M. Hunter, *The Missing Peace: The Search for Nonviolent Alternatives in United States History* (Kitchener, Ont.: Pandora Press, 2001). Juhnke, a Mennonite, teaches at Bethel College in North Newton, Kansas; Hunter teaches at Earlham College, a Quaker school in Richmond, Indiana.

11. In an insightful essay in *Fides et Historia*, William Vance Trollinger cites Juhnke and Hunter's work to argue that, because Christians are so diverse in their ideological commitments, the monolithic notion of Christian scholarship needs to be made more complicated, accounting for various Christian perspectives (including the Anabaptist perspective) rather than assuming a single Christian perspective. More specifically, Trollinger reminds us that Juhnke and Hunter's historical perspective will likely be rejected by Christians who are committed to the notion that the United States's wars have been redemptive. See William Vance Trollinger, "Faith, History, and the Conference on Faith and History," *Fides et Historia* 23 (2001): 1-10.

12. In some ways, education is more accurately described as a professional discipline, though of the three categories in this book, it probably fits best with the social sciences. Due to space considerations, disciplines in the natural sciences (e.g., biology, chemistry, and physics) and various professional disciplines (e.g., nursing, law, and engineering) are absent from this volume. Their absence should not be interpreted to mean that scholarship in these disciplines cannot be distinctively Anabaptist.

13. As Shirley Hershey Showalter notes in her conclusion to this volume, this definition of scholarship is relatively broad, for it includes nonspecialists as a possible audience. As Showalter also notes, this definition parallels the broadened understanding of scholarship advocated by Ernest L. Boyer, a 1948 graduate of Messiah Bible College and the former president of the Carnegie Foundation for the Advancement of Teaching, in his book, *Scholarship Reconsidered: Priorities of the Professoriate* (Princeton, N.J.: Carnegie Foundation for the Advancement of Teaching, 1990).

14. It should be acknowledged, of course, that all of these scholars are more than Anabaptists. Some are women, some are men, some are Canadians, some are U.S. citizens, some are ethnic Mennonites, some are relatively recent converts to the Anabaptist tradition. To assume that being a committed Anabaptist always trumps these other identities in a person's scholarship would be to assume too much, which is why the contributors to this volume were asked to embed their vocational choices, their intellectual interests, and their scholarly contributions in the context of personal narratives. The results reflect not only Anabaptist commitments, but also human complexity, which is as it should be.

Minding the Church

1: Literature

The Notebook in My Back Pocket

Jeff Gundy

"Now it's fine if the truth is real to you, but if it's not, it's you that are left out and not the truth."—John Howard Yoder[1]

"I am too local a creature to take the truth unless or until by God it happens to me."— William Stafford[2]

These two statements have been banging around in my head for years. Clearly they conflict on several levels, but we might begin by noting the difference in pronouns. The first addresses a *you* who is presumably flirting with misguided individualism, if not apostasy or heresy, and it implies that the author, the *I* who does not name himself, has a solid grip on "the truth" and how to find it. The second statement locates the issues differently, within the authorial *I*. It confesses the difficulty of believing what does not *feel* real, rather than instructing others on the need to accept some particular version of the truth.

Let me suggest that the first statement represents the natural stance of the scholar, the theologian, the historian, the literary critic: a stance that claims objective knowledge, that analyzes and interprets, instructs and corrects. The second is the stance of the artist, the poet: it testifies to inner experience, speaks without apparent concern for consequences, and insists that the personal cannot be ignored; in fact, it suggests that the personal is in some way the *measure* of the truth.

I know both of these positions from the inside, and the rewards and risks they involve. I *believe* in both of them, even as I know they conflict with each other. As a teacher and scholar I spend most of my working life trying to learn and transmit what seems true and real by more or less objective or at least external standards—ways of reading and interpreting literary texts, ways of writing effective prose and poetry, particular readings of history and tradition and the whole blooming, buzzing world. I am accustomed to evaluating students according to how well they have learned such information and practices, applying standards that may not be easily quantifiable but are not merely subjective either. I write pages of what I hope is carefully reasoned and convincing argumentative prose.

But as important and valuable as these ways of operating are, for a long time they have not seemed entirely sufficient to me. And so, through all my days of planning and talking and grading, through the jammed, splintered weeks when I haul books and papers home every night, I carry a notebook just small enough to fit into my back pocket. While I'm about my earthly, timely, responsible duties, other possibilities thread themselves around and behind the regular routine. A little phrase overheard, an image out of the expected on a familiar street, a new slant of light, a stray impulse during a lecture, and something else begins to happen.

The language of poetry happens as it will, and engages the truths I accept intellectually in strange and sometimes disconcerting ways. Surely being a poet in modern America is a curious, sideways venture in itself. Being a Mennonite poet employed by a church-related college contributes other sorts of dissonance, as does being an intellectual in a tradition long suspicious of book learning. Yet somehow I have found myself dancing and swerving through a life that includes all of these polarities, unwilling or unable to yield to any of them, to choose one or another pole. I want to be a poet *and* an American *and* a teacher *and* an intellectual *and* a Mennonite. What's more, I want to be *good* at them all, not necessarily by everyone's lights, but by my own at least. Let me discuss further, trying to be faithful to these multiple allegiances by mixing abstraction and personal narrative as I go.

Poetry, Religion, Oppositions, Contraries ...

Many poets would argue that their art is entangled with the world but not subject to it, as it is concerned with but not merely answerable to ethics and even religion. "I cannot be a saint, and I would like to be," writes the poet David Brendan Hopes. "Yahweh and Apollo make absolute demands. You can serve two great masters only if you intend to cheat them both. I am a poet."³

Is Hopes right about this choice? Menno Simons, Conrad Grebel, and Dirk Phillips probably would have agreed with him—and known exactly which master a good Christian must choose. Yet surely Dante and Milton and George Herbert and John Donne would have dismissed as absurd the idea that poetry was not compatible with Christianity. Their fellow poet William Blake might have understood Hopes, but I suspect he would have put the opposition differently. "Without contraries is no progression," he claimed in his passionate and heretical "Marriage of Heaven and Hell," daring to suggest that the "contraries" of reason and energy, love and hate, were necessary oppositions and that conventional codes of "good" and "evil" were disastrously misaligned human constructions.⁴

I first read Blake, along with William Butler Yeats and Theodore Roethke and other such heterodox poets, early in my career at Goshen College. The course, taught by Nick Lindsay, was titled something like "Poetry and the Tradition," and gossip had it that Lindsay had hijacked the class from another professor who would have taught it with more, or at least a different, emphasis on tradition. But it was marvelous, scary, exhilarating to wander through the words and rhythms, to encounter language whose intensity rivaled that of the Bible itself. In those years I fell in love with beautiful images and dangerous ideas, and among all my other betrayals I have never lost those allegiances.

What is a good Mennonite boy doing reading Blake anyway, that supreme individualist and free-thinker who wrote "I must create my own system or be enslaved by another man's"? After all, my tradition teaches *Gelassenheit* and discipleship and community discernment, and at least on my good days I still believe in all of those things. Blake sat naked in his garden, talking with spiritual beings, and wrote long wild poems challenging every orthodoxy of his day.

Good Anabaptist fathers and mothers can hardly be blamed for trying to keep their sons and daughters away from such texts and ideas. Surely the last fifty years or so have been a great and dangerous experiment for many U.S. Anabaptists, as we have moved back into the urban, educated, sophisticated world from our long rural exile. For generations my own ancestors have been farmers and preachers; in the last two generations, quite suddenly, we have moved from the fields into the cities and the professions. The process is bound to be transformational; what shape will the changes take? I hope and believe, still, that somehow I am living in the world without being entirely of it—but my version of that equation is radically different from my father's, never mind my ancestors two or three more generations back, who squabbled and schismed over wedding rings and farm implements.

Remember, though, that not only the intellectuals and fringe members are moving away from long-standing traditions. My home church in Illinois held meetings in the mid-1960s to discuss whether women really had to wear coverings to church; somehow it was decided they might be optional, and within a few months all but a few women had abandoned them.

When we talk about tradition and heritage we are talking about a moving target, after all. We choose among a welter of stories and traditions and histories, consciously or not. To know those traditions is risky, but to be ignorant of them, or to take a sketchy selection as the whole, is not safe either. Beyond the obvious dangers of a little knowledge lies, we must hope, the possibility of another harbor, one that we can reach only by daring to learn all that we can, by exploring the world with all the rigor and clarity and wild hope that we can muster.

Growing Up

I grew up safe and well, mainly, on the Illinois prairie, less terrorized and more privileged than most, but gifted with the indigenous midwestern disease: thinking that real life must be somewhere else. Boredom seemed the greatest danger of the flat landscape, the endless grid of corn and bean fields, square section roads and small towns. Yet against the boredom, I remember wonder. At the beauty and pain of the world, surely, but even more at the sheer strange inevitability of things: that I should be *this* I, in this body, in this place, that there should be this particular set of things in the universe instead of any other, instead of nothing. That wonder still lingers.

My parents' farm was four miles from Flanagan, Illinois, a farm town with about one thousand residents. Mennonites were well-known in the area, a long-standing minority group, mostly assimilated in terms of dress and technology; for considerable stretches of time it was possible to feel quite normal. I had good friends, as well as some rivals and enemies, among my Lutheran, Methodist, and Catholic schoolmates.

Religion was a category, and it mattered, but even during the Vietnam War we did not come to blows over it, though during World War I someone had splashed yellow paint on the Flanagan Mennonite Church just down the road. In the 1960s the radio and television brought us the world, and some of the boys went off to war and didn't come back, but still we remained distanced from much of the terror and strangeness of the time. In spring 1968, my sophomore year in high school, with Robert Kennedy and Martin Luther King both murdered and riots in cities all over America, the thing I brooded on most was whether I would letter in track. I did, barely.

In the church youth meetings we debated "going C.O." versus refusing to register at all; many of the men had done Civilian Public Service or noncombatant service, and we heard their stories. We learned some church and Mennonite history, especially in the classes preparing for baptism, but not much about our particular church; only many years later would I hear that Waldo Mennonite had begun as the Gridley Prairie Amish congregation. The plain, nearly square sanctuary was often full in those years, with big families and the many children of farmers who would mostly, like me, go off to college and not come back.

Church mattered, but so did school. Earlier prohibitions against organized sports had eased in my father's childhood, and I played football and basketball and baseball, though with more passion than skill. Too much of a jock to be considered a total nerd, I also read compulsively, mostly not great literature but science fiction and sports stories and whatever else I could find. Nose buried in a book, my parents described me, a little uneasily.

For a first son like me, with younger siblings crowded around, reading was a shield and an escape from a daily routine that seemed safe but mundane. Four miles out of town, four miles from church, we were connected to the community and extended families on both sides but were also our own social and economic unit. We children worked with our parents, walking beans in the summer, gathering eggs before supper all year round, trying our best to weasel out of chores.

My parents, high school sweethearts, had only one year of college between them, but they assumed their children would go. I was the first of six, and although I was a lazy student I did well on tests. A cousin was at Goshen College, four hours away—just about right—and a brief visit convinced me it was a lot more interesting than Flanagan. I didn't seriously consider anywhere else.

I headed off to college with a cheap twelve-string guitar, an equally cheap stereo for my folk and rock records, an area rug and a few books, knowing almost nothing except that I wanted to be some kind of rebel. I considered myself a pacifist and was fascinated by things of the spirit, but I found most public piety embarrassing or annoying. I had no idea what I would do with my life, but I was ready for a change: I left my letter jacket at home, quit shaving, and played no organized sports for the first time since eighth grade. I knew a few people from church camps and youth conventions, and college seemed a bit like camp at first, but it went on and on. It was stimulating, sometimes stressful, but so much more absorbing and congenial than high school that before long I couldn't imagine going home again except to visit. Summer work was plentiful in Goshen, and for the next six years, except for a brief foray to Hawaii with a friend and a study-service term in Jamaica, it was where I lived.

At Goshen I also found myself for the first time in a community dominated by Mennonites. In Flanagan we were known and mostly tolerated, but in Goshen being Mennonite was weirdly normal. It was flattering and encouraging, although also disconcerting to discover others whose pedigrees far outclassed my own. I felt underprepared for the school work at first, but eventually discovered that I could manage it and still have time for fun.

Especially strange was the sense of being at the middle of something, however minor. The big College Mennonite Church, with its domed ceiling and circular sanctuary, seemed designed to demonstrate that this was it, the center, if hardly the origin. The names of great men, some of them still present, were spoken reverently and their great works remembered: Oyer, Hershberger, Burkholder, and of course Harold S. Bender, longtime administrator and Mennonite authority, author of the magisterial "Anabaptist Vision" essay which in midcentury had helped define Mennonites to themselves and others as a people committed to discipleship, nonresistance, and the believers church.[5]

Before long I found myself gravitating toward the English Department, where the books and conversations were strange, challenging, often fascinating. Two of the least conventional professors on campus,

Jack Dueck and Nick Lindsay, became special mentors. Lindsay had been imported from South Carolina to preach the gospel of beauty and poetry as he'd inherited it from his famous father, the poet, visionary, and eccentric Vachel Lindsay. He was gnarly and impassioned and wonderfully unpredictable; after a dazzling five-minute oration on Tiew, the god of Tuesday, or the mating habits of songbirds, he'd shrug suddenly and say, "Ah, or else it isn't," and we'd go on.

Dueck was a Canadian Mennonite Brethren with a fine tenor voice who made us sing "Oh, What a Beautiful Morning" on dark winter mornings. He loved staging events to disrupt classroom routines. Once he collected a set of essay exams on fire imagery, dropped them into the wastebasket, and lit them on fire. When we read Solzhenitsyn he had the police come in and take him away in handcuffs.

It was wonderful to meet men and women who were not coaches nor farmers nor housewives, and to listen to them say daring, challenging, finely tuned things about books and language and life. Besides Dueck and Lindsay—neither of whom would be full-time faculty members for long—there were other fine, supportive professors. In the English Department were Ervin Beck, Sara Hartzler, Wilbur Birky, John Fisher, and Dan Hess. Historians John Oyer and Alan Kreider made me consider majoring in history, and Mary Oyer taught me more than I thought I wanted to know about art and music. The imposing, impressive, enigmatic J. Lawrence Burkholder was the president—from a few hints here and there, we suspected the borders of his thinking might not be as narrow as certain members of the constituency would hope.

As the Vietnam War slowly ground to its end, the overall atmosphere at Goshen was a curious mixture of tolerance and rigidity, radicalism and caution. Harold Bender had died in 1962, but the long-standing tension between progressive and conservative forces which he had both survived and helped to perpetuate was still a reality. As I learned to know it, Goshen seemed to be a place existing always on sufferance, constantly scrutinized by suspicious, powerful outside forces who had to be kept happy (or at least in the dark) to avoid another debacle like the mid-1920s closing of the college.

In those years it seemed that life among the Visionaries required a certain kind of cunning, a mix of concealment and assertion that may be part of the essence of poetry, which is at once so private and so dependent upon an audience. I had bought a green notebook early in my first year, mainly to record my laments about a young woman I wished would take me as seriously as I took myself. Before long I was writing all I could, taking poetry classes, checking anthologies out of the library to browse, discovering poets of all periods and kinds. I published a few poems in campus periodicals and church magazines, then two little chapbooks with the college's Pinchpenny Press—excellent experience, though publishing a full-length book would take me almost another twenty years.

MENNONITE WRITING?

Nowhere in my reading could I find even one Mennonite poet whose work was taken seriously beyond the church periodicals. Lindsay was a South Carolina Presbyterian, a far cry from Mennonite, and too quirky to place much of his own work in the literary establishment. The Canadian Rudy Wiebe was just about the only serious Mennonite writer I knew of, and his short tenure at Goshen had ended before I arrived. I read his earnest *Peace Shall Destroy Many* and the sweeping, Faulknerian *The Blue Mountains of China*, which I found sometimes exhilarating and sometimes impenetrable. Both were impressive, but I could not figure out what use to make of them in writing my own poems. I discovered and loved William Stafford's gentle yet tough poems, but knew only dimly that he had peace-church connections and sympathies.

I had registered as a conscientious objector but drew a high draft number and was not drafted. Having decided not to get a high school teaching certificate, I decided on graduate school almost by default. When I went off to Indiana University, after a year of work in a sash and door factory, I assumed that being Mennonite would have little to do with the poems I wrote. The story of my particular tribe of Illinois Mennonites seemed not crucial or interesting even to other Mennonites, and for years I assumed that my life had been too placid and uneventful to mine for much material—"pathological normalcy," I took to calling it in grad school. There were plenty of subjects in the natural world, in relationships, in politics. Only years later would I be ready to learn my own history in depth and try to make literature out of it.

Into the World?

Indiana University (IU) was huge; even the small city of Bloomington was bigger than anywhere I'd ever lived. My wife Marlyce (Martens) and I had met and married during college, and she had plans to finish her undergraduate degree. Because IU gave no assistantships to new grad students, we lived meagerly on our savings and part-time jobs the first year. Our apartment in campus housing was small, cold, and ugly, and the hide-a-bed we slept on got a little less comfortable every night. It was a good half-hour walk to class when it was too snowy to ride my bike; I couldn't accustom myself to paying bus fare. A few acquaintances from Goshen helped ease us into the local life, but it was a long year, though I did well enough in my literature courses and poetry workshops and began to make some friends.

The poets at Indiana University were capable and genial, although after my years with Nick they seemed a bit bland. I didn't know what to think when I got a poem back with "nice" in the margin; from Nick, "nice" would have been the deepest insult. They talked about things like line breaks and imagistic coherence; they did not veer off into long expositions on the Norse gods or ask whether a poem would cheer the slaves, horrify the despots, or praise the earth. On a visit back to Goshen I found myself telling a friend, "Some of those people don't even believe that there *is* a true nature of the universe!"

Eventually I understood that it was not so odd to concentrate on matters of craft in poetry workshops, that it was Lindsay and Dueck—and maybe me—who were the eccentrics. From the steady scholars and diverse students in the department I learned a great deal. A stream of visitors came through campus, too: Robert Bly, Alice Walker, Marge Piercy, Gary Snyder. I was too shy to talk much to them, but they were an entrance into the world of people who actually wrote books.

Near the end of my first year, partly because the creative writing program led only to a master's degree, I applied for the Ph.D. program in literature and a teaching assistantship. Over the next three years I compiled a set of poems titled "The Candidate for Lint" for my master's thesis, finished my course work, and took qualifying exams. I taught literature and composition classes, then was asked to teach some creative writing courses. I even won some local prizes and began to get a few poems accepted by magazines that had nothing to do with Mennonites.

Back to the Mennonite World

The offer to teach at Hesston College came unexpectedly, via a phone call late one Saturday night in spring 1980, just as I had finished my dissertation proposal ("Versions of the Self in Modern Poetry": not much Mennonite about it, although one of my subject poets was William Stafford, whom I learned was a World War II conscientious objector with Brethren connections, and another was Robert Bly, active in resistance to the Vietnam War.)

I accepted quickly—in those days, any kind of full-time academic job was hard to pass up—but with many qualms. I wasn't sure I could finish my dissertation while teaching, or what Hesston (a two-year college with many students in vocational programs) would be like. I wasn't sure that I could be orthodox enough to stay out of trouble with the Mennonite Board of Education, which controlled Hesston as it did Goshen. But the four years there went well; I slogged away at the dissertation in the summers, and Roger Mitchell, my director, was patient and helpful. I taught a range of general education and English classes, learned from experienced and canny teachers like Jim Mininger and John Lederach, and discovered that I positively liked talking about a wide variety of issues and subjects with students. (I also learned that, as the teacher, I could control the discussion and my own role in it well enough to stay mostly out of trouble.)

I kept writing poems and managed to get some of them published in magazines. We bought a tiny house and fixed it up, and our first child, Nathan, was born at the end of our first year in Hesston. Benjamin followed two and a half years later. Marlyce worked in several offices at the college, but mostly stayed at home after the children were born. We had less discretionary income than ever, but those were good days.

In December 1983 we drove back to Bloomington for the dissertation defense. Nathan was a toddler and Ben just two months old; after dinner, Marlyce took them back to the hotel while I stayed up late with Roger Mitchell and a few friends, talking poetry. When I finally went to bed, I lay awake for hours, wondering if this would change my life.

We began to think that living closer to at least one set of family would be nice, and I yearned to teach more literature and upper-level courses. One spring day my mother sent a clipping from the *Mennonite Weekly Review*—Bluffton College was advertising for an English professor. My younger brother Gregg had gone to Bluffton, partly because unlike Goshen they had a football team, and my three youngest siblings had followed. It seemed reasonable enough to follow them, and somewhat to my surprise I was invited to come. In August 1984 we moved into the rambling gray house on South Lawn Avenue, two blocks from the college, that is still home.

Bluffton College was treading water in the mid-1980s, burdened by debts from underfunded building projects, its student body shrinking into the 500s. The campus was scenic but a bit shabby. The teaching load was heavy, and few faculty found the time to do serious research. Yet there were many good people around, students and faculty, and we quickly felt we belonged. Over the next years the college recovered and grew, carving out a distinctive niche as a church-related college which is closely related to the General Conference Mennonite Church yet independently owned and operated. The Bluffton history of being intentionally Anabaptist while attracting mostly non-Mennonite students has created a unique atmosphere, committed yet tolerant, that I found congenial from the start.

When I came to Bluffton in the mid-1980s I had plans to revise and publish my dissertation, but other projects kept intervening. I continued writing poems and sending them out, acquiring a fat folder of rejection slips and a smaller file of acceptances. Eventually a small press published a chapbook, *Surrendering to the Real Things*, in 1986, and my first full-length collection of poems, *Inquiries*, appeared in 1992. A second collection, *Flatlands*, followed in 1995. I also published a few essays on contemporary poetry in literary journals and anthologies, and did some conference presentations; I wrote many book reviews, including a series of essay-reviews for *Georgia Review*.[6]

But in the last fifteen years much of my scholarly work has shifted toward Mennonite subjects—especially literature—and been published in journals like *Mennonite Quarterly Review*, *Mennonite Life*, and *Conrad Grebel Review*. One spur has been my ongoing friendship with Mennonite theologian and Bluffton College religion professor J. Denny Weaver, who convinced me that I ought to be doing research on Mennonite literature for Mennonite periodicals. Weaver helped to establish the Bluffton College Study Center, which provides generous support for summer research on Anabaptist-related subjects.

Work on Mennonite literature has been made both easier and richer by the flowering of Mennonite writing in the United States during the last two decades, when a number of fine writers with some Mennonite background or connection have become increasingly well known. Poets who began to write independently of each other, widely scattered across the country, began to meet at conferences and workshops and to form a loose network. Some of these writers, especially Keith Ratzlaff, Jean Janzen, Dallas Wiebe, and Julia Kasdorf, became my treasured friends and critics, even as I tried to write about their work.

The flowering of Mennonite writing in Canada, which began somewhat earlier, also provided models of work that engaged Mennonite traditions and was successful as serious literature. Among many fine writers and critics, I found poets Di Brandt and Patrick Friesen and critic and editor Hildi Froese Tiessen especially valuable as authors and colleagues. A conference on "Mennonite/s Writing in Canada" organized by Tiessen at Conrad Grebel College in 1990 was a milestone in the maturation of Canadian Mennonite writing, and a similar but even larger conference at Goshen College in 1997 was equally significant for American Mennonite writers and scholars.

As Mennonite writers began to carve out careers for themselves, it became possible to imagine a role within the larger literary culture and within the church culture as well. Interestingly, their success in the general literary culture made the church pay more attention to them. Intellectuals, academics, and church leaders have begun to quote poets, invite writers to speak, offer attention and praise. Yet the relation between the church and its artists remains complicated.

Many within the church are still suspicious of the arts, and the near adulation that some writers have received can be almost as disconcerting as indifference or hostility. I have had many conversations with my compadres about our ambivalent and sometimes tortuous relations with the church.[7] Those relations have been relatively easy for me in Bluffton, where I am a member of the progressive and open-minded First Mennonite congregation, but many others have fled or been chased to the fringes of the church, if not beyond.

All through this period I have periodically vowed to abandon footnotes entirely. I haven't yet managed that, but in hopes of reaching a wider Mennonite audience, I did begin writing less academic prose. A summer research project on my great-grandparents George and Clara Strubhar, midcentury Mennonite church leaders in central Illinois, became the seed for my 1995 prose book *A Community of Memory: My*

Days with George and Clara.[8] The book explores the history of the Gundy and Strubhar families (Amish-Mennonites of Swiss origin) in the United States through a series of first-person narratives. Currently a second set of essays on my mother's ancestors and a 1999 trip to Europe is underway, with the working title "Scattering Point," after the creek that begins on the home place in Illinois. And poems continue to emerge; a new collection, *Rhapsody with Dark Matter*, appeared in fall 2000.[9]

LAST THOUGHTS

I have come to accept that trying to be a Mennonite poet and writer will never, and need never, be too easy. In the great dance some of us are meant to be organizers and sustainers and defenders of the tradition, and others to be restless and dissatisfied and clearers of the underbrush. Some of us may play more than one role; no writer can exist for long stuck in a rigid position. And so I have written pieces that I believe are plentifully appreciative of Mennonite traditions and practices, and defended and written about and taught texts that are deeply critical. Surely it is within those complexities and ambivalences and contradictions that the real work happens.

By the time I've filled one of my little notebooks it will be dog-eared from its time in various pockets, water-stained, the cover ratty and taped around the fold. Much of what's in it may be notes on lectures and talks, along with stray thoughts, phone numbers, addresses, and drawings for bookshelves. I start from the back with such things. But from the front I start with the lines that might be the beginnings of a poem. Sometimes they add up to something.

I heard it suggested recently that only great artists manage to disentangle what is truly personal, truly *theirs*, from the welter of ideas and styles in which we are all immersed. It struck me as scary but true in a personal sense, because I often feel, and fear, that my own work is merely a reflection of the times rather than something authentically my own. Of course, such fears reflect the American individualism of which Anabaptism is rightly skeptical; better, perhaps, to seek to be the voice of the community than to quest after some illusory individuality.

This is one more dualism that I yearn to refuse. After many trials and errors I have come to believe that the only way I can truly serve my community is to be as fiercely individual as I can manage. What worse betrayal of the community than mere acceptance of what the least imaginative and most authoritarian within it would have us be and do?

This may also be bad theology. I can offer only the defense of scoundrels and poets: I'm not a theologian.

Perhaps one more literary allusion may be helpful: F. Scott Fitzgerald once wrote that "the test of a first-rate intelligence is the ability to hold two opposed ideas in the mind at the same time, and still retain the ability to function. One should, for example, be able to see that things are hopeless and yet be determined to make them otherwise."[10]

Even on my good days there are more than two opposed ideas in my head, as there are at least half a dozen things it seems I ought to be about, all of them worthy: teaching, writing, spending time with my family, keeping up the house and garden, reading, pursuing peace and justice, saving the earth, praising God with all my heart and soul and strength. If we cannot serve two masters, how can we serve six, or ten, or twenty? The world is full of things that need doing, and the one I feel most called to do is to create things made of words that aspire toward truth and beauty. Is this sensible, or practical? It would not have occurred to many of my kith and kin even to ask the question, but I believe beyond all doubt that the answer is yes.

Notes

1. Goshen College Convocation Address, October 22, 1973. Quoted in *Goshen College Maple Leaf* (1974), 5.

2. William Stafford, "It Is the Time You Think," *Stories That Could Be True: New and Collected Poems* (New York: Harper & Row, 1977), 55.

3. David B. Hopes, *A Childhood in the Milky Way: Becoming a Poet in Ohio* (Akron, Ohio: University of Akron Press, 1999), x-xi.

4. William Blake, "The Marriage of Heaven and Hell," in *Jerusalem, Selected Poems, and Prose*, ed. Hazard Adams (New York: Holt, Rinehart and Winston, 1970), 124.

5. Harold S. Bender, *The Anabaptist Vision* (Scottdale, Pa.: Herald Press, 1944).

6. See Jeff Gundy, *Inquiries: Poems* (Huron, Ohio: Bottom Dog Press, 1992); and Jeff Gundy, *Flatlands* (Cleveland, Ohio: Cleveland State University Poetry Center, 1995).

7. For some of my earlier thoughts on these issues and others, see the essays "U.S. Mennonite Poetry and Poets: Beyond Dr. Johnson's Dog," *Mennonite Quarterly Review* 71 (1997): 5-41; "In Praise of the Lurkers (Who Come Out to Speak)," *Mennonite Quarterly Review* 72 (1998): 503-10; and "(In)visible Cities, (F)acts of Power,

(Hmm)ility, Fathers and (M)Others: Anabaptism, Postmodernity, and Mennonite Writing," in *Anabaptists and Postmodernity*, ed. Susan Biesecker-Mast and Gerald Biesecker-Mast (Telford, Pa.: Pandora Press U.S./Herald Press, 2000), 175-90. I recommend the entire October 1998 special issue of *Mennonite Quarterly Review*, also published as *The Migrant Muse*, to anyone interested in Mennonite literature. Also of special interest are essays by Julia Kasdorf and Scott Holland on these issues; see, for example, Julia Kasdorf, "Bakhtin, Boundaries and Bodies," *Mennonite Quarterly Review* 71 (1997): 169-88, and Scott Holland, "Theology Is a Kind of Writing: The Emergence of Theopoetics," *Mennonite Quarterly Review* 71 (1997): 227-41.

8. Jeff Gundy, *A Community of Memory: My Days with George and Clara* (Urbana, Ill.: University of Illinois Press, 1996).

9. Jeff Gundy, *Rhapsody with Dark Matter* (Huron, Ohio: Bottom Dog Press, 2000).

10. F. Scott Fitzgerald, "The Crack-Up," in *The Art of the Personal Essay: An Anthology from the Classical Era to the Present*, ed. Phillip Lopate (New York: Anchor/Doubleday, 1994), 520.

2: Philosophy

What Does Athens Have to Do with Zurich? Reflections on Life as an Anabaptist Philosopher[1]

Caleb Miller

I WAS RAISED IN THE HOME OF A BEACHY AMISH MINISTER in Kansas. But contrary to the stereotypes this may conjure, careful reasoning about important questions was a valued practice in my family. My father modeled this at home and in the community, and I enjoyed many vigorous theological and political discussions with both friends and family. I learned along the way that I had something of a knack for logical *argument*—in both senses of the word!

My specific interest in the discipline of philosophy arose during the two years between my graduation from high school and my matriculation at college. During that time, at the urging of my father, I read most of the published works of Francis Schaeffer. In Schaeffer's writings, I encountered some of the big questions of life and existence: What can we know and how can we know it? What is the nature of ultimate reality? How does God relate to his creation? Are there moral absolutes?

I was inspired by the idea that Christian faith could provide the answers to these questions and impressed by the power of logical reasoning to clarify and illuminate them. In time I came to believe I was meant to be a philosopher and sensed a calling to this work. My study of philosophy as an undergraduate student only confirmed that sense.

My Anabaptist Background

The Beachy Amish community that nurtured me both taught and exemplified the best of the Anabaptist tradition. I learned the importance of the church as an alternative community, mutually accountable and committed to following Christ. Although the Anabaptist tradition is unfortunately fraught with examples of abusive and destructive church discipline, the discipline that I observed seemed to me, on the whole, constructive and motivated by humility and grace. While there was an earnestness about Anabaptist distinctives, I grew up with the awareness that we Anabaptists were part of a much larger Christian family and that our primary identity was as Christians. Our Anabaptism was justified because, and to the extent that, it made us more faithful followers of Christ. When I left that community to attend Drake University at the age of twenty-one, I took that sense of a broader Christian identity with me.

This sense that I was a Christian first, an Anabaptist Christian second, benefited me greatly at Drake; it enabled me to find common cause with other Christians in a setting almost completely devoid of Anabaptists. At the same time, it partly obscured the significance of my Anabaptist commitments, a significance that became clearer to me in time.

In those years of intense involvement, first with InterVarsity Christian Fellowship, then with Gordon-Conwell Theological Seminary, two evangelical institutions that I continue to admire greatly, I came to see that my Anabaptist differences with fellow Christians were more important (at least more important to me) than I had expected. Although I expected to encounter differences over such issues as pacifism, believers baptism, and free will, I was unprepared for the degree to which concessions to personal weakness and practical "necessity" figured in assessments of what could be expected of Christians.

More specifically, I was unprepared for such statements as "I know I should be doing . . . but I'm just not there yet," or "That can't be what God wants us to do, because it just wouldn't work." In a similar vein, the Reformed tradition that dominated InterVarsity and Gordon-Conwell introduced me to the idea of a "cultural mandate," according to which any vocation is a Christian vocation if it is required for the flourishing of a culture. I was not initially prepared for the view that the requirements of a culture, even a culture opposed to God's purposes, might trump what seemed otherwise to be the counsel of Christ and the Scriptures.

My encounter with such ideas helped me appreciate that, despite my commitment to embrace other Christians as brothers and sisters, my Anabaptist convictions were nonetheless very important to my faith.

Philosophy and Christianity

Historically speaking, the relationship between Christianity and philosophy has been a checkered one. The early centuries of the Christian faith reveal both a strong *antipathy between* Christianity and the recognized philosophies of the day and the Christian *appropriation of* Greco-Roman philosophical concepts and insights. And while medieval philosophy was dominated by a self-consciously Christian perspective on almost everything, the modern period (beginning with Rene Descartes in the seventeenth century) has seen philosophy become much more secular and less supportive of Christianity. Even so, the influence of the design argument for the existence of God was so great in the eighteenth and early nineteenth centuries that atheism was extremely rare among philosophers in the English-speaking world.

All of that changed with the 1859 publication of Charles Darwin's *Origin of the Species*. Darwin was widely interpreted as offering an intellectually respectable alternative to divine design. As a result, the first half of the twentieth century was perhaps the most thoroughly atheistic and secular chapter of philosophic history. The discipline of philosophy, especially in the English-speaking world, was during this time pervasively hostile to religious faith in general and to Christianity in particular. In 1960, there were only a handful of members of the American Philosophical Association (APA) who openly admitted to being Christians.

This has changed dramatically in recent years. Both the number and influence of Christians in philosophy have soared. The Society of Christian Philosophers (SCP) is now by far the largest subgroup of the APA, and its quarterly journal, *Faith and Philosophy*, publishes outstanding articles on the whole range of philosophical issues. It is not unusual to see sessions at APA meetings on explicitly Christian questions and themes. What's more, many of the participants at those sessions, and many of the authors published in *Faith and Philosophy*, are not Christians. Atheists and agnostics have undertaken to write sympathetically on such topics as the Christian doctrine of the incarnation,[2] substitutionary atonement,[3] and Christian pacifism.[4]

There have been a number of high-profile conversions to Christianity among influential philosophers in their mature philosophic years, and it's safe to say that the influence of Christians in philosophy has been out of proportion to their numbers.[5] Indeed, one philosopher was heard to complain about the "Christian Mafia" controlling the APA.[6] Although that comment should sound a cautionary note to Christians tempted by triumphalism, it is not indicative of the relations between Christian philosophers and their non-Christian counterparts, which are generally quite good. Instead, it offers a dramatic, if exaggerated, indication of how much things have changed.

How did this remarkable revival of interest in, and influence of, Christianity in philosophy come about? There are, of course, many factors, but I think two influences are especially worth mentioning.

The first is rarely acknowledged but, I am convinced, crucial. I mentioned above that my interest in philosophy was spurred by reading Francis Schaeffer. It turns out that I am far from alone in that respect. Most professional Christian philosophers are aware of the philosophic limitations of Schaeffer's work, but many of them will admit, if pressed, that they were originally inspired to study philosophy by reading his work. My evidence for this is only anecdotal, but I am convinced that the increased number of Christians in philosophy today is due in large part to the inspiration that Schaeffer provided.

The second and more widely acknowledged influence is that of Alvin Plantinga, an American philosopher from Christianity's Reformed tradition. Plantinga entered the profession in the early 1960s when Christianity was either despised or ignored by almost everyone in the discipline. Some of the few Christian sympathizers who remained were preoccupied with trying to reformulate the faith to make it palatable to their secular colleagues. They were found conceding such claims as that belief in God is nonsense, but suggesting that it might nevertheless be *important* nonsense.[7]

Plantinga, a very serious Christian, thought the attitudes of both the secular detractors of Christianity and its accommodationist defenders were wrongheaded. He was convinced that influential arguments against theism and Christian faith were not cogent, and that the accommodationist strategy of Christians diminished the faith without contributing to its plausibility. So his entire career was intentionally, often explicitly, undertaken from the perspective of Christian faith.

Although he never thought it important to offer arguments *for* Christian faith (or even theism), he has devoted himself to rebutting philosophical objections to belief in God and to Christian belief, to correcting philosophic misunderstandings and misrepresentations of Christianity, and to reflecting philosophically on the implications of Christian faith. Along the way, his influence completely transformed the way philosophers think about the problem of evil and the rationality of belief in God and made major contributions to epistemology, metaphysics, and philosophy of language.

In 1983, Plantinga presented an address titled "Advice to Christian Philosophers" when he was inaugurated to the John A. O'Brien Chair of Philosophy at the University of Notre Dame.[8] The advice he offered was to take a less defensive posture in philosophy.

Up to this point, self-consciously religious philosophy by Christians was mostly concerned with defending theism. When Christians dealt with other matters in philosophy, they tended to accept the terms of the debate dictated by the leading lights of secular philosophy. It was time, Plantinga said, for a little more "Christian boldness." It was time, he said, for Christian philosophers to take seriously the fact that they were not only members of a profession dominated by opponents of the faith but that they were also (and more importantly) members of the Christian church. The defensive battles were important, he acknowledged, but it was time to move beyond them by staking out and developing explicitly Christian answers to philosophic problems and by taking up philosophic problems that were motivated by Christian belief.

Christian philosophers have heeded his advice. There is now a burgeoning literature of such explicitly Christian philosophy.

My Career as a Philosopher

From the beginning I have seen pursuit of philosophy as an important expression of my Christian faith. Indeed, I have seen my career in philosophy as the ministry to which God has called me. I have also seen my Anabaptist beliefs as essential to my understanding of Christian faith. However, it was some years before I came to see my work in philosophy as motivated by the Anabaptist elements of my faith.

In the beginning, the questions that interested me were important to almost any worldview. Moreover, the Christian resources for responding to them seemed to me to be found in the common elements of ecumenical orthodoxy rather than in any distinctively Anabaptist insight. As a result, the philosophy to which I initially gravitated did not reflect any specifically Anabaptist themes.[9]

It might seem that ethics would be a good area of philosophy to find distinctively Anabaptist insights. But although I believed ethical issues to be crucial and embraced Anabaptist ethical positions, even becoming something of a peace activist during seminary and graduate school, this did not seem to me to be a fruitful area to channel my scholarly efforts.

First of all, some of the characteristically Anabaptist ethical positions appeared to me almost completely indefensible apart from appeals to the Christian Scriptures. Therefore, defending such positions seemed to me more appropriate for persons in biblical studies, theology, or theological ethics than for those of us in philosophy. From my perspective, the most important philosophical contribution to these arguments would be in defending the Christian faith *in general*. Any argument for pacifism, for example, that did not assume the truth of Christianity did not seem to be convincing, even to me.

Another reason for my reticence to pursue an Anabaptist research program in ethics stemmed from the fact that, in certain ways that traditional Anabaptist ethics departed from the mainstream of Western ethical theory, I did not accept the traditional Anabaptist side of the argument. Clearly, not everything about my Anabaptist upbringing had taken hold in my beliefs.

I was taught a two-kingdom ethic according to which the moral duties of Christians were different from those of secular society in general and from those of secular government in particular. It may therefore surprise readers familiar with my writings that I was formerly unpersuaded by this approach to ethics. First of all, this approach struck me as self-serving, for it required sacrifices on the part of others (e.g., in national defense and law enforcement) from which it absolved Christians. Further, it seemed to me logically incoherent to hold that some people (e.g., police officers) were obligated, under certain circumstances, to exercise lethal force, while simultaneously insisting that *all people* ought to serve Christ, a service that required the complete renunciation of lethal force. All in all, I found it much more plausible that, while not everyone would likely recognize or abide by Christian ethical standards, everyone was, in fact, obligated to do whatever Christian ethics required of people.

My views started to change, however, when I began to teach ethics at Goshen College. Since I was teaching a course called "Christian Ethics" at a Mennonite college, I thought it incumbent upon me to give the traditional Anabaptist view a fair hearing. So even though I had rejected it myself (and was under the impression that it no longer dominated even Mennonite ethics), I tried to explain the motivations behind a traditional two-kingdom view as sympathetically as possible—and I was surprised to find that some of my students found the case for this ethical stance quite persuasive!

Of course, I also thought it important to point out what I regarded as its chief drawbacks, i.e., the considerations that had initially led me to reject it. But when I set about trying to clarify those objections, I found that they did not "argue well." In short, I concluded that my objections were not as cogent as I had assumed they were, that they all depended upon false assumptions or invalid inferences.

At about the same time, I encountered colleagues at Goshen College—for instance, John D. Roth and Theron Schlabach—who espoused and clearly articulated a two-kingdom Anabaptist ethic. The process took several years, but I finally came to the conclusion that a two-kingdom ethic was an intellectually defensible position to hold.

Indeed, as I thought more about it, I eventually concluded that a two-kingdom Anabaptist ethic beheld some insights that were quite promising for addressing some long-standing problems of moral theory. Since Immanuel Kant's writings in the eighteenth century, the prevailing assumption has been that any genuinely *moral* obligation applies equally to all people at all times, and to think otherwise is to be arbitrary and irrational (let's call this "Kantian universalism"). But the growing awareness of cultural diversity in mores has cast some doubt on this assumption.

The Kantian universalist is required to say, when there are incompatibilities between the mores of two different cultures, that one of the cultures is wrong. But given the depth and range of such differences, such an accounting for them seems to suggest a sort of moral skepticism, according to which a given person's cultural limitations make it very difficult for him or her to know anything about what the moral truth is.

In response to this skepticism, two major alternatives have emerged: (1) subjective moral *relativism*, according to which moral duties are determined by human moral attitudes or beliefs; and (2) moral *anti-real-*

ism, according to which there aren't really any moral duties, only variable human attitudes toward human actions. But these alternatives have seemed even less plausible than Kantian universalism to most moral theorists.

But traditional Anabaptist ethics has room for—indeed it insists upon—*variability* in moral obligation from community to community, namely, the differences between the obligations of the Christian community and those of the pre-Christian Hebrew community, as well as the differences between Christian obligation and those of the secular state. Yet according to two-kingdom Anabaptist ethics (and unlike the two options above), those differences do not depend upon the subjective attitudes and beliefs about the matters in question. My suggestion (developed more fully elsewhere) is that the principles underlying Anabaptist explanations of those differences can be applied to make sense of other differences in moral obligation between communities *without* subjectivist, anti-realist, or skeptical implications.[10]

The reception of my moral theoretic views among philosophic colleagues has been encouraging, even if their favorable reception has not often been accompanied by a willingness to accept distinctively Anabaptist applications of them. I have concluded that, given the uniqueness of my Anabaptist perspective, it is likely that I can contribute much more significantly to philosophy by writing on moral theory than by writing on epistemology.

Although I do not think that Anabaptism offers a *unique* philosophical view in other areas of philosophy, I do think that my Anabaptist orientation and upbringing have given me an importantly different perspective on some issues from those of most of my philosophic colleagues. For instance, my home community's emphases on *humility* and *Gelassenheit* (submission, or "yieldedness") were quite different from the ideals that have long dominated Western intellectual traditions. Moreover, the relative cultural isolation of the Anabaptist/Amish tradition that nourished me kept it largely insulated from the prevailing winds of Western culture and Western intellectual history. That combination of different values and relative insulation has imbued me with a perspective on philosophic issues that, in some instance, is quite different from the mainstream.

I'll mention two such issues: (1) the issue of certainty and (2) the controversy between realism and anti-realism. I'll discuss these issues in order and point out what I take to be the connection between them, as well as what I take to be their relationship to humility and *Gelassenheit*.

Certainty

Although I have always valued the effort to get things right, it has never occurred to me that we should expect to achieve certainty about most of our beliefs. It seems obvious to me that, despite our best efforts to get it right, we typically remain susceptible to error. But for a very long time in the Western philosophical tradition (and in Western culture more generally), there has been an almost obsessive preoccupation with *certainty*. So foreign was this preoccupation to my upbringing that it took me some time to recognize its pervasiveness in the history of philosophy, the general idea being that the only kind of belief worth having is one about which we can be justifiably certain.

The modern version of this preoccupation was instigated by two seventeenth-century philosophers, Rene Descartes and John Locke. Despite the famous differences between these two men, they actually agreed on a great deal. They agreed that *knowledge* was only of truths that were indubitable and certain, i.e., such that we can't doubt them and that they cannot be false. Both Descartes and Locke thought that the foundations of such infallible knowledge of the absolute truth were to be found in the infallible data of introspection. The only other beliefs that could be known, according to Locke and Descartes, were those that followed self-evidently from these foundational ones.

In retrospect, it seems obvious this project was doomed to failure. The problem is that very little of human interest follows *self-evidently* from the data of introspection. In particular, it seems that nothing about God or the external sensible world is logically entailed by any combination of such foundations. It eventually became clear to moderns that our knowledge of the external world could never be infallible. The sensible response to that realization would have been to acknowledge that we would have to make do with less than we might have wished. The human mind has its limits. Moreover, human sin tends to undermine the reliability of our judgments, not least judgments about our cognitive powers. It would have been the wise and humble thing to admit that virtually everything we take ourselves to know remains susceptible to error. Unfortunately, the historical response has often been quite different.

Realism and Anti-Realism

Understanding that response will help us to understand the second issue on which I think my Anabaptist background provides a helpful perspective. One of the most important controversies in contemporary philosophy is that between *realism* and *anti-realism*. Realism is the view that reality is what it is *independently* of our thoughts about it. Anti-realism is the view that what reality itself is *depends upon* our cognitive attitudes toward it.

While anti-realism seems to me overwhelmingly implausible, it claims many prominent adherents. The best explanation for that fact is, I think, related to the failure in the quest for certainty outlined above. To oversimplify somewhat, modernity began with the complete confidence that we could be the cognitive masters of absolute reality, i.e., that we could have infallible knowledge of what reality was. To preserve the illusion of our mastery, philosophers have adjusted and readjusted our notion of reality so that we can still be its cognitive masters, until we have arrived at the Orwellian illusion that reality is only what we think it is.

The deepest reason for the influence of this view, as I see it, is what William Alston calls an "intolerance of vulnerability." Alston, who is one of the leading defenders of realism, writes, "This vulnerability to the outside world, this 'subjection' to stubborn, unyielding facts beyond our thought, experience, and discourse, seems powerfully repugnant, even intolerable to many." He further describes this attitude as "insisting on human autonomy and control and refusing to be subservient to that on which our being and our fate depends."[11]

Here, then, we see the relationship between this philosophical debate and Gelassenheit. I would argue that the *acceptance* of our dependence upon what is beyond our control is the very soul of Gelassenheit, whereas insisting on the control of that on which our fate depends is its very antithesis.

While both anti-realism and the quest for infallible certainty are, I think, utterly wrongheaded, they have exhibited a surprising resilience in philosophy. But as a philosopher, I have never found either view even remotely tempting, a fact I attribute to my Anabaptist background. Schooled as I was on the importance of humility and Gelassenheit, it has always seemed to me astonishingly audacious to aspire to infallibility, and a bit nutty to think that the existence or properties of mountains and stars somehow depend upon our cognitive attitudes toward them.

In the past several years, I have deployed my background in epistemology and what I take to be the insights of an Anabaptist perspective to criticize and explain the acceptance of anti-realism. Very little of this work has been published yet, but I expect more of it to be coming out in the relatively near future. Unlike my work on moral theory, I do not regard this work on realism and anti-realism to be *uniquely* Anabaptist. But I do think that a characteristically Anabaptist appreciation of the importance of humility and Gelassenheit, especially in their Amish forms, is both helpful in avoiding the temptations that give rise to anti-realism and insightful in explaining anti-realism's hold on us.

Lessons for Anabaptists?

As noted earlier, one of the biggest stories of philosophy at the end of the twentieth century was the reemergence of the influence and respectability of Christian philosophy. But Alvin Plantinga, the central figure in this reemergence, has been almost completely indifferent to respectability. Indeed, he viewed the effort by professing Christians to be respected in philosophy as perhaps their biggest problem.

There is a lesson there that should not be lost on Anabaptists. The lesson is that the effort to accommodate Christianity to worldviews that prevail in the academy, in order to gain respectability among adherents of such worldviews, is often self-defeating.

One problem is that these worldviews are often at odds with Christianity. The attempt to accommodate them thus tends to undermine Christianity by incorporating elements at odds with it. But the effort also fails to enhance respectability because it subjects Christianity to standards it is ill equipped to meet. Secularism, for example, will almost always satisfy its own standards of acceptability better than Christianity will. As a Christian, I am also convinced that Christianity has the truth on its side. We undermine that advantage by attempting to water it down.

A second lesson from the recent experience of Christianity in philosophy relates to the fact that this resurgence of Christian influence happened in *philosophy*. Why is that? One reason, I am convinced, is that philosophers recognize the importance of logical reasoning and are able to see and accept the consequences of such reasoning. For instance, Plantinga succeeded in convincing most philosophers that the existence of evil is logically consistent with the existence of God, not because philosophers liked that consequence, but because they recognized the cogency of his arguments.

Although controversy over substantive questions pervades philosophy, there is actually a great deal of consensus about whether particular arguments are cogent. Indeed, as a result of the work of Christian philosophers, a great many atheist philosophers were convinced that some of their favorite arguments against theism were unsound. To be sure, it didn't convince many of them to espouse Christianity, but it nonetheless made philosophy much less hostile to theism in general and to Christianity in particular.

Logical argument is not the only or even the primary tool for honest truth-seeking, but it is a crucial one. It is one that is especially helpful where there is controversy among people about what the truth is. When we recognize that a belief of ours entails the truth of something we don't yet believe, we are faced with a choice: we can either give up our belief, or we can adopt its consequence.

In other words, logical argument is a means by which others can point out the implications of our beliefs and so hold us accountable for them in light of their fuller significance. Contrary to what some have argued, then, logical reasoning is not coercive. For unlike coercion or indoctrination, for a person to be persuaded by a logical argument, she has to become convinced *by her own lights* that the conclusion in question follows from premises that she holds.

In sum, logical reasoning is a gift of God not to be spurned. God gave us the capacity to reason logically so that we would know what truths are implied by the truths we already believe and to recognize falsehoods among our beliefs by understanding their more obviously false implications. If we reason properly, we enhance our ability to believe the truth and avoid error. If we really believe in Christianity and in an Anabaptist version of it, we should expect that subjecting our beliefs to logical analysis will be likely to make the truth of what we believe even clearer. Moreover, as a community that professes to value mutual accountability, we should welcome the use of reason as a means of accounting to each other for our beliefs.

Again, logical reasoning is not the only or even the primary means of honest truth-seeking, but it is an important one. It is also one that Anabaptists are perhaps too reticent to employ.

Notes

1. This title is an allusion to Tertullian, the early church father who regarded philosophy as an enemy of the Christian faith. At the end of a diatribe against philosophy as the source of heresy, Tertullian wrote: "What indeed has Athens to do with Jerusalem? What concord is there between the Academy and the Church? What between heretics and Christians?" Tertullian, *The Prescription Against Heretics,* trans. Peter Holmes, *Christian Classics Ethereal Library*; available from http://www.ccel.org/fathers2/ANF-03/anf03-24.htm#P3125_1133921.

2. Aaron Edidin and Calvin Normore, "Ockham on Prophecy," *International Journal for the Philosophy of Religion* 13 (1982): 179-89.

3. David Lewis, "Do We Believe in Penal Substitution?" *Philosophical Papers* 26 (1997): 203-10.

4. Evan Fales, "Are Christians Obliged to be Pacifists?" *Faith and Philosophy* 11 (1994): 298-301.

5. Two collections of testimonials by Christian philosophers have been published, about half of each by philosophers who converted during their philosophic careers. See Thomas V. Morris, ed., *God and the Philosophers: The Reconciliation of Faith and Reason* (New York: Oxford University Press, 1994); and Kelly James Clark, *Philosophers Who Believe: The Spiritual Journeys of Eleven Leading Thinkers* (Downers Grove, Ill.: InterVarsity Press, 1993).

6. Recounted in Merold Westphal, "Taking Plantinga Seriously: Advice to Christian Philosophers," *Faith and Philosophy* 16 (1999): 173.

7. For the development of such a suggestion, see Thomas McPherson, "Religion as the Inexpressible," in *New Essays in Philosophical Theology*, ed. Antony Flew and Alasdair MacIntyre (London: SCM Press, 1955), 131-43.

8. Alvin Plantinga, "Advice to Christian Philosophers," *Faith and Philosophy* 1 (1984): 253-71.

9. For instance, my dissertation was in the area of epistemology. The theory I defended was inspired by a theistic worldview, but it was not explicitly or uniquely Christian, much less Anabaptist, in its motivation or its significance.

10. For a development of some of these views, see "An Anabaptist Theory of Moral Obligation," *Mennonite Quarterly Review* 71 (1997): 571-93; "Creation, Redemption and Virtue," *Faith and Philosophy* 16 (1999): 368-77; "Character-Dependent Duty: An Anabaptist Approach to Ethics," *Faith and Philosophy* 17 (2000): 293-305.

11. All quotations in this paragraph are from William P. Alston, *A Realist Conception of Truth* (Ithaca, N.Y.: Cornell University Press, 1996), 264.

3: Rhetoric

Seeking the Rhetoric of Jesus

Susan Biesecker-Mast

I COME TO THE QUESTIONS POSED BY THIS VOLUME from a somewhat different background than one might expect. Whereas one might anticipate that I was an Anabaptist first and a scholar second, just the opposite was the case.[1] Before beginning my graduate studies I had never heard of Anabaptism. Indeed, I was poring over Aristotle's *Rhetoric* before I was even a Christian. I thus went through much of my graduate studies (not to mention all of college, high school, and elementary school) without giving a thought to how my studies were impacting my faith—never mind how my faith might impact my scholarship. Not only did these questions fail to trouble me, they never even occurred to me.

The fact that I came to Anabaptism late has been significant for me personally, and therefore important for the way in which I think about the relationship between my scholarship and my faith. That being the case, I want to begin by recounting my story.

So, You Grew Up in Chicago. . . .

A lot of people, many of them Mennonite, do not like "the Mennonite game" because they understand it to be an exclusionary ritual. As the spouse of an ethnic Mennonite, I can appreciate that critique whenever an ethnic Mennonite who has just established my husband's genealogy turns to me and asks, "So, where are you from?" and I have to answer, "Chicago." My response typically has the same disappointing effect: to bring a warm and easy conversation to a sudden stall. Still, even as I appreciate the problems with "the Mennonite game," I also like hearing others play it. I enjoy hearing the names run across lines that stretch out and then intersect, then split and join again into an endless web of generations, until finally and inevitably some (however distant) link is made to the one with whom the game is being played.

It is hard for me to be more than a spectator to this game, because my own roots are in a rather different tradition—namely, that deeply American tradition in which one sets off, often alone (or with one's nuclear family), usually for a better job and, in so doing, leaves the past and all the relations within it behind.

My parents each grew up in a Chicago suburb, one on the north side and the other on the south. There they were raised to worship God, study hard, work even harder, and above all seek a better life. To these ends my mother got confirmed in her Catholic church, my father went to the Methodist church, and both were the first in their families to go to college. My parents met at Bradley University in Peoria, Illinois, and their blind date was, by all accounts, the occasion for love at first sight. They got married while they were still students and had my brother within the first year of their marriage. A year and a half later my sister was born. By my parents' tenth anniversary my mother had borne three children, the family had moved ten times, and my father had gone from selling pots and pans door-to-door to designing washer and dryer parts to selling fasteners all over the Midwest.

From what I can tell, those were fast years in which my parents did not talk much about the fact that they came from different religious backgrounds. Perhaps that is why my childhood religious experience (my brother's and sister's, too) was disjointed. Each of us was baptized in the Catholic Church but, as far as I know, never attended a Catholic church.[2] I do remember that we went to a Methodist church for a while when I was little. I also remember that we often went to church Christmas Eve. I recall that I felt strange when we did go to church, because I did not have much of an idea about what to do or say in Sunday school.

By the time we moved to Inverness, a suburb that was then on the outermost edges of the greater Chicago area, my family was no longer attending church. My parents never said why we stopped going. It felt to me that they had simply decided that we did not need church anymore.

In some ways Inverness was a wonderful place to grow up. Our yard was large and there were bushes and trees all around. I loved to climb those trees and make forts in the bushes. Also, the roads within Inverness were quiet and winding. They were wonderful for long and relaxing bike rides. Importantly, the schools near Inverness were excellent. I was encouraged at home to study hard and was prepared well at school for my college studies.

But Inverness also had its disadvantages. The bushes around our yard were not planted for playing; they were planted for privacy. They were effective. In fact, they were so effective that in the eleven years I lived there I never once saw the old woman who lived next door.

I suppose that the large yards were designed to give each family plenty of greenery to enjoy. But the effect I remember most was that the houses—and thus the people—were far apart from one another.

Finally, the roads that passed between the subdivisions were wide and busy, which made traversing the several miles to town too dangerous for a child. During the school year these barriers, distances, and divisions did not seem significant. But during the summertime, when friends from school disappeared into their subsection of the development, Inverness could feel rather isolating.

The Un-Altar Call

About the time I was solidly into adolescence—I was just finishing eighth grade and was not looking forward to three long summer months in Inverness—my best friend told me about a youth program in which her older brother was participating. Scores of teenagers from our area were getting together every Thursday night for outdoor games and rock music. Of course, by this time the bushes in our yard and the forts I had built in them did not hold much interest for me. But lots of teens, many of them male, surely did.

I had a wonderful time that summer. Every Thursday evening I joined a couple hundred other youth at a local park where, organized into our standing teams, we would play poison ball or some other low-skill outdoor game for a couple of hours. Then, as the summer sun began to set, we would head over to the YMCA gym, where a portable stage had been erected, folding chairs had been set out, and a rock band was beginning to play. We would find our seats with our teammates and, after a while, the music would fade into a skit that would dissipate into a cartoon slide show that would prepare us for a message brought by the youth leader. He was a youth pastor, I now realize, though we never called him that.

As I said, I had a wonderful time. I thoroughly enjoyed being with all those young people, playing games and listening to the music. But I was often unsure of what to make of the Christian message that always brought those evenings to a close. To be sure, my uncertainty was largely due to the fact that I had not had much experience with church. But I was also confused because the whole approach of the youth program was so subtle. It was not clearly identified as a Christian youth ministry; the leader was not called a "pastor," we never heard a "sermon," and we never sang any hymns. As an adolescent who, before going to sleep, had often prayed to a God who was a mystery, this youth program was absolutely intriguing, but also a bit frightening.

Over the course of that summer and into the next school year, I became deeply involved in the program. Rarely missing a Thursday night, I became a regular member of the "core" of my team. I also started attending Sunday worship at the youth program's parent "church."

Toward the end of the summer before my sophomore year, I went to a Thursday night gathering, as usual. I played an outdoor game, as usual, and enjoyed the music and gleaned some insight from the cartoon slide show. Then I settled in for the message. The youth leader, as always, gave a good message—about self-improvement, I think. Then all the lights went out on the stage and suddenly we were immersed in darkness, except for the red exit sign above the double doors. The youth pastor continued. He asked us all to close our eyes and bow our heads and ask ourselves this question: Has Jesus come into your heart and made you a Christian? He repeated the question several times, as if to help us consider it carefully.

I did not want to hear this question. It was not a question I wanted to answer. But there it was, repeated, no less. For a good ten minutes or so I tried to put off the question. I sat there in the dark, waiting for the lights to come back on. Some time later the youth pastor gave us further instruction. He said that those of us who had found Jesus in our hearts could leave, but that the rest of us were to stay.

Apparently, I could not just wait it out. He was going to make me stay there until I answered this question. So I closed my eyes and bowed my head, and I searched my heart. After what seemed like a stretch of time just this side of eternity, I gave up looking because it had become clear to me that Jesus was not in there. Finally, I opened my eyes and made my way in the dark to that red exit sign.

I never went back to that youth program or its parent "church." I stopped going, not because I thought the ministry was untrue but because I believed that I had been forsaken. Jesus had not come into my heart. Clearly, I was not a Christian.

Saved by the Body

In 1987 I started graduate school at the University of Pittsburgh, where I met a peculiar person. In seminars where we were studying Freud, Marx, Nietzsche, Lacan, and Derrida (theorists who, especially in the 1980s, were viewed as wholly critical of religious belief), I came to know a young man who was intense not only about the readings and discussions but about Christianity. Odder still, he belonged to some small Christian sect I had never heard of before.

We got to be friends. Over the course of several months, our friendship grew as we spent many late nights at the twenty-four-hour diner, talking about rhetoric, social theory, and the Anabaptists. The first two topics interested me greatly. The last one did not. Perhaps that was partly because Anabaptism seemed to include the commitment that a believer, when faced with violent intruders threatening to harm the person's dearest ones, would not use a gun to stop them. I had never met anyone with such strange and deeply held principles.

As peculiar as I thought he was, I also found myself becoming attracted to him. Late one night, after an engaging discussion about the material in one of our seminars, I asked if I might kiss him. He said yes, and that was great. And then he had a question for me: would I go to church with him? That was not the question I wanted to hear. My turn away from the church was not some casual retreat. I left because I understood myself to have been forsaken, and that was painful. Now this person I was falling in love with was, to my mind, asking me to discover all over again that Jesus was not within me.

I went.

As it turned out my return to church went well. The congregation, which was small, was friendly. I enjoyed getting to know them. I also enjoyed listening to them sing. I would have liked to join them, but I could not sing the words. I felt that if I sang the words I would be lying and that God would know it. Although I still felt estranged from Christianity, I continued to go to the Pittsburgh Mennonite Church (PMC) with Gerald. In spring 1991, Gerald and I were married by the pastor at PMC. By that time I was serving on at least one church committee and was making a regular practice of engaging in the lively exchanges that were characteristic of our congregational business meetings.

Not long after we were married—and after about two years of worship leading, lots of business meetings, great discussions in our small group, and wonderful fellowship meals—it occurred to me that I should become a member of that church. I thought the time had come for me to say publicly what I believed was already true—that I was committed to that body. John Stahl-Wert, our pastor, seemed pleased with my decision and asked me to meet with him once a week for several weeks in preparation for membership.

At our first meeting John presented me with a choice: to be taken into membership by confession of faith alone or also by baptism. John knew I had been baptized as a baby, and he therefore said that I did not have to be baptized for membership at PMC. But he added that he recommended it.

This choice made me anxious. I knew that I felt a strong commitment to PMC, but I was having no more luck as an adult than I had had as a teenager in finding Jesus inside. As far as I could tell, he still had not come into my heart.

John gave me time to consider this choice. In fact, several meetings and some important study and much discussion passed before he asked me again.

Of course, he eventually returned to the question, and when he did I had a question for him. Can a person be a Christian even if Jesus has never come, even if she cannot find Jesus inside?

I will never forget his answer. He said that if I were to come into membership, I would not do so alone. He reminded me that we were going to ask the congregation, the body of believers, the body of Christ, whether to take me into their membership, their body, Christ's body. He asked me to trust their decision and, if they said yes, to let them carry me forward, let them bring Christ to me.

I was baptized in the Pittsburgh Mennonite Church in spring 1992. Jesus finally came to me in the faces and faith of that body of believers. And by their action and in their midst, I was saved.

What Has This Got to Do with Rhetoric?

Now, almost ten years since my baptism, I find myself to be not only a member of a Mennonite church but also a faculty member at a Mennonite college who focuses her scholarly efforts on questions related to the church and even enthusiastically assents to pacifism. I have been through quite a transformation.

How does human transformation like that happen? I believe this is a rhetorical question. As Aristotle instructs us, rhetoric is the art of persuasion. It is an art, he teaches us, because it can be learned and theorized but cannot be reduced to a formula. It is about persuasion because it seeks transformation without coercion. So to study rhetoric is to study how human beings transform their world by discourse and how they are themselves transformed by discourse.[3]

Over time rhetoric has met with widely divergent receptions. In ancient Greece, where Western rhetoric got its start, rhetoric initially enjoyed a good reputation. As the art of crafting discourse capable of moving the *polis* toward some collective action, rhetoric was seen as a valuable and practical art central to the functioning of the Athenian democracy. Later, when the highly styled rhetorics of some famous rhetoricians came to be linked with the downfall of Athens, rhetoric developed a bad reputation as the discourse of self-interested individuals seeking to beguile audiences for personal gain.[4] Importantly, a cursory view of the history of rhetoric suggests that whenever rhetoric has been understood primarily as an art of persuasion that makes democratic decision-making possible, it is highly valued. However, when it is seen as the stylizing of a discourse designed to benefit the rhetorician, it tends to be derided.

In graduate school I learned that rhetoric is best understood as that practical art central to the workings of a vital democracy. However, I also learned that any good rhetorician pays attention to style—that is, to the manner in which a case is made. A good rhetorician will do that because he or she will know that the manner of speaking matters as much as the content of what is spoken. Indeed, a good rhetorician will go even so far as to say that style is also a kind of content.

To study the content and style of a discourse is crucial to understanding how discourse impacts human beings. But that is not enough. An understanding of context and purpose is also crucial. We must consider context because that is always where the rhetorician looks for appeals. The rhetorician must begin where the audience is.

In addition, context is crucial for understanding whether a change has occurred. If we do not know where an audience's members began, we cannot judge whether they have been moved.

Finally, we must understand the rhetorician's purpose. Since rhetoric is discourse by which human beings seek to change their world, we can only appreciate their effort when we have an idea of their aim.

My purpose in offering this brief summary of the definition, history, and critique of rhetoric is to make a simple point: namely, that rhetoric is the discourse of the possible.[5] It is such because it always begins where we are, with the here-and-now, yet always seeks to move us elsewhere. Rhetoric must begin with the world as we know it, because only then can rhetoric make any sense to us. Yet it must also always seek to make that world otherwise, because only then can it be the discourse of transformation.

From the time I began the course work for my doctoral degree to the time I got my first full-time teaching job, I sought to better understand rhetoric as the discourse of the possible by studying the discourses of social movements. I began with the rhetoric of the Sophists, fifth-century B.C.E. teachers and practitioners of rhetoric whose rhetorical skill helped to transform Athens from a culture ruled by blood relations to one governed by the polis. Later, I studied the rhetoric of American women's movements. In my dissertation I sought to discern whether popular feminist books published in the early 1990s by feminists like Gloria Steinem, Naomi Wolf, Susan Faludi, and Marilyn French were truly discourses of the possible—that is, discourses seeking to change patriarchal culture into relations of equality between men and women.

But then my research took a turn.

During the summer before Gerald and I moved to Ohio to begin our first full-time teaching positions, we spent a month in Holmes County, Ohio, with Gerald's parents. Over the course of that month I became thoroughly fascinated by the interactions that tourism was enabling between the Amish and middle Americans. A whole host of questions about the impact that tourism was having on Amish and Mennonite communities in Holmes County interested me. However, most compelling to me was the question of what impact the Amish and Mennonites of Holmes County might be having on middle America. Thus inspired by what I believe to be the potent, if subtle, witness of these communities in Holmes County, my research has come to engage some additional questions. In addition to asking *how* a rhetorical discourse seeks to make change by way of its appeals and style, I now find myself also asking what change *ought to be* advocated and what strategies *ought to be* employed.

I believe the answer to the first question is best found in the life and teachings of Jesus. Further, I believe that the most compelling interpretation of his life and teachings can be found in the work of John Howard Yoder. Indeed, I believe Yoder was right when he argued that we ought to take the life and teachings of Jesus so seriously as to live according to them—according to, as he put it, "the politics of Jesus."[6]

The politics of Jesus, I understand Yoder to have argued, call us to recognize that the world is not the kingdom of God and, at the same time, to live each day as if it were. Thus, rather than allow our faith either to be separated from our daily living or to be integrated into it, we should live in the full recognition that the world goes 'round by greed and violence; yet we should choose to live by generosity and peace.

To live by generosity and peace is to live in faith. And, of course, to live in faith is to live the impossible.

In a nutshell, then, since becoming an Anabaptist my scholarship has taken a turn toward trying to understand how the impossible is made possible or how the kingdom of God is articulated in human discourse or, finally, what is the rhetoric of Jesus.

I believe I will spend the rest of my days trying to answer this riddle. Still, I cannot help wondering whether I may already have been given some clues about it in the differences between my experience in the suburban Chicago youth ministry and at Pittsburgh Mennonite Church.

A Rhetoric of Jesus?

At the time I stopped attending the youth group and church in suburban Chicago, I was not altogether sure why I felt compelled to leave. I knew it had something to do with the fact that I experienced their "unaltar call" as evidence that Jesus was not interested in me. But now as I think more about it, I believe there was more to it than that. Indeed, I believe my leaving had to do with the manner in which that ministry was done.

Although I did not think about it much at the time, I remember that I was aware that the ministry had begun only after extensive market research had been conducted. That research was said to have revealed that there were a lot of people in the Chicago suburbs who were interested in God but were put off by church.

In response, this youth and adult ministry was developed to offer God without church. We never sang hymns or referred to the youth or lead minister as "pastors." We never met in a church building and never sat in pews. Even during the worship service on Sunday mornings we never heard a "sermon," but rather a message that sounded like a keynote speech appropriate for a self-improvement seminar.

Importantly, I never thought of the people who gathered for those worship services as a "church," because we did not function as a body. Rather, we were a gathering of individuals seeking insight for our particular lives from our un-pastor.

The youth group did not function as a body either. When we "gathered" on Thursday nights, we always did so first as members of teams competing aggressively against one another to earn team points in the hope that we would be declared the winners at the end of the month. Although I am sure that there was some group cohesion within the core of the team, I also recall that the primary purpose of our gatherings was to memorize biblical passages—again, to earn points. Our sense of belonging owed much to our drive to win.

In a context such as this, where the primary rhetorical strategy was to seem un-churchly, it is not altogether surprising that I was ill prepared for the un-pastor's un-altar call. It came to me as a shock, because it did not fit into the context of outdoor games, rock music, and self-help discourse.

Before the call, the discourse was all about making us feel comfortable, as if participating in the youth group and attending worship on Sunday were just like playing a sport at the high school, going to a concert of your favorite rock group, or watching Phil Donahue. Whether we were scoring team points, clapping to the beat of the music, or sitting in the movie theater seats on Sunday morning, the emphasis was on the familiar. Then, suddenly, all was unfamiliar as we were asked to decide whether we belonged to God.

At Pittsburgh Mennonite Church, my experience was altogether different. PMC was a church formed by a group of believers who came together out of a desire for fellowship, not in response to a market analysis. This was a body of believers that understood itself to be about serving others, not about having its desires met. At PMC the emphasis was not on the familiar; the pastor's focus was not on making us always feel comfortable. In fact, the contrary was probably more often the case, as John regularly asked us in his sermons to question our habits and examine our assumptions.

In short, this was a congregation that made no sense except as a body. Everything it did it did as a body, whether it was doing its work in commissions, sharing regular fellowship meals, working through differences of opinion at business meetings, or anticipating the coming year at the annual church retreat. Especially significant for me, this was a congregation that believed in a kind of conversion that did not require that I find Jesus inside, but instead placed its trust in a deliberate process of studying the Sermon on the Mount with the pastor, learning about the Anabaptists in a membership Sunday school class, and being carried forth to the baptismal waters by the gathered body, the body of Christ.

If I were only a rhetorical critic and not a Christian, I would conclude from this contrast that both methods of evangelism were successful, since both methods seemed to result in genuine conversions. Indeed, I might even conclude that the method used by the Chicago unchurch was far more successful than the one used by PMC. Whereas the Chicago ministry has since become a megachurch drawing tens of thousands of people every Sunday, PMC is a robust but comparatively tiny congregation.

Yet because I am a Christian as well as a rhetorical critic—and, moreover, a Christian who reads the Bible from the perspective of the peace-church tradition—I must draw another conclusion. That is, that while PMC's manner of evangelism may not have produced as many conversions, I believe it to be a far better effort. Although I do not fully understand what the rhetoric of Jesus is, I suspect that if I ever do, I'll remember having heard it first at PMC. Further, I expect that it will be, like the rhetoric of PMC, a rhetoric that is embodied in the gathered believers, forthright in its witness to the kingdom of God yet nonresistant in its evangelism.[7]

THE CHURCH AND SCHOLARSHIP

I opened this essay by claiming that my coming to Anabaptism late has been significant for my scholarship. Indeed, that was my initial justification for recounting my faith story. I made that claim because I think that coming to rhetoric before coming to Anabaptism has shaped the way I tend to think of the relationship between faith and scholarship. Since I was already well into serious study of rhetoric before I became a Christian, I did not tend to ask myself how my scholarship impacted my faith. Instead, I tended to ask how my scholarship might be enriched by my faith.

Also at the beginning of this essay, I mentioned that although I cannot play the Mennonite game well, I still enjoy hearing others play it. What I enjoy about it is the truth that it speaks about the extent to which all of us, whether or not we are ethnic Mennonites, may make sense of ourselves, our faith, and our commitments through the complex web of relations from which we have come and within which we are being transformed. Although I never expect to discover, like so many ethnic Mennonites probably have, that my parents are second cousins, I also no longer live either physically or spiritually in a place designed to produce the experience of isolation. Thus, if I ever do arrive at a fuller understanding of the rhetoric of Jesus, I expect that I will do so through the church. Just as the only way I could find Jesus was through the body, so too will I only come to understand his rhetoric through the body. How could it be otherwise?

So, if I were to draw any conclusion about the relationship between scholarship and faith, perhaps it would be this: Bringing wisdom to the church is not the primary task of faithful scholarship; rather *being in the church* is the first condition for the possibility of doing faithful scholarship.

Notes

1. Significantly, five other contributors to this volume (Terry Brensinger, Polly Ann Brown, Perry Bush, Jay McDermond, and David Mosley) also come to it in a similar way—as people who did not grow up Anabaptist.

2. I say "as far as I know" because I cannot remember ever attending a Catholic church; as both of my parents are no longer living, I cannot ask them.

3. Aristotle, *On Rhetoric: A Theory of Civic Discourse*, trans. George A. Kennedy (New York: Oxford University Press, 1991).

4. This view of rhetoric is reiterated today whenever social commentators refer to "mere rhetoric"—that is, discourse used, typically by politicians, to mislead the people for their own political gain.

5. I am borrowing this notion of rhetoric as the discourse of the possible from

John Poulakos, "Rhetoric, the Sophists, and the Possible," *Communication Monographs* 51 (1984): 215-26.

6. See especially John Howard Yoder, *The Politics of Jesus* (Grand Rapids, Mich.: William B. Eerdmans, 1972).

7. For an essay developing this notion of a nonresistant evangelism, see my "The Aporetic Witness" in *Practicing Truth: Confident Witness in Our Pluralistic World*, ed. David W. Shenk and Linford Stutzman (Scottdale, Pa.: Herald Press, 1999), 130-47.

4: History

Anabaptist Visions at the Library of Congress (and Other Tales from the Edge of Evangelicalism)

Perry Bush

*T*HOSE OF US WRITING MENNONITE AND BRETHREN IN CHRIST HISTORY do so in the shadow of giants. By virtue of my position teaching history at Bluffton College, for example, I inherit the weighty mantle of such luminaries as C. Henry Smith, the dean of Mennonite historians in the early part of the twentieth century, of Robert Kreider and his sparkling intellect, and of John Unruh, whose book *The Plains Across* was once named as a finalist for the Pulitzer Prize.[1] There were—and are—giants elsewhere: at Goshen College, Bethel College, Conrad Grebel College, Fresno Pacific University, Eastern Mennonite University, and of course Messiah College, where Morris Sider, for much of the past three decades, has produced close to a book a year on the Brethren in Christ.

A major reason that this small corner of the historical terrain has housed such a comparatively strong array of academic talent has to do with the powerful role that history has played in twentieth-century Mennonite self-understandings. The examples are many: Harold S. Bender's monumental "Anabaptist Vision," Guy Hershberger's *War, Peace, and Nonresistance*, the recent Mennonite Experience in America and Mennonite Experience in Canada series.[2]

Through such vehicles North American Mennonites have seized upon their past as a way of reconstructing their future. Long before postmodernist theoreticians legitimated such an enterprise, Mennonite historians discarded any pretense of a supposedly pure, complete objectivity. Instead, over what is now nearly a century of historical writing, they set out with determination and talent to create a usable past.[3]

When I began to enter the Mennonite academic world as a graduate student, it was partly the explicit nature of this scholarly scheme that attracted me. This was an agenda that lent itself perfectly to the guilt-ridden, evangelical political activist I was then. Uncovering usable pasts for a socially engaged church was the only way that I could legitimate the life of the mind that I thought socially irresponsible but was unable to turn away from. I encountered various Anabaptist visions in the glow of the reading room at the Library of Congress and embraced them like long-lost friends. A dozen years later such an agenda possesses me still.

Inheritances

I was born and raised in Southern California, and in an evangelical subculture so enveloping that the best way I can relay its power is to merely talk in code. I was like a little lost sheep that had gone astray, until I met the Good Shepherd who gathered me home. At one point in my early teen years, I made a personal decision for Christ, and I was saved—born again. I read the Four Spiritual Laws and thrilled to the tones of "How Great Thou Art" with the Billy Graham crusades that flickered across the static radiance of our new-model color TV set.

I absorbed my theology from C. S. Lewis's Narnia tales. I huddled in the balcony of Lake Avenue Congregational Church in Pasadena and heard thunderous sermons of God's wrath and Christ's grace from Pastor Jacobs. I fell in love with sweet Jesus in the company of my teenage church fellowship group, where we chimed along in harmony with every guitar chord ("I am the resurrection"—clap—"and the life"—clap-clap-clap-clap). While I have sojourned some years now away from my high school fellowship group, I retain an evangelical theology so deeply ingrained that I could wake up from deep sleep and sing, without much thinking, every word of "I've Been Redeemed."

I was also raised by a gentle academic father who had earned a Ph.D. in Semitic Languages and for thirty-three years taught Old Testament at the thoroughly evangelical Fuller Seminary in Pasadena. Hence I received a kind of privileged education that comes so naturally to children of academics. From a young age, my brother, sister, and I learned to question established verities, discuss issues, and float ideas. We unconsciously absorbed the assumptions and practices of intellectual life. I remember my father was once ticketed on a California freeway as we drove home from church—not for driving too fast, but because he was driving too slowly, too immersed in the discussion we were all having over the content of the pastor's sermon that morning.

At an equally young age I watched as my father and a few of his seminary friends began to model a kind of evangelical peace activism for their students and also, less consciously, for their children.[4] The group members all visited regularly and filled our dinner table with discussions of war, nonviolence, and Martin Luther King. On Wednesday noons they led a small group of students to the steps of the Pasadena post office to vigil silently with the Quakers, holding up a sign that read "Fuller Students and Faculty Against the War in Vietnam."

At some point in these same years, my father was removed from his position as teacher of an adult Sunday school class at the Lake Avenue Church, at least partly because of the questions he had raised with his class regarding the war. My mother cried with angry humiliation, and we searched for another church.

In the early 1970s, my parents made a principled decision not to join the white flight out of Pasadena when a local judge ordered the desegregation of the schools. Instead, they bought a home in a racially mixed neighborhood, fully expecting to lose money on it.[5] We kids were bused across town to combustible, racially mixed schools. There we suffered, endured, and ultimately benefited from a painful and particularly American kind of education that occurred without formal instruction in the hallways and schoolyards.

In the years to come I learned a number of lessons: about systemic causes of injustice, about the poisonous legacy of racial hatred, and about how to develop my own kind of nonviolent survival techniques. My siblings, many of my friends, and I also learned to regard with bemused contempt the kind of instinctive fear of all black people we observed in many other suburban whites. At home, I began to ask pointed questions about the kind of social arrangements that could produce these kinds of injustices, and my father fed me old copies of *The Other Side*, the *Post-American* (later, *Sojourners*) and a new book by an activist named Ron Sider entitled *Rich Christians in an Age of Hunger*.[6]

Altogether, these experiences left me with a number of inheritances that were central in both my intellectual and spiritual development. Sometime during my junior year in high school, for example, the protagonist of one of the short stories I wrote (in the first person, no less) hotly declared himself a pacifist. I began to apply such concepts to my evangelical tradition, and when I did, I found it wanting. The sweet Jesus we sang love songs to at church, I was coming to realize, had something to say not just about the quality of my Quiet Time or whether I drank or smoked, but also about the way I acted in the world with respect to other matters. I was blessed with a marvelous pastor at our Presbyterian church who preached simple living from the pulpit—and dared to model it in a wealthy suburb. Our youth group engaged in fundraisers for World Vision. But I heard little in my evangelical subculture about matters of war or injustice, and I had read enough of the Bible to begin to ask why not. When I went to college, these kinds of questions would fester even more.

Berkeley and Georgia

I arrived in Berkeley in the fall of 1978, after spending a dilatory year and a half at two different state universities and with the vague feeling that the time had come to settle down and get serious about academic matters. Berkeley not only provided the kind of academic rigor that I had anticipated, but much more. Away at a large, impersonal university, I quickly immersed myself in familiar elements of my evangelical subculture. I grew involved with InterVarsity Christian Fellowship and Berkeley's First Presbyterian Church.

At the same time, I moved along with the currents of student activism that still persisted. We picketed post offices in 1980 following President Carter's reintroduction of draft registration. I also became increasingly involved with a growing antinuclear movement, particularly with the efforts along these lines of an intentional Christian community I discovered down in the flats of west Berkeley.

The major developments for me in college were intellectual ones. As professors today, we scratch our heads about how to awaken intellectual hunger in many of our students. It is a maddeningly elusive goal and, while none of us has found the formula, I do know that it happened to me, both inside and outside of class.

My major, political science, seemed largely tedious. I only realized later, when it was too late to change undergraduate fields, that I liked politics more than political science, and what I really loved was history. Still, there were high points: an intense seminar in Marx, for example, and masterful lectures by Berkeley historians Charles Sellers and Lawrence Levine. I began to read fiendishly and to push myself. An advisor once told me not to take all three courses in my major, because it would be too demanding. So I enrolled in elementary Arabic, just because I thought it was beautiful. I lost myself in a lengthy honors thesis on the Student Nonviolent Coordinating Committee. Outside of class I took in visiting speakers like the economist John Kenneth Galbraith, the Watergate prosecutor Leon Jaworski, and novelist James Baldwin.

After college I moved to Americus, Georgia, for a year's voluntary service with Habitat for Humanity. Less than eight years old in the early 1980s, Habitat was at the time small and obscure. "International headquarters" was a converted one-story house on a side street in a small town, staffed by maybe a dozen volunteers living together in four small houses along the same street. I loved it. We built the small homes for the working poor, sold them at no interest in the African-American community where we lived, and used the payments to build more.

These were the "economics of Jesus," Millard Fuller proclaimed, telling us that these homes were nothing less than "demonstration plots of God's kingdom." I found the whole idea fantastic. Here was a living model of the church fleshed out in the world that I had been abstractly theorizing about.

It was there in Americus that I encountered Mennonites for the first time. The Lancaster Mennonite Conference had established a Voluntary Service unit there, and these young people my age were a regular part of our little community of Habitat volunteers. Between these Mennonites and me there were grounds for a wide variety of contrary impressions. With my long hair, rock music, and California slang, I must have seemed to them like I had floated down from outer space. To me, these Mennonites appeared to me quaintly innocent but with a slightly daunting ethnic-conservative cast. They all seemed to come from places like Kreiderton or Souderville in Pennsylvania. The young women wore some kind of fishnet hairpiece on their heads. (Was I really insensitive enough to warmly assure my new friends that I thought their hair covering seemed "kind of funky"?)

Despite these dissimilarities, we became good friends, these Mennos and I: we joined together in worksite high jinks, after-work basketball games, and pecan harvests on the streets of Americus. But I also found myself attracted to their tradition. While their theology appeared just as evangelical as mine, my Mennonite friends casually informed me that they had learned their pacifism at their church. Imagine that! Except for the ethnic aftertaste and the hairpiece thing, I thought to myself, these Mennonites had a remarkable tradition.

In fall 1982 I returned to California to spend several years in what I envisioned as another little manifestation of God's kingdom, with that intentional Christian community in the flats of west Berkeley. It was a deeply enriching experience in some ways and a bit of an alienating one in others. I lived with and grew to love this small set of self-described radical Christians, an affection that has lasted, in some cases, nearly two decades now. The worship leaders strummed guitars beautifully and led me to an intensity and joy of Christian worship that I have never quite encountered since. We painted houses together in a crew called "Pacem Painters," shared our funds in a common pot, and lived simply with an eye to world economic injustice. Some of us were packed off to jail together in marvelously moving acts of Christian civil disobedience at the Lockheed plant in Sunnyvale, California, and at the Lawrence Livermore Labs, the major development facility for America's next generation of nuclear weaponry.

At the same time, I couldn't escape a growing sense of discomfort with the sharp little hierarchies in that small community of two dozen people, only gradually recognizing the kinds of broken relationships that would lead to the community's collapse within a few years.

Intellectually at this time I rooted myself in the theological traditions underpinning our effort and others like them: Dorothy Day and the Catholic workers, the Berrigan brothers and Thomas Merton, the writings of Jim Wallis and the folks at Sojourners. It wasn't until much later that I realized the extent to which our community—and certainly myself—had absorbed Anabaptist theology. While we would regularly leaflet the workers heading into the Lockheed plant with messages of Christian peacemaking, I remember a gnawing sense of theological discomfort. Why should these people listen to us, I wondered? We have a different ethic than they do; we are citizens of another kingdom. I wasn't sure how I justified speaking to the Lockheed workers at all.

When my intentional community finally fragmented, I found myself working as a full-time house painter and a part-time antinuclear activist. There was too much painting and not enough politics; for me, at least, painting houses seemed like a prescription for meaninglessness. In a sense of quiet desperation I sent off applications to graduate programs in the only academic field I could envision myself becoming absorbed in. I would go off and study history.

Anabaptist Visions at the Library of Congress

In fall 1985 my new spouse and I packed our worldly possessions into a Honda Civic and drove to Pittsburgh, so I could begin graduate study in U.S. social history at Carnegie Mellon University. At the time, I wasn't quite sure what social history was; I had come to Carnegie Mellon principally because it had offered me admission and a substantial fellowship. I also arrived feeling no small amount of guilt about my apparent abandonment of "the movement"; how could one justify the pursuit of a Ph.D. with Reagan pursuing mad warfare in Central America and the country seemingly edging closer to the brink of nuclear destruction? I determined that I would not completely sell out my old ideals, that I would find some way of harnessing history to the work of the church.

After several years of intensive course work and a battery of qualifying exams, I began to approach the question of a dissertation topic. By this time we were living in Washington, D.C., where my spouse, Elysia, had landed a job teaching sixth grade in a bilingual (Spanish/English) public school, primarily to refugee children from Central America. We had a small apartment near the school, in the neighborhood of Mt. Pleasant. I played with my wife's students at school functions and regularly encountered them on the street. I also heard stories from Elysia about the kinds of murder and oppression their families had fled from and the kinds of personal emotional toll they paid. Yet our government insisted that these were economic refugees and tried to deport them. They would only have qualified for asylum as political refugees had they suffered the same treatment from a government like Cuba's.

That was the context that informed me as I daily rode my bike down to the Library of Congress on Capitol Hill to search for a subject I could build a book on. I wanted to see where evangelical theology and antimilitarist politics came together.

In the 1980s, conservative evangelicals had entered American politics big-time, but had allied themselves with what I thought were entirely the wrong kind of people. Calling themselves the "Moral Majority," these evangelicals devoted themselves to the service of political forces engaged in a massive military buildup and a concentration of the national wealth at the upper end of the economic spectrum.[7]

But did it have to be this way? I knew enough about my evangelical tradition to realize that something was askew. This was a tradition, after all, that had entered American history calling for a radical upheaval of the prevailing socio-economic order (what else did calls for the immediate emancipation of slaves signify?) and whose ultimate model, Jesus of Nazareth, had called his followers to be peacemakers.[8] Even though I knew I had moved to the edge of my old subculture, what my fellow evangelicals needed, I figured, was a more appropriate usable past.

I began looking first for what I called an "evangelical left." I realize now that I could have found such a movement had I investigated U.S. society in the 1840s or the 1890s, but I was a twentieth-century historian particularly fixated on the 1960s. The only "evangelical left" I could find functioning then was little more than a collection of evangelical seminarians writing letters to each other, and the stalwart social historians on my dissertation committee (Peter Stearns, Lizabeth Cohen, and principally John Modell) were dubious. So I cast about some more.

Somehow I thought to look at conscientious objectors in World War II, which led me directly to a systematic reading about the historic peace churches. Soon I began delving into matters Mennonite, just selecting whatever book next grabbed my interest as I proceeded through the subject index in the card catalog at the Library of Congress. I read widely but eclectically: E. K. Francis's writings on Canadian Mennonites in the High Plains; Melvin Gingerich's massive study of Mennonite Civilian Public Service; theological writings by Gordon Kaufman and John Howard Yoder.

I soon realized that I was onto something, though at first it took me a while to straighten it out. Mennonites offer a fairly complex initiation rite to the outside scholar, with their complex array of MCs, GCs, Mennonite Brethren, Brethren in Christ, Mennonite Brethren in Christ, Mennonites Defenseless and Evangelical, and forty dozen Amish groups arranged by bumper colors. The distinction between the Mennonite General Conference and the General Conference Mennonites stumped me for a solid week. But Mennonites carefully cited their sources, and the citations spoke to promising archival resources, with specific letters, other church records, and even draft census materials.

As I continued, I found myself in fundamental agreement with Anabaptist theology. Reading Hershberger and Bender's articulation of two-kingdom theology, I found myself saying, "Of course, that's what I've been saying for years." It reminded me of the intellectual troubles I had encountered in leafleting the workers at Lockheed. Why should we expect them to listen to us? We have a different ethic than they do. But then I followed avidly as people like Hershberger and Yoder solved my own theological quandary for me. We witness to the state, they said, because Christ is Lord. God had expectations not just for how the church should act in the world, but also everyone else, *including* the state.

If this was all so, that God didn't have two moralities, two kingdoms, but one, then how else could the state learn of proper behavior except through the voice of God's people? Because of Christ's Lordship, Christians should challenge rulers (read the MC Johnstown Statement of 1961) to "find the highest possible values within their own relative frames of reference. In doing so, the Christian may and can rightfully speak to decisions which the Christian ethic will not permit him to carry out."[9] I had never planned to abandon my activism, but from then on I felt I could speak to the state with more theological consistency.

Moreover, here was a Christian community, I realized, whose lived theology managed to bridge that divide I had found so troubling in my younger days. To be sure, in any honest encounter with Mennonites (or for that matter, with anyone else) one is sure to come across contradictions, inconsistencies, and many, many shades of gray. I quickly discovered, for example, that the Mennonite record on conscientious objection in various American wars was a good deal less than a hundred percent. (To further complicate the picture, I discovered that many of the Mennonite servicemen of World War II were just as filled with Christian devotion as Mennonite objectors.[10])

To a Mennonite who has long ago taken peace commitments for granted, such a story may signify a failure of the church. But to an evangelical like myself, whose own tradition had easily surrendered any critical distance it had with a war-making state, the record of a majority of church youth opting for another way than war seemed truly remarkable. Mennonites had a theology as inherently conservative as any I had known in my youth, but out of it (and maybe because of it) they managed to speak meaningfully about peace to the state and to match their convictions with their actions. By the later twentieth century, North American Mennonites had even managed to go beyond strict considerations of peace and begun to address relevant matters of justice.

Finally, I encountered a rich and exciting intellectual community. This hit home for me most directly when I picked up, in the reading room at the Library of Congress, the festschrift to Guy Hershberger entitled *Kingdom, Cross, and Community*.[11] As I read it, I discovered that here was a group of scholars from a variety of disciplines—history, sociology, theology—caught up in a marvelous intellectual engagement, debating with each other, refining each other's concepts, working from the same shared tradition, and reshaping it into a vehicle that could carry the church forward.

Joining the Community

So I decided I was going to write a dissertation not just on Mennonite pacifism in the twentieth-century United States, but also more generally on the Mennonite relation to the state, which reinforced this pacifism. With an eye to the shortcomings of my own tradition, I wanted to discover how it was that this ethno-religious group had managed to hold on to this crucial tenet of their theology (a tenet that became increasingly central to their identity) even while undergoing an extensive process of acculturation. If I could tell that kind of story and tell it well, not only could such a project help me with prosaic matters like a job (and even, someday, with tenure), but also it might even provide some kind of a usable past to non-Mennonite evangelicals. This project grew first into a prospectus, then into a dissertation, and finally, after years of revision, into a published book.[12]

In short order this project plunged me into the Mennonite academic community that I found so potently illustrated in the Hershberger festschrift. When I ventured to Goshen to do dissertation research, Leonard Gross plucked my name out of a college newsletter and invited me into his home for a month. The same thing happened when I had a request for housing placed on a bulletin board at Bethel College, the result being weeks of Jim and Anna Juhnke's stimulating hospitality. Archivists gave me space to work, handed me piles of documents, and loaned me keys so I could work late at night. Back at home in D.C., Elysia and I began attending Hyattsville Mennonite Church.

Years later, I made the deliberate decision to leave one tenure-track position for another at Bluffton, to more effectively and purposefully participate in this Mennonite scholarly community. I did so because I found myself along the same track as my Mennonite academic colleagues: I wanted to help create a usable past for the health and maintenance of the church. By telling the story of the past in the way that we do, we can shape the direction the church heads into the future.

In the end, while I nurtured the (apparently fruitless) hope that my book on Mennonite pacifism could offer a usable past that my fellow evangelicals could approximate, I also meant it as a pointed reminder to Mennonites of their remarkable peace tradition, in hopes they would be further led to carefully preserve and renew it in an uncertain future. Since then I've completed a second book, describing how one Mennonite college (namely, Bluffton) has for a century navigated its way between the poles of secularization on one side and a careless "evangelicalization" on the other.[13] I told this story in the frank hope that this college will continue to steer such a path, and in such a manner that it could perhaps serve as a model for others.

In the decade or so since I've finished my dissertation and begun teaching, I have done some broader thinking about the differences my own Anabaptist commitments might make in how I approach the different narratives of larger U.S. history. For instance, concerns about justice that my Anabaptist concerns have reinforced inform the way I read the civil rights movement and, specifically, the career of Martin Luther King.

In teaching students both on well-manicured, secluded campuses and also, particularly, in several, less-sheltered state penitentiaries, I am periodically struck by student comments indicating the degree to which King has been utterly assimilated and rendered into a popular, harmless national symbol by American pop culture. Such an assimilation is functional for a nation wedded to a myth of progressive race relations, in which (the popular consensus agrees) all racial problems have largely been solved and racial justice achieved.

Of course, such an assertion rests on nothing more than a compilation of historical and sociological poppycock. If we as a people ever really do want to take the necessary and difficult steps to remove the poison of racism from our society (a questionable proposition in itself), I have argued that the first step might be to toss out this myth of progressive race relations and recapture something of the radical political and economic vision of Martin Luther King Jr.[14]

In applying my own Anabaptist thinking to the study of history, I have repeatedly found my Mennonite colleagues offering helpful clues. Some years ago John Howard Yoder challenged pacifist historians to begin to map out how differently U.S. history might look if viewed through the lens of nonviolence. Jim Juhnke is perhaps the most influential of the scholars who took up Yoder's call. His book, *The Missing Peace,* now serves as a foundation stone for those of us re-visioning American history in nonviolent ways.[15]

Through my own reading, thinking, and borrowing, I have stapled together a conceptualization of the demands and practices of modern, total war that has proved paradigmatic in the way I understand much of modern U.S. history. While influenced by my reading of historians like Ronald Schaffer and Michael Sherry, this process was also greatly aided by several generations of students in a course I've taught repeatedly titled "War and Peace in American History." Briefly summarized, I have come to understand the repression or co-optation of dissent at home, and the accompanying destruction of civilians abroad, as necessary by-products of modern industrial warfare.[16]

My view of economic issues provides another example of how my acceptance of the Anabaptist tradition shapes the way I do history. In the same way that Mennonites have begun to integrate issues of justice as central in their vocabularies, I have come to realize the centrality of economic justice issues in U.S. history. Out of this rethinking, I've done some writing designed to nudge my old evangelical community to return to a commitment to economic justice that was once central in their own tradition. For much of their history in the United States, I argue, many in the revivalist tradition reverberated to a kind of "evangelical populism" before carelessly allowing themselves to be seduced and co-opted by the advocates of free-market economics in the later twentieth century. It is time, I suggest, to try to recapture this older tradition.[17]

In this open advocacy of writing history to offer usable pasts, we must, of course, remain cognizant of the kinds of hazards that Marsden and others have articulated and which David Weaver-Zercher has ably highlighted in his introduction to this book. In our scholarship we must play obediently by all the honored rules of the academic game—not, for example, enlisting God as a special extra-historical agent in our stories (as comforting as such an enterprise might be to the Mennonite ego).

There are other dangers, too. In constructing histories carefully tailored to the needs of the present, we run the risk of getting the story wrong in ways we might not have otherwise. In my book on Mennonite pacifism, for example, I held up Mennonites as a premier example of a conservative Christian group that, through dedication to bedrock concepts such as peace and service, has been almost uniquely able to resist the bulldozing power of mainstream American culture with all its seductions. I came to such conclusions honestly back then, still surprised at the depth of Mennonite fidelity to peacemaking and service. Yet if I were to write the same book today (after a seven-year sojourn in Menno country), I might revise my estimate regarding the degree to which Mennonites have resisted acculturation and temper my claims of Mennonite uniqueness.

In this observation I am merely echoing what postmodern theorists have been quick to remind us for several decades now—that all scholars write out of particular contexts and that we must continually acknowledge our potential biases.[18] The charge seems especially pertinent to those of us engaged in constructing usable pasts, however. In tailoring our history to the needs of the present we seem especially prone to being captured by it. And so we must repeatedly step back and issue (as I mean to do here) our own declarations of intellectual independence.

Today I am repeatedly reminded of the pleasure I take in my craft. Reading and writing history is inherently satisfying. I love the way that historians deduce cause and effect relationships out of the seeming disorder and mayhem of the past. There is a kind of magnifying glass quality that appears when we look at the past, for the closer and more carefully we look the more complex and surprising everything appears. I love the way that skilled historians can spin this complexity into an alluring and exciting web of narrative. I hope to continue to sharpen my own still-developing skills along these lines.

At the same time, I can do no other but continue to approach the past out of my own context. I am an evangelical Christian who has come, with some joy and appreciation, to place myself in the Anabaptist tradition. Because of what I understand Christian faith to demand, I will continue along a parallel path as an activist: for peace, for justice, for a more equitable sharing of the world's resources, for lifestyles that tread more lightly on the earth. Christians engage in this kind of activism because of our determination to reflect the presence of our risen Lord, who loved mercy and hated injustice. If history cannot be used to speak to agendas such as this, then what on earth is history for?

NOTES

1. John D. Unruh Jr., *The Plains Across: The Overland Emigrants and the Trans-Mississippi West, 1840-60* (Urbana, Ill.: University of Illinois Press, 1979).

2. Harold S. Bender, *The Anabaptist Vision* (Scottdale, Pa.: Herald Press, 1944); and Guy Franklin Hershberger, *War, Peace, and Nonresistance* (Scottdale, Pa.: Herald Press, 1944).

3. One of the first sustained analyses of Mennonite historians creating a usable past is Rodney James Sawatsky, "History and Ideology: American Mennonite Identity Definition Through History" (Ph.D. diss., Princeton University, 1977).

4. I remember this small circle of dissidents consisting of my father, Lew Smedes, Mel White, and the ringleader, a young ethics professor named Jim Morgan. George Marsden has briefly touched on the influence of Jim Morgan at the Fuller Seminary of the 1960s. See George M. Marsden, *Reforming Fundamentalism: Fuller Seminary and the New Evangelicalism* (Grand Rapids, Mich.: Eerdmans, 1987), 254.

5. It was a beautiful home, too, with two stories, four bedrooms, a large yard, and a pool. It is indicative of the extent of white racial fears to note that my parents were able to buy it for a relative pittance. As it turned out, after a few years the racial hysteria subsided. Baby boomers hit their prime home-buying years, southern California real estate prices shot skyward, and my folks made a fair pile of money from the house. One cannot usually count on such a direct pecuniary benefit ensuing from a stand for conscience, but it's nice when it happens.

6. Ronald J. Sider, *Rich Christians in an Age of Hunger: A Biblical Study* (Downers Grove, Ill.: InterVarsity Press, 1977).

7. I was cognizant then, as I am now, that evangelical Christians ranged across the political spectrum and that the Moral Majority did not fully represent the complexity of evangelical political thought. There were, of course, a wide number of non-Anabaptist evangelicals who were chagrined by the rise of the religious right (indeed, it was precisely such people who had raised me). At the same time, there seems little denying, then or now, a clear political trend. Evangelicals rather convincingly swung to the Republican Party in the 1980 elections and have continued to support the party of Reagan with their votes. So central have evangelicals become to Republican political success that they have become a kind of "base vote" for the Republican Party, its political foundation from which it reaches out to other voters in an attempt to broaden its political coalition. See Richard V. Pierard's "Cacophony on Capitol Hill: Evangelical Voices in Politics" and Michael Johnston's "The 'New Christian Right' in American Politics," both in *The Political Role of Religion in the United States*, ed. Stephen D. Johnson and Joseph B. Tamney (Boulder, Colo.: Westview

Press, 1986), 72, 132-33, and Albert J. Menendez, *Evangelicals at the Ballot Box* (Amherst, N.Y.: Prometheus Books, 1996).

8. See, for example, Nathan O. Hatch, *The Democratization of American Christianity* (New Haven, Conn.: Yale University Press, 1989), 49-113, and William R. Sutton, *Journeymen for Jesus: Evangelical Artisans Confront Capitalism in Jacksonian Baltimore* (University Park, Pa.: Pennsylvania State University Press, 1998).

9. "The Christian Witness to the State: A Declaration of Christian Purpose and Commitment," adopted by the Mennonite General Conference, Johnstown, Pa., August 23, 1961.

10. See Perry Bush, "Military Service, Religious Faith, and Acculturation: Mennonite G.I.s and Their Church, 1941-1945," *Mennonite Quarterly Review* 67 (1993): 261-82.

11. John Richard Burkholder and Calvin Redekop, ed., *Kingdom, Cross, and Community: Essays on Mennonite Themes in Honor of Guy F. Hershberger* (Scottdale, Pa.: Herald Press, 1976).

12. Perry Bush, *Two Kingdoms, Two Loyalties: Mennonite Pacifism in Modern America* (Baltimore, Md.: Johns Hopkins University Press, 1998).

13. Perry Bush, *Dancing with the Kobzar: Bluffton College and Mennonite Higher Education, 1899-1999* (Telford, Pa.: Pandora Press U.S., 2000).

14. See Perry Bush, "Can Martin Luther King Be Rescued from the Taming of Pop Culture?" *Gospel Herald*, January 20, 1998, 1-3.

15. See John Howard Yoder, "The Burden and the Discipline of Evangelical Revisionism," in *Nonviolent America: History through the Eyes of Peace*, ed. Louise Hawkley and James C. Juhnke (North Newton, Kan.: Bethel College, 1993), 21-37; James C. Juhnke and Carol M. Hunter, *The Missing Peace: The Search for Nonviolent Alternatives in United States History* (Kitchener, Ont.: Pandora Press, 2001).

16. For a brief summary of this conceptualization, see *Two Kingdoms, Two Loyalties*, 13-19.

17. See Perry Bush, "Economic Justice and the Evangelical Historian," *Fides et Historia* 23 (2001): 11-27.

18. Treatments of postmodernism that I have found to be helpful include Anna Green and Kathleen Troup, "The Challenges of Poststructuralism/Postmodernism," and Judith Walkowitz, "Science and the Séance: Transgressions of Gender and Genre," both in *The Houses of History: A Critical Reader in Twentieth-Century History and Theory*, ed. Anna Green and Kathleen Troup (New York: New York University Press, 1999), 297-325, and J. Denny Weaver, *Anabaptist Theology in the Face of Postmodernity: A Proposal for the Third Millennium* (Telford, Pa.: Pandora Press U.S., 2000), 17-48.

5: Music

Professing the Question

David L. Mosley

My mouth shall speak of wisdom;
And the meditation of my heart shall be of understanding.
I will incline mine ear to a parable:
I will open my dark saying upon the harp.—Psalm 49: 3-4 (KJV)

In his *Republic* Plato claims that only two activities are necessary for the education of young men: gymnastics and music. Of course, Plato and his fellow Greeks understood these disciplines in a far broader way than they are presently construed. While gymnastics involved physical training and athletic competitions (including contests that survive in our summer Olympics), they also involved attention to posture, disciplined breathing, and grace in movement—perhaps not unlike the ideas behind *tai chi*. Music, or *mousike* (literally, having to do with the Muses in ancient Greek), referred to the verbal recitation of poetry accompanied by performance on the lyre and sometimes by dancing. But the study of music also included the manipulation of numbers and the investigation of the heavens, inasmuch as the ancient Greeks assumed human music to be analogous, albeit inferior, to the expression of the celestial music of the planets—the "music of the spheres."

While my own early education in the Louisville, Kentucky, public schools bore little resemblance to life in Plato's academy, the things that disciplined my youth were nevertheless music and gymnastics—or, to be more precise, the French horn and football. As I reflect upon these activities and their subsequent influence on my career, I realize that the rehearsal room and practice field taught me much about striving with others toward a common goal. These disciplines fostered in me respect for hard work and a sense of responsibility for more than just myself.

Also obvious to me now is that my participation in both music and athletics insured I would never be fully at home in either context. After all, what self-respecting jock gets up early on Saturday morning following Friday night's game to rehearse a Mozart symphony with the civic youth orchestra? And what serious young musician continues to compromise his future as a performer after suffering broken hands and smashed fingers?

Needless to say, my friends did not understand, and my coaches and conductors were even more incredulous. While I was an active participant in both worlds I remained something of an outsider in each, and as an outsider I soon took up the position of observer. This combination of standing in the middle and watching is one I still occupy today as a scholar who works across disciplines, as a professor who teaches in more than one department, and as a nonethnic Mennonite who teaches at Goshen College.

A Question Posed

The other event that shaped my adolescence and echoes—sometimes deafeningly—through my adult life was my involvement in the charismatic Christian movement of the late 1960s and early 1970s. While there is much to be said for a Christianity that emphasizes exuberance and jubilation in the Lord, I experienced a dark side of the charismatic movement. Focused as it is upon the gifts of the Holy Spirit as outlined in 1 Corinthians 12, a charismatic faith places a premium on outward manifestations of God's presence in one's life. As a youngster of ten I was initially puzzled by the ecstatic states I witnessed, and before long I felt guilty that I did not have them myself. Soon I began to manufacture them to gain acceptance and approval from family and friends, the result being that I eventually grew cynical about their very integrity—and my own.

At the heart of the charismatic Christianity to which I was exposed is the doctrine of conversion, a public surrender of one's self to Jesus in a moment of extreme emotionality, after which one's life is never to be the same. As I recall the sermons and altar calls of my adolescence, the waving of arms and the speaking in tongues, I also relive the guilt, the pressure, the anxiety, and the seeming sham of it all. Most of all I recall the shame I felt then (and still feel today) because I allowed myself to be coerced into conversion. This is the first time I have written about this experience; the words come slowly and the self-examination is close to crippling.

A great irony in all this is that my own words—words that were misunderstood—initiated my parents' involvement in the charismatic movement. When a traveling evangelist came to our church, I was struck by how frequently she used the word *Jesus* in her sermons and in her conversations. At the dinner table the night after the first service, I innocently asked, "Why does Mrs. _____ use the word *Jesus* so much?"

What I was expressing was simply surprise at the frequency of this word in her speech. What my parents heard was a call to reorient their lives and the life of our family.

For many years I succeeded in avoiding any reflection upon this period of my life. Indeed, it passed quickly enough and within five or six years my parents returned to a spirituality that is still central to their identity but is no longer expressed in terms of charismatic worship and the doctrine of conversion. I am convinced, however, that the questions posed by this time—questions about the efficacy of language, the nature of the relationship between the significance of words and their articulation, and the whole idea of ecstatic utterance—not only shape my identity as a person of faith but also my work as a professor and scholar.

So as not to paint a picture of victimization (which is not my intent) nor to suggest an atmosphere of unresolved antagonism between my parents and me (which is not the case), I also wish to emphasize two of the many areas in which my childhood and adolescence were positively shaped by my home life and its general atmosphere.

My mother was, and is, a consummately skilled church musician. She is an excellent organist with a knowledge and mastery of much of the instrument's vast repertoire. She is also an inspiring choral conductor with a particular gift for working with children's voices. The worship experiences she plans are theologically sound and aesthetically coherent.

Since all of this and more is demanded of our church musicians on a weekly basis, we must never take them for granted. The rich musical environment in which I grew up, both at home and in the church, likely had as much influence on my developing musicianship and musical understanding as did my excellent experiences in school, in private study, and in the civic youth orchestra.

While my mother created an environment in which my musicianship could flourish, my father, a physician who regularly worked sixty-hour weeks, also made significant contributions. One specific instance, I believe, is quite telling.

As a football player and child of the 1960s and 1970s, I sometimes watched games on television. More than that, I read about the game—its strategy, its history, and its great players. And sometimes I listened on the radio. One Saturday afternoon my father showed me a way to map the various plays of the game on a single sheet of paper for each quarter. It involved laying out the "field" on the page and then graphing, by means of various kinds of lines, the different "plays" of the game.

I was immediately fascinated. I could both track the plays successively, in time, and see the entire fifteen-minute quarter synoptically, at a single glance. There is no doubt that my subsequent fascination with structuralist modes of inquiry—which involve mapping cultural and aesthetic expressions in terms of *syntagma* and *paradigm*—grew directly from this single experience.

By the time I entered Vanderbilt University two knee operations had curtailed most of my athletic activity, and I embarked upon an interdisciplinary degree in literature and music, a degree devoted to words and sounds. Once again, I had placed myself in a position between two disciplines; I studied in two departments, fully at home in neither. I then earned a master's degree in music performance from the Eastman School of Music and a doctoral degree from Emory University's Graduate Institute of the Liberal Arts, where I again worked along interdisciplinary lines in the fields of literature, musicology, and philosophy.

In all these years of school I was constantly looking at the relationship between music and language, that complex interrelationship between sound and sense involved in any verbal human expression. I had turned the spiritual and existential quandaries of my childhood into the academic questions of my young adulthood: the potential inherent in language for *misprision* (i.e., the separation that sometimes exists between the sound of words and their meaning), the conundrum of speaking in tongues, and the phenomenon of ecstatic utterance as embodied in music and especially expressed in song.

All of my reading and writing were devoted to teasing apart the seemingly symbiotic relationship between the sound of words and their meaning in poetry and song. Yet instead of answering my question, this work was leading me further away from any real resolution of the matter. At the same time, a rather troubling darkness was beginning to cast its shadow.

The Silence of Sheol

The theoretical framework I discovered in graduate school and have used in subsequent scholarly work is known as *semiotics*, or the theory of signs. Semiotics is based upon an approach to language that separates the sounds of words from their meanings. As described by Ferdinand Saussure and Charles Sanders Peirce, this theory of words as signs claims there is no necessary relationship between a word, or phoneme, say <tree>, and that thing that grows in the ground possessing roots, a trunk, branches, and leaves.

This, of course, is not a new idea. Philosophers of language since Plato have debated the nature of signs and the seemingly arbitrary relationship between words and the meaning assigned to them. Still, the developments in semiology, and the limits to which such brilliant scholars as Umberto Eco and Jacques Derrida have pushed it, have important, and sometimes daunting, implications. For it is one thing to claim that the relationship between words and their significance is arbitrary and founded on convention; it is entirely another to call into question the efficacy of language itself, to reduce its status from that which makes us human to a game in which one competitor tries to outwit and out-maneuver another, as if in a contest.

The Frenchman Jacques Derrida plays an especially insidious game with the language of texts. In his work *Of Grammatology* Derrida insists that all texts are based upon the specious notion that language is capable of communicating in univocal fashion, thereby conveying a singular meaning or presence.[1]

Derrida's theory of "deconstruction" is an effort to show that this assumption of *presence* in language is in fact based upon an *absence* of unequivocal meaning. In short, there is a false foundation beneath every expression and, if one is clever enough, the weak spot in the foundation can be probed and prodded until the text eventually comes tumbling down under the weight of its own incorrect assumptions. Derrida calls this weak place in the foundation, this assumed presence which is really an absence, an *aporia*—a Greek term meaning "opening."[2]

As a method of literary criticism, deconstruction is capable of teaching us things about texts that we might not otherwise discover. Indeed, it has provided a wonderful rationale for a whole generation of scholars to revisit canonical works already possessing long pedigrees of explication and write about them all over again with a "new and improved" scholarly apparatus. But while it is hard to deny the fruitfulness of this endeavor, the effect it had on me during this time was not a happy one.

Soon after the publication of my dissertation I began to experience periods of decreased energy, feelings of anxiety and hopelessness, and most troubling of all, the inability to comprehend more than a paragraph of what I was reading for more than two or three minutes. I had difficulty formulating sentences, and it seemed the words I needed were locked behind a door to which I had no key. I had frequent dreams in which I, or more often persons I cared for, were in danger. If I could only speak they would be saved. In the dream I would often struggle mightily, yet no words would come. I would awaken from the dream, sometimes with my jaw clamped tightly shut, sometimes screaming. These periods would eventually pass and I would return to reading and writing as before.

I know now that, clinically speaking, I was experiencing symptoms of depression. What I am still learning is that I was also entering into the wasteland, an area of existence devoid of significance, an area in which the soul itself experiences utter silence and destitution. Authors from Dante to William Styron have written about this experience eloquently, and sometimes romantically. Mythologically speaking, it is the wasteland Parsifal must enter and conquer in his quest for the Holy Grail. Yet my experience had no romance associated with it. Indeed the word *romance* is derived from an old French term meaning story, and there seemed absolutely nothing that could be turned into a story from my time in the aporetic wasteland.

I now understand this time not only in terms of psychology and brain chemistry, but also in terms of spirituality. I had fallen into what the Old Testament calls *Sheol*, a place beneath this world, a realm marked by silence. I also understand that my experience of voicelessness was directly related to my attempts to avoid the questions of my youth. My efforts to escape the horns of the dilemma with respect to words and their articulation took the form of analysis, speculation, and intellectual activity as it treated music on the page. I managed to ignore the fact that these musical texts had life only when they were embodied in time, given both voice and a presence.

There was nothing wrong with my approach in and of itself, but with respect to my soul and its question about meaning, I made little headway. I spent my time teasing apart the complex tangle of words and sounds in the song compositions of Franz Schubert, Robert Schumann, and Gustav Mahler, in the poetry and prose of James Joyce and Dylan Thomas, and in the philosophical works of Friedrich Nietzsche. While this work was fascinating and fruitful, I was doing nothing to restore the wholeness of the Logos, the Word made flesh. I was doing nothing to seek out the Word that saves us from the aporia, the opening that can lead to meaninglessness.

The Abyss as Means or End

Of course, Jacques Derrida was not the first person to employ the term *aporia*. Indeed, the use of the term is as old as Western philosophy itself and was first used in descriptions of Socrates's method of teaching.

Socrates described himself as a "gadfly," pestering people with questions to make them reassess their inherited ideas about what constituted a good or virtuous life: truth, beauty, and goodness. Using his famous "Socratic method," Socrates would pose to his listener a question that encouraged the listener to state his or her understanding of one of life's essential ideas. Socrates would then begin to question his listener's definition and, after a sustained dialogue, these questions would start to lay bare the misunderstanding of his conversation partner.

At the point the one being questioned realized the error in his or her beliefs, Socrates succeeded in inducing the state of aporia, meaning the recognition of ignorance, of an opening into which wisdom might enter.[3] Importantly, Socrates would not then provide his answers or attempt to impart his knowledge to his conversation partner, for he believed that it was in this aporetic state that the person's *soul* might speak to him or her.

Of course, Socrates's use of aporia was far different from its employment by Derrida. For whereas deconstruction takes the exposure of the aporia (or absence) in a text as the *end* of the process, Socrates employed the inducement of a state of aporia as a *means to an end*—the admission of ignorance that is the first step toward understanding.

So as not to be misunderstood, semiotics, structuralism, and deconstruction were not the cause of my entrance into the abyss. They were simply the wrong ideas at that time. Nor am I at all interested in psychologizing my situation and blaming my family, my church, or the charismatic movement. I am not the victim in this story; rather, I have been blessed with the gift of a sustaining question by which to orient the life of my soul and the life of my mind. Indeed, my question about meaning invites, even demands, that I continuously strive toward the integration of my spiritual quest with my vocation.

Professing the Question

Curiously, and sometimes maddeningly, little of my difficulty manifested itself at work. I may have been more or less taciturn, more or less eloquent in my lectures, but I was nonetheless granted the grace to teach, to make music, and to interact in meaningful ways with my students and colleagues.

I refer to this state of affairs as grace-filled because I have come to see that the way I live my question is the very essence of my vocation as a professor, especially at a church-related liberal arts college. While my scholarly work may not always translate directly into the classroom, my constant reading and writing insures that I understand the question about language, meaning, and its embodiment more fully. And because of a sustained dialogue about these questions with colleagues outside of my own institution, I am able to interact with my students in a more informed, coherent, and articulate fashion.

It is my contention that the role of the professor/scholar in a church-related institution of higher education is to model the manner in which questions can become the basis for a way of life. By living with the questions and submitting to their discipline, we show students ways they might make their own quandaries the basis for life of both mind and soul. By living with the questions we can make the questions themselves holy, or, as Karlfried Dürckheim puts it, "transparent to transcendence."[4] By contemplating the questions, literally bringing them before God in the temple, they inform both our pedagogy and our scholarly activity, and we can make of them a source of wisdom.

The 1896-97 catalogue for the Elkhart Institute, the institution that was soon to become Goshen College, contains a statement that I have found to be quite instructive in this regard. The mission statement reads, in part, that the aim of the Elkhart Institute is "to aid the young mind in attaining wisdom, without which knowledge fails to be a blessing." Indeed, wisdom is the goal.

Embodied Answers

Recent years have allowed me to explore a new kind of embodied scholarship in the form of conducting. Although I came to the activity with real misgivings (as a professional hornist I had spent twenty-some years sitting in the back of orchestras complaining about conductors), the wisdom of my wife, along with her endless encouragement, convinced me that this was an opportunity worth exploring.

I would argue that my work as a conductor, or the work of any performer or composer in an educational setting, constitutes a kind of *embodied* scholarship. The time spent bringing one's performance skills to bear upon a musical text leads to a kind of physical understanding and acquisition of the work. Like most conductors, I spend many more hours analyzing and preparing a score, testing different tempos, and experimenting with gestures than I do rehearsing it or conducting it in a performance. I have discovered that I cannot fully comprehend the music or successfully communicate it to the performers without this intense physical involvement.

The role of the body in understanding ourselves and our world is the topic of a recent book, *Philosophy in the Flesh: The Embodied Mind and its Challenge to Western Thought.* Authors George Lakoff and Mark Johnson claim that human reason "is inextricably tied to our bodies and the peculiarities of our brains," and they continue to argue that our entire understanding of reality "begins with and crucially depends on our bodies."[5] My time spent in analysis, research, and reflection on musical texts is a form of scholarly activity that results, not primarily in conference papers and published articles, but in a creative activity that involves the whole person—the intellect, the emotions, and the body. Moreover, this creative activity depends upon a meaningful interaction with a community—the audience. As I often tell my ensembles, this kind of inspired and expressive music-making can be a form of service.

There are two narratives, one from Greek mythology and one from the Old Testament, that offer similar explanations of what I believe to be the essential wisdom of music. More than that, they provide answers to my own questions about language, the relationship between words and their articulation, and the idea of ecstatic utterance.

In Greek mythology, Orpheus, son of the muse Calliope, is able to give form to the otherwise chaotic emotional experience of the human being by means of singing and playing the lyre. Within the Judeo-Christian tradition, David is similarly able to sooth the troubled soul of Saul, likewise by the integration of words and music embodied in performance. It is this power of music to create order and significance out of what is seemingly inchoate and meaningless that I care about most and attempt to convey to my students.

Susanne Langer writes insightfully about this aspect of music in her book, *Philosophy in a New Key*. "Music is not self-expression," writes Langer, "but *formulation* and *representation* of emotions, moods, mental tensions and resolutions—a 'logical picture' of sentient, responsive life, a source of insight.... Not communication but insight is the gift of music; in a very naive phrase, knowledge of 'how feelings go'.... Music is our myth of the inner life."[6] Though it was first published nearly sixty years ago, Langer's book remains the best explanation of the meaning of music and its significance that I have found.

The wisdom of music as source of insight and the true significance of ecstatic utterance have coalesced for me when singing the Psalms. When I sing Psalm 141 slowly—"Lord, I cry unto thee: make haste unto me; give ear unto my voice..."; when I sing aware of the inspiration and exhalation of breath singing involves—"Let my prayer be set forth before thee as incense; and the lifting up of my hands as the evening sacrifice..."; when I pay attention to diction and the movement of my mouth—"Set a watch, O Lord, before my mouth; keep the door of my lips. Incline not my heart to any evil thing..."; and when I recall that by singing this psalm in this manner I enter into communion with all those who have sung the Psalms since the days of ancient Israel—"O God, the Lord: in thee is my trust; leave not my soul destitute...."—the experience is a balm for my soul (Psalm 141:1-4a, 8, KJV).

There was no room for such a song of supplication in the charismatic movement of my adolescence. Neither is there room for it (nor for the other psalms of lament and desperation) in today's contemporary Christian music. When lamentation and supplication are eliminated from worship, an essential movement of the soul is sealed off.

The sound of words and their meaning have come into correspondence for me when I have had the opportunity to sing the Lord's Prayer in communion with others in a high-ceilinged room. At these times I am no longer aware of my own individual voice, but rather of the one voice into which it is absorbed. These have been times of grace and healing. At these times I am no longer a spectator, nor even an individual, but in some very physical and spirit-filled sense I am connected to the song and to my soul.

The singing of "psalms and hymns and spiritual songs" (Eph. 5:19) allows me to experience sacred language in the fullest sense. This embodied experience of ecstatic utterance places me outside quotidian reality and its concerns. Indeed, it allows me to stand outside myself—which is the literal meaning of ecstasy—and at the same time brings my mind, my body, and my spirit into closer communion with God. Walter Ong, a brilliant Jesuit scholar, writes with both authority and insight about this kind of experience in his *Orality and Literacy*: "Because in its physical constitution as sound, the spoken word proceeds from the human interior and manifests human beings to one another as conscious interiors, as persons, the spoken word forms human beings into close-knit groups."[7]

These close-knit groups of individuals relating to one another as conscious interiors is, for me, an admittedly abstract but nevertheless compelling description of what the church might be: people called together by the incarnate Word and living life, both individually and as a community, in conformity to its discipline. Ong continues, "The spoken word is always an event, a movement in time, completely lacking in the thing-like repose of the written or printed word. . . . God the Father speaks his Son: he does not inscribe him. Jesus, the Word of God, left nothing in writing."[8] Our conformity to the incarnate Word "spoken" into existence by God has to do both with our efforts to hear that Word—to comprehend its meaning for our world—and to attune our lives, day by day, to its resonance.

Notes

1. Jacques Derrida, *Of Grammatology*, trans. Gayatri Chakravorty Spivak (Baltimore, Md.: Johns Hopkins University Press, 1976).

2. Some may see my summary of Derrida's deconstructive method as lacking nuance, and they may be right. But it is precisely because of deconstruction's tendency

to submit texts and their meaning to labyrinthine interrogation that their presence and ability to speak univocally to the reader is undermined.

3. Frederick A. G. Beck, *Greek Education, 450-350 B.C.* (New York: Barnes and Noble, 1964), 193.

4. Alphonse Goettmann, *Dialogue on the Path of Initiation: The Life and Thought of Karlfried Graf Dürckheim*, trans. Theodore and Rebecca Nottingham (Nottingham Electronic Publishing, 1998), 40.

5. George Lakoff and Mark Johnson, *Philosophy in the Flesh: The Embodied Mind and its Challenge to Western Thought* (New York: Basic Books, 1999), 17.

6. Susanne Langer, *Philosophy in a New Key: A Study in the Symbolism of Reason, Rite, and Art* (Cambridge, Mass.: Harvard University Press, 1942) 222, 244-45. The emphases are Langer's.

7. Walter Ong, *Orality and Literacy: The Technologizing of the Word* (New York and London: Methuen, 1982), 74.

8. Ibid., 75.

6: Sociology

Select Your Mother Carefully: Reflections on a Sociological Journey

Donald B. Kraybill

As A SOCIOLOGIST WHO CONTENDS THAT ideas and behavior are shaped by social forces, I naturally assume that scholars, despite their professional training, are not immune to social influences. In other words, scholarship is always biographical, reflecting in various ways the experiences and values of the scholar.

While this seems rather obvious to me, it is nevertheless true that scholarship sometimes appears to be cloaked in neutrality and cool objectivity. It is not. My own scholarship has been shaped by my social context, more specifically, by the ferment created by crisscrossing social forces: I was a Cold War American raised in a peace church; I was a white, Pennsylvania German farm boy studying sociology at an urban university in a largely African-American community; I was a pastor preaching the importance of sacred authorities and divine revelation while learning about the social construction of beliefs and behavior.

Born a few weeks after atomic bombs leveled Hiroshima and Nagasaki, I grew up on this side of the nuclear divide. As a child of the Cold War, I remember crawling into my mother's bed in the early 1950s because of nightmares in which Russians were coming down our street to take us away. I graduated from high school in 1963 and was in college during the Civil Rights Movement, Vietnam War protests, and all the other social turbulence of the 1960s. The Cold War rhetoric that sliced the world into two camps and the social upheaval of the Sixties persuaded me that the peacemaking message of the Mennonite Church was both relevant and timely.

Sectarian Ferment

I grew up in a Mennonite family in Lancaster County, Pennsylvania, during a time of rapid social change. The Mennonite community of my childhood embodied what sociologists call a "sectarian" subculture—a community that draws sharp lines between itself and the larger society to ward off contaminating influences and unwanted values.

As a sectarian culture, the Mennonite Church in eastern Pennsylvania exhibited firm behavioral expectations in the 1950s, many (though not all) related to dress. Women could not cut their hair, and young couples who wore wedding rings were chastised by the church. Televison was strictly forbidden; indeed, its nonuse was a condition of church membership. Musical instruments were not permitted in worship services, higher education was suspect, and practicing law was considered unbecoming for a disciple of Christ. Although many of these traditional boundaries were crumbling as I came of age—a result of urbanization, industrialization, higher education, and the experience of young Mennonites in Civilian Public Service during World War II—they nonetheless forged my world view, especially my understanding of the relationship between the church and the larger society.

In retrospect, it is not insignificant that many traditional Mennonite ideas and practices were in flux as I grew to adulthood. Some of these challenges to tradition resulted in long, passionate debates over issues that outsiders might have considered trivial. Could men wear long, "worldly" ties, should they keep the traditional bow tie, or should they wear no ties at all? (This issue was not at all trivial to me: I remember my father calling me back into the house one evening as I headed out the door and insisting that I remove the long tie that I was wearing without his permission.)

Other changes were less controversial but, in the long run, no less consequential. Indeed, the most sweeping change then underway in my community was the demise of our agricultural social base. Within three generations, the percentage of farming households in my extended family plummeted from 100 percent to 3.7 percent. All of my uncles and aunts grew up on a farm, but only one of their twenty-seven combined children (i.e., my cousins) became involved in farming. While I was the first in my extended family to pursue higher education and receive a Ph.D., many of my cousins soon became involved in higher education and, instead of staying home on the farm, scattered around the globe.

Coming of age in a sectarian context that was undergoing rapid social change no doubt stirred my sociological sensitivities and curiosity. Indeed, such ferment often produces sociologists in ethnic and minority groups, for members of such groups soon develop an acute awareness of group boundaries, social change, and the power relations between majority and minority groups. As a result of these sensitivities, groups on society's margins—Jews, African-Americans, and Hispanics, for example—have long produced a disproportionate number of social scientists. The same can be said for Mennonites, of which I am just one example.

But beyond the impetus provided by its sectarianism, the Mennonite Church molded my convictions, views, and even my career choices in numerous other ways. In high school I joined the Future Farmers of America with the plan of studying dairy husbandry at Penn State University. However, sometime during my senior year at Lancaster Mennonite High School, my Bible doctrine teacher (a local Mennonite bishop) urged me to consider "helping people rather than milking cows." I took his advice seriously and consequently entered Millersville State College (now Millersville University), hoping to learn how to help people as a way of expressing my Christian convictions. For despite all the heated discussions about coverings, long ties, and plain suits, I had been deeply touched by many caring people in the church. I had learned to love the church and wanted to serve God through its ministries.

Eager to serve others, I decided to study social work at Millersville—a course of study that required some sociology courses as prerequisites. I soon got hooked on sociology because, for the first time in my life, I discovered a battery of concepts—culture, assimilation, norms, conflict, ethnic group, and social change—that helped me to understand myself, my people, and all the social changes that had engulfed my Mennonite community in the late 1950s and early 1960s.

My fascination with social science flourished even more when, after two years, I transferred to Eastern Mennonite College (now University) and completed a double major in theology and sociology. The intersection of theological and sociological studies stirred my imagination and piqued my curiosity, and it continues to do so today. At Eastern Mennonite I received my first exposure to Anabaptist history and theology, both of which helped me to understand my religious heritage and its values from a broader historical and international perspective. Until that time my religious consciousness had primarily been shaped by my experience in two Mennonite congregations, both in Lancaster County. Now for the first time I discovered Anabaptist scholarship and serious scholars working in the context of the church.

My interest and appreciation for the church continued to grow, and after graduating from Eastern Mennonite I returned to Lancaster County to work as a director of Mennonite Voluntary Service. Before long I was ordained as an assistant pastor in a nearby Mennonite congregation, but my vocational pursuits would soon take me elsewhere.

The Social Construction of Reality

After three years of administrative work I was eager for new intellectual challenges. Without precise vocational goals, I decided to study social science to learn more about social and organizational behavior, entering a Ph.D. program at Temple University. Still, I continued to serve as a part-time pastor. I soon found myself reading Marx and Weber on the train during my daily commutes to Philadelphia, and reading Jesus on Saturday nights in preparation for my sermons the next morning.

Eventually, the intellectual gulf became too wide and the work of pastoring amid a Ph.D. program too demanding, so I decided to concentrate all of my efforts on my graduate studies. I served as a research assistant to John A. Hostetler, then the leading scholar of Amish and Hutterite societies. This experience introduced me to the scholarly study of Anabaptist communities which eventually became a focus of my research and writing.

In graduate school Peter Berger had the most important influence on my intellectual development. Berger's book *The Social Construction of Reality* (1966), which he co-authored with Thomas Luckmann, helped me to understand that human beliefs, values, and perceptions are socially constructed in the course of human interaction.[1]

I read and reread *The Social Construction of Reality*; it had a profound impact on how I understood everything, including my faith. Clearly more than any other thinker Berger helped me to see the world in a new and entirely different way. Because of his religious background, he too was struggling with how to reconcile his faith commitments with sociological realities, and I sensed an affinity with his spirit. I conversed with him only once, for three minutes in an elevator at a professional conference, but his writings changed the way I came to view virtually everything in the world.

Grasping the radical implications of the socially constructed character of human beliefs created an intellectual crisis for me that, interestingly, took me back to the root of my Christian faith—Jesus. Viewing beliefs as constructs of social interaction weakened some of the revelatory legitimacy of doctrinal understandings (of Christ, the Trinity, heaven, hell, etc.), for according to the sociology of knowledge, human understandings—whether religious, political, or social—reflect the social, economic, and political interests of particular communities and are sustained to the extent they remain plausible amid changing social settings.

If this was true (and I believed it was), could we be sure of anything? That question led me back to Jesus. Despite all the scholarly debates about which of his sayings were genuine and which details of his life were trustworthy, the historical evidence was rather clear and uncontested: there was such a person who lived and was crucified in Palestine. In the jargon of sociology, the reality of God had been operationalized in an empirical form, a historical person.

Returning to Jesus through Berger, I found myself in company with the early Anabaptists, who had taken Jesus seriously as they sought to follow him in life. About the same time, in the mid-1970s, I was reading John Howard Yoder's *The Politics of Jesus* and discovered that he too was exploring the social and political consequences of the life and teachings of Jesus.[2]

The confluence of these factors—sociology, Berger, Yoder, and Jesus—led to my writing *The Upside-Down Kingdom*, a sociologically informed reading of the synoptic gospels.[3] In writing the book I was trying to interpret Jesus from an Anabaptist perspective by using the tools of sociology; I was also hoping to translate Yoder into everyday language. *The Upside-Down Kingdom* did not break any new ground in terms of New Testament scholarship; rather, it was a creative interpretation of the synoptic gospels through sociological lenses. And, of course, it was also a sermon! To my surprise, it received a warm welcome from a wide audience far beyond Anabaptist circles and continues to be read in its third edition.

Beyond Berger I have also been shaped by Max Weber's "radical perspectivism."[4] Simply put, how we see and interpret the world is profoundly shaped by our socioeconomic location. Our social context, in other words, frames and filters our view of reality.

Students, faculty, administrators, and janitors all view a college from different perspectives. More generally, upper- and lower-class persons, whites and Latinos, men and women, Amish and Catholics see the world and interpret the same events through very different lenses. Social context and location color our perceptions of reality—not only our perceived reality, but our scholarship as well. As David Weaver-Zercher notes in his introduction to this volume, all scholarship is shaped by interests of many types, and it is also "interested." Thanks to the contributions of postmodern theorists, the days of positivism and feigned neutrality are gone.

Intriguing Questions

Shaped by my own experiences, my work has explored several key questions from several different angles: What is the relation between the church and the larger society, between the culture of the church and mass culture, and between subgroups and the dominant society? How do groups create symbolic boundaries and manage them to deter assimilation—that is, to prevent being swallowed up by the larger society? This focus on intergroup relations and cultural subgroups within mass society likely reflects my formative experience growing up in a Mennonite subculture that was undergoing rapid social change.

Another theme that has occupied my attention has been the relationship of the individual to the collectivity; for instance, how are individual rights appropriately balanced with collective concerns without suffocating the individual? A related issue is the extent to which social behavior results from individual autonomy or, on the other hand, is produced by social and cultural forces that go unnoticed. These themes, while important for any society, likely loom large on my screen because they were key issues in the church during my formative years. Additionally, how much control is appropriate for the church to exercise over the individual? If individualism runs rampant, will it become cancerous for the common good—not only in the church but in the larger society as well?

A third persistent theme in my work is how the beliefs of a group are constructed, how they change, and how groups are able to persuade their members to adopt the group's corporate creed. Berger talks of "plausibility structures," the patterns of social organization that lend credibility to a particular set of beliefs.[5] I am particularly interested in how meaning is constructed through social interaction and how it attains credibility. The bulk of my most recent work is indebted to the "sociology of culture," which seeks to understand how cultural values, symbols, beliefs, and practices are created by human communities, and how symbolic codes and their meanings are reconstructed and preserved over time. Robert Wuthnow's work in the sociology of religion and Robert Bellah's writing on community—especially his *Habits of the Heart*—have influenced my understandings of religious communities.[6]

More recently I have become interested in ritual activities and the way in which ritual formulas organize human behavior, reinforce boundaries, and reaffirm beliefs. Again, my interest in ritual has surely been cultivated by my experiences with ritual in the life of the church, e.g., footwashing and communion. In all of these ways the intellectual questions and research topics that I have explored have been driven, often implicitly, by the cultural and religious perspectives that shaped my worldview as an Anabaptist Christian. In short, my scholarly interests, the topics I select, and the way I study and interpret them have clearly been molded by the values bestowed upon me by the church and my participation in it.

Research Agenda

The values of the Christian faith and the heritage of Anabaptism have clearly funneled my scholarly interests and perspectives in many ways—from the topics I study to how I interpret the data I gather. As a scholar, I have always felt supported by the church and have never experienced any churchly restraints on my work, at least in any official way. Similarly, I have never experienced any constraint from officials at the colleges where I have taught. Still, I have constantly been aware that addressing certain topics would carry political risks both within the church and beyond. I have therefore often considered the political impact of a given research topic before proceeding, but any constraints were self-imposed by my own assessment of risk.

My scholarship has never followed a systematic plan. The projects that I undertake change as new issues arise and as I develop new interests. In retrospect, my work can be placed into three basic categories: (1) books that sought to help the church more effectively engage the broader culture; (2) books that enabled church members in Anabaptist churches to better understand their own heritage; (3) books that aided persons outside of Anabaptist circles to understand Anabaptist peoples and their practices, most of which included an indirect critique of the dominant North American culture. I've selected an illustrative book in each of the three categories for brief comments.

One of my early books that aided the church in engaging the broader culture was *Facing Nuclear War*.[7] This text, which provided an assessment of the nuclear threat and suggested possible Christian responses, was primarily addressed to Christians within the Anabaptist tradition and focused on a major issue that I wrestled with personally in the early 1980s. Rather than breaking new scholarly ground, *Facing Nuclear War* sought to motivate Christians to act in the face of a possible nuclear holocaust.

I would place *The Upside-Down Kingdom* in the second category—that is, as a book that helped Anabaptists to better understand their own heritage.[8] Although *The Upside-Down Kingdom* enjoyed broad circulation beyond Anabaptist circles, it served to remind church members how Anabaptists read Scripture and to consider some of the implications of taking Jesus' life and witness seriously.

Amish Gatekeeping

My books on Amish society fall into the third category above, for they interpret Amish culture to the broader public (and, secondarily, to scholars of Anabaptist societies). In these works I have tried to interpret Amish values and practices from within the culture and history of Amish society.

The Riddle of Amish Culture is the best known of these books.[9] In this and other books I have argued that seemingly odd Old Order practices (e.g., riding in cars but not driving them) are not inconsistent or hypocritical, but are indeed reasonable solutions to issues confronting the Amish. In other words, these and other practices, which are often perplexing to outsiders, have an internal cultural logic that makes sense within the social context and historical framework of Amish culture.

In addition to being a fascinating research topic, the Amish have provided me with a platform to offer a social critique of mass society. In certain ways I have used the Old Orders as a foil to get the attention of outside readers and, once I've gotten their attention, to critique practices and values in contemporary U.S. culture. In *The Riddle of Amish Culture*, the last chapter simulates a dialogue between Amish values and those of mainstream America. Although that short chapter contains a message I really wanted to say all along, the hard research and tedious scholarship that produced the book's first eleven chapters helped earn me the right, so to speak, to engage in cultural criticism of the larger society.

The Amish enable me to speak indirectly about many issues arising from my own Anabaptist convictions—issues related to the integrity of adult baptism, the importance of community and accountability, the balance between individualism and collective welfare, and the role and contribution of a counterculture in mass society. Through my Amish-related research I have also been able to address many issues that have broad relevance for the larger society: the impact of technology on social relations, the role of community in shaping identity, the social sources of happiness and human satisfaction, and the value of tradition.

Although it's difficult to identify all the psycho-cultural forces that pull one toward a particular subject, I suspect that I am largely attracted to the Amish because of my own disenchantment with certain aspects of contemporary culture. The specialization, individualism, and mobility of contemporary life fray the social fabric in ways that fragment human experience and produce discontinuity. Amish social organization, on the other hand, constraining and restrictive as it is, provides a social home characterized by wholeness, stability, and continuity—all of which contribute to human well-being and happiness.

Based on ethnographic observations, not survey data, I believe that Amish people on average are happier than your typical technologically pampered American. And so I am intrigued by these people who have fashioned livable, satisfying communities amid modern America.

My role vis-à-vis the Amish themselves is often a delicate and sensitive one. I have always felt a warm welcome from them, and have been refused an interview only once in fifteen years. Nonetheless, I frequently struggle with two issues in my Amish-related research: Amish "dirty wash" and public "gatekeeping."

How much of their dirty wash should I expose, knowing that it might injure some people? Can I be a responsible scholar if I do not describe and interpret their culture with honesty and integrity? I have access to considerable information about Amish individuals. A perennial question is when and how I reveal information in ways that are accurate but not injurious to Amish individuals or the community as a whole.

I also struggle with my gatekeeping role. Members of the news media frequently ask me for information about and access to Amish persons. How do I supply information that is correct without creating awkward situations for the Amish themselves? And how much access to individual Amish persons should I provide for media representatives?

I have generally not given names of Amish persons to reporters (though on a few occasions I have accompanied reporters to Amish homes). Generally, I have spoken with the press but have not provided them direct access to Amish contacts. Some of this is driven by my desire to shield the Amish from meddlesome reporters. But it is also driven by scholarly self-interest, since my standing within the Amish would quickly diminish if I opened the gate of access to a continuous stream of reporters and cameras. In any event, my research on the Amish often casts me in a sensitive role that requires both wisdom and discretion.

On Humility and Mothers

Because I often take existing information and present it in new and creative ways, I really view myself more as an interpreter, guide, and translator than as a scholar devoted to producing "new knowledge." In any case, I have thoroughly enjoyed my career in sociology because it has offered me freedom to explore a wide variety of topics and questions with a consistent disciplinary focus and orientation. My sociological vocation has allowed me to serve the church in nontraditional ways and has given me ample freedom to address a host of issues.

In addition to the intellectual pleasure of doing research, sociology has also nourished in me a profound sense of humility and empathy. I increasingly appreciate the limits to what we know and how we come to know it. Sociology often underscores the "unintended consequences" of collective action, the fact that despite our best attempts, our glorious rhetoric about planning, and our best strategic decision making, we often cannot anticipate the long-term effects of individual and collective decisions.

Sociology has also taught me humility because I realize that much of who I am has been bestowed upon me by my family and my birthright culture. Peter Berger once remarked that it is important to select one's mother carefully, underlining the powerful impact that our social location at birth plays in our later position in society and our general well-being. My "mother"—my social location at birth—has shaped me in many ways, granting me privileges that many people in this world cannot even imagine.

Weber's radical perspectivism and his emphasis on *verstehen*—sympathetic understanding—have together taught me the importance of trying to grasp how the world looks from diverse social positions, and why various actors come to see the world the way they do. These virtues of the sociological perspective—humility and empathy—coincide with what I understand to be fundamental claims of the Christian gospel as well. And so, happily for me, disciplinary and gospel perspectives complement and enrich one another in profoundly satisfying ways.

Notes

1. Peter L. Berger and Thomas Luckmann, *The Social Construction of Reality: A Treatise in the Sociology of Knowledge* (Garden City, N.Y.: Doubleday, 1966). Among Berger's many other books the following have been formative for my thinking: Peter L. Berger, *The Sacred Canopy: Elements of a Sociological Theory of Religion* (Garden City, N.Y.: Doubleday, 1967); Peter L. Berger, Brigitte Berger, and Hansfried Kellner, *The Homeless Mind: Modernization and Consciousness* (New York: Random House, 1973); Peter L. Berger, *Facing Up to Modernity: Excursions in Society, Politics, and Religion* (New York: Basic Books, 1977); and Peter L. Berger, *The Heretical Imperative: Contemporary Possibilities of Religious Affirmation* (Garden City, N.Y.: Anchor Press, 1979).

2. John Howard Yoder, *The Politics of Jesus* (Grand Rapids, Mich.: Eerdmans, 1972).

3. Donald B. Kraybill, *The Upside-Down Kingdom* (Scottdale, Pa.: Herald Press, 1978, 1990).

4. See Stephen Kalberg, "Max Weber's Types of Rationality: Cornerstones for the Analysis of Rationalization Processes in History," *American Journal of Sociology* 85 (1980): 1145-79.

5. See Berger, *The Sacred Canopy*, 45-47.

6. See Robert Wuthnow, *Producing the Sacred: An Essay on Public Religion* (Urbana, Ill.: University of Illinois Press, 1994); and Robert N. Bellah, et al., *Habits of*

the Heart: Individualism and Commitment in American Life (Berkeley, Calif.: University of California Press, 1985).

7. Donald B. Kraybill, *Facing Nuclear War: A Plea for Christian Witness* (Scottdale, Pa.: Herald Press, 1982). I would also place in this category Donald B. Kraybill, *Our Star-Spangled Faith* (Scottdale, Pa.: Herald Press, 1976) and Donald B. Kraybill and Phyllis Pellman Good, *The Perils of Professionalism: Essays on Christian Faith and Professionalism* (Scottdale, Pa.: Herald Press, 1982).

8. I would also include in this category Donald B. Kraybill, *Mennonite Education: Issues, Facts, and Changes* (Scottdale, Pa.: Herald Press, 1978); Leo Driedger and Donald B. Kraybill, *Mennonite Peacemaking: From Quietism to Activism* (Scottdale, Pa.: Herald Press, 1994); Willard M. Swartley and Donald B. Kraybill, *Building Communities of Compassion: Mennonite Mutual Aid in Theory and Practice* (Scottdale, Pa.: Herald Press, 1998); and Donald B. Kraybill and C. Nelson Hostetter, *Anabaptist World USA* (Scottdale, Pa.: Herald Press, 2001).

9. Donald B. Kraybill, *The Riddle of Amish Culture* (Baltimore, Md.: Johns Hopkins University Press, 1989, 2001). Other books in this category include Donald B. Kraybill, *The Puzzles of Amish Life* (Intercourse, Pa.: Good Books, 1990); Donald B. Kraybill and Marc A. Olshan, ed., *The Amish Struggle with Modernity* (Hanover, N.H.: University Press of New England, 1994); Donald B. Kraybill, ed., *The Amish and the State* (Baltimore, Md.: Johns Hopkins University Press, 1993); Donald B. Kraybill and Steven M. Nolt, *Amish Enterprise: From Plows to Profits* (Baltimore, Md.: Johns Hopkins University Press, 1995); Donald B. Kraybill, *Old Order Amish: Their Enduring Way of Life* (Baltimore, Md.: Johns Hopkins University Press, 1993); and Donald B. Kraybill and Carl F. Bowman, *On the Backroad to Heaven: Old Order Hutterites, Mennonites, Amish, and Brethren* (Baltimore, Md.: Johns Hopkins University Press, 2001).

7: Psychology

Anabaptism and Psychology: From Above and Below

Alvin C. Dueck

As A SCHOLAR I WAS BORN FROM THE WOMB of a people. My nurture came through emigration stories, family gatherings, Ukrainian foods, Saturday German school, and Mennonite educational institutions. My people have a memory that stretches back several thousand years; the Hebrews are their ancestors. In their midst I learned a language—a vocabulary and a grammar—that has consciously and unconsciously shaped my construal of the self, of community, of healing and health. The people beyond the bounds of our neighborhood viewed the world differently; at least it seemed they did. My identity, then, was shaped from below—by a this-worldly community hardly different in form (though certainly in substance) from most other ethnic subcultures.

My understanding of the Mennonite community has changed over the years, however, and so has my understanding of and relationship to psychology. In my early years, this relationship was compartmentalized, even conflicted. For while my Mennonite community viewed the discipline of psychology the same way they viewed Canadian society—as foreign and threatening—I myself was intrigued with psychological studies. I would therefore characterize these years as a time of enchantment with the discipline and increasing embarrassment with my heritage.

Later, after completing my doctoral studies and while teaching at a small Mennonite Brethren liberal arts college, I discovered anew my Anabaptist heritage, and I began to explore its implications for psychology and psychotherapy. This was an exhilarating time, with new understandings and new directions taking shape.

More recently, yet another direction has emerged. My faith has become more confessional and my understanding of the discipline more linguistic in nature; correspondingly, I have begun to focus on the interaction of Anabaptism and psychology with postmodernity.

Segregated and Conflicted

From my childhood through the end of graduate school, I viewed my Mennonite people as strictly sectarian. Much like the early church father Tertullian, they believed that Jerusalem had nothing to do with Athens—and that faithful Christians should therefore have nothing to do with "the world." Needless to say, most church members at that time viewed psychology as a "worldly" profession. That I should study it was a crossing of boundaries.

Surprisingly, my interest in psychology was piqued not in a university setting but in a small Mennonite Brethren Bible school in southern Manitoba. The introductory textbook to psychology was hopelessly out-of-date, and the course was offered only to help us evangelize more effectively. But I was intrigued—and I wondered how I might connect my course in First Corinthians with the beginning course in psychology.

For the next ten years I tacked back and forth between psychology, on the one hand, and theology and pastoral work on the other. When I enrolled at the University of Winnipeg I did so concurrently at the Mennonite Brethren Bible College. While in doctoral studies, I pastored a small congregation. I must confess that, during this time, my religious commitments and my psychological convictions traveled mainly on separate tracks. While there was some exchange between the two, neither was truly influenced by the other.

Even after I left graduate school my worlds remained largely disconnected. On the one hand, I remained active in the church; on the other, I grew as a professional. Looking back it is clear, however, that my spiritual development did not keep pace with my immersion in the psychological world of research and teaching.

In retrospect I realize that the social movement in cultures proceeds primarily from the village to the city—from particular to universal—and seldom the reverse. Accordingly, when I entered the university and was taught the more universal language of philosophy and psychology, there was no question as to which language carried more weight; the wider and more public language ruled and interpreted my ethnic Mennonite language.

I felt this disjuncture acutely. My mother did not understand psychology, period. And it seemed to me that the discourse of psychology of religion, for example, was incapable of grasping the richness of my religious heritage. (The categories of "projection" and "unconscious forces" seem thin indeed when applied to the thickness of personal faith.) It was only after the recovery of my Anabaptist theological heritage that I was finally able to *both* find a place for psychological perspectives *and* be faithful to my ethnoreligious vision of reality.

On Returning Home

Anabaptist Christians are not simply an ethnic people. Rather, they are a people who point beyond themselves to a story they believe to be true. The story of the God who makes covenants, is manifest in the person of Jesus Christ, and continues to be present in the Spirit, is not a story this community invented. It is a narrative which carries authority from beyond, a story to which the community may hold itself accountable. In that sense, baptism, Bible school, church conferences, and church publications nurtured me (not just ethnic particularities), and the ten-year period after my doctoral studies served as a homecoming. On returning home I embraced this thick piety, recognizing that new life was a gift of God. This too is my community, and to that extent I was (and am) born from above.

During my graduate studies, which I concluded in 1974, I had been silent about my Anabaptist heritage ("ethnic embarrassment" is what my sociologist friends would be ready to call it). It became evident to me, however, that a significant change had occurred when, in a postgraduate seminar at Yale University in 1983, I introduced myself as a Mennonite psychologist and shared my story. The sixteenth-century Anabaptist radicals, with their rejection of infant baptism and their call to follow Christ unto death, were my forebears, I said. I talked about our communal heritage, about our long migrations replete with illness, privation, and death, and about my own childhood in an ethnic Canadian Mennonite community.

Thankfully, the small group of scholars did not exile me. Rather, they were intrigued. What might be a Mennonite perspective on Freud, Erikson, and Jung? they wondered. When I realized that Marxists, feminists, and African-Americans wrote their psychologies from their thick particularities, I began to write more self-consciously as an Anabaptist.

Over the years I had taken numerous Mennonite history courses, but it was only after my doctoral work was completed—and after long hours of dialogue with colleagues in sociology, history, and theology at Tabor College (1974-1978) and later at Fresno Pacific University (1979-1984)—that my Anabaptist heritage took on relevance for my work in psychology. And so a book emerged in which I wrote self-consciously as an Anabaptist, a book I entitled *Between Jerusalem and Athens: Ethical Perspectives on Culture, Religion, and Psychotherapy*.[1]

Using the idea of "the reign of God" as an ethical culture, I argued in this work that the church was an alternative community for the Christian psychologist and that the Christian therapist was called to be a radical disciple. Beginning with the reign of God creates a context, I said, from which to interpret modern (and postmodern) cultures. Moreover, the reign of God serves as an ethical guide for therapeutic objectives. Indeed, being committed to the Christian community relativizes the professional community and gives the Christian psychologist a communal identity. Following Christ may even move a psychologist to provide therapeutic services to underserved populations or work toward reconciliation where there has been violent injury.

Formative stories

On my return home, our Anabaptist stories assumed new significance: stories about Conrad Grebel, Menno Simons, Dirk Phillips, and later, Elizabeth Simons; stories about Eduard Wuest, P. M. Friesen, and J. B. Toews, men who shaped the identity of my own tribe of Mennonites, the Mennonite Brethren; and stories about my own family's emigration from the Ukraine, about our difficult years in southern Manitoba, and about the death of my father. After years of immersion in scientific rationalism, it's little surprise that I now wondered whether such stories were not as significant for understanding human nature as science claimed to be. Perhaps therapy could be understood as the hearing and telling of stories, and not only as the application of scientific findings. Moreover, perhaps a therapist's *own* story was critical to therapeutic dialogue and healing. In any case, the Anabaptist story of suffering, tolerance, prophetic critique, communal life, and costly discipleship began to influence the way I viewed the character of the therapist.

Whether rooted in Switzerland or the Ukraine, the Mennonite story is a story of suffering, and so I, as a psychologist, have reflected on suffering. After all, I have parents whose loved ones were murdered on the Ukrainian steppes, a grandfather who died a decade after arriving in Canada, a mother whose husband drowned shortly after their marriage, and a father-in-law who screamed through the night after viewing the movie *Dr. Zhivago*. Few psychologists have reflected on the effects on those Mennonite fathers and mothers who survived the 1920s holocaust in Russian villages like Chortitza and Halbstadt. What secrets did those quiet grandmothers carry, and what anger did those grandfathers barely contain?

I know Mennonites are capable of suffering, but can we face the nature of our own suffering? We have a theological language for suffering, but do we have a psychological vocabulary that describes the personal and interpersonal effects of such trauma? I wish it weren't so, but all too often I am told such a vocabulary is irrelevant.

It was these stories of suffering that became more meaningful when, in 1999, our daughter gave birth to a baby with Trisomy 13, a major chromosomal malformation. The child arrived blind, deaf, with double cleft palate, malfunctioning kidneys, and shrunken brain. We grieved Nathaniel Dovano's short life. I wished not to shrink from the face of death, and so I wrote to understand the God who suffers with us.

Nathaniel Dovano
Nathaniel Dovano,
you came to us across waters
dark and foreboding.
So long we waited
to see and hear you,
But you came silently,
no crying you made.
Your small unformed mouth
gasping for air.
Your heart beating strong,
beginning to fail.

When, O God, will the day come when
an infant will live more than a few hours,
and a great-grandfather will live out his years?

You know broken bodies,
Those stretched on a cross,
Those buried in unmarked graves,
Those disfigured by extra genes,
Those unable to give birth.

Something is awry in this world you have created
when the innocent suffer,
when the unborn are maimed,
when some grieve an infant loss,
and others yearn for a child. . . .

Is it you Lord?
Is it you who comes to us this day
with cleft palate
and weakened heart?

Yes, resurrected bodies are not whole.
Your nail scarred hands and feet
are not a perfect body.

Nathaniel Dovano Smith,
Show us the way
to the disabled God you mirror.
Teach us on this sixth day of creation
to say "It is good."

Confronting individualism

During my years at Tabor and Fresno Pacific, I began to conceive of the relationship between Christianity and psychology in terms of theological ethics, a conception that was no doubt nourished by a year of theological studies with John Howard Yoder and Stanley Hauerwas. My concern in this regard was not to engage in one more psychological interpretation of religion; to the contrary, I found myself moving in the opposite direction. Two key questions emerged during this time: What contribution could an Anabaptist theological perspective make in understanding the psyche? And what psychological research or theories were compatible with an Anabaptist perspective?

In a related way, my involvement in an intentional community (Fellowship of Hope, 1978-1979) and an intentional neighborhood (1979-1998) increased my appreciation for the communal aspects of my Mennonite heritage—the result being a growing critique of psychology and psychotherapy as overly individualistic. Psychological individualism is most evident in the assumption that the resources for change lie within the individual rather than in any collectivity larger than the individual.[2] I admit that I was much enamored with Carl Rogers in the late 1960s, for in contrast to what seemed to me to be a claustrophobic ethnicity, Rogers's psychological gospel of "grace" was refreshing.[3] However, after living in various forms of Christian community for the past thirty years, recovering the communal dimensions of my heritage, and observing the destructive effects of individualism, I have reconsidered the value of that approach. In the process, I have found much support for a more communal perspective in psychology.[4] Correspondingly, I have found myself looking at the Christian community in hopes that the church might be an ethically discerning and healing community.

Social location

During this return home, I have also become sensitized to the particularity of my discipline. I cannot help but think that my Anabaptist heritage (and its ethnic particularity) predisposed me to be more aware of issues of power and ideology. In time I came to realize that psychology itself is a form of ideology. Too often its proponents fail to recognize their particularity.

Long before I realized that psychology was an indigenous social construction, I had heard about the "cargo cult." Missionary converts discovered that, when the Western missionary prayed, the answer came by ship. But the product that was exported from the West was not only the gospel but a way of life, a culture.

The discipline of psychology reflects American culture, and it too has been exported. Since American psychology emerged largely on native soil, its mode of psychotherapy is largely pragmatic in orientation, scientific in methodology, and individualistic in its guiding assumptions—and, despite our best intentions, not wholly applicable to other cultures. One example will suffice: I once heard a psychologist recently returned from China lament that the Chinese did not use psychological inventories, and it occurred to me that, instead of lamenting that fact, we should be asking how it was possible that the Chinese did not need our psychological instruments. Behind the guise of universality I sensed a particularity, and as a Mennonite I knew about particularity.

To help my students recognize the situatedness of psychology, I have taken classes to Mexico (1978, 1981) and Guatemala (1999, 2000) in immersion programs. In the latter country we listened as simple people talked about the pain and suffering they experienced from thirty-plus years of civil war. We also listened to psychologists who were seeking to contextualize their work to this setting, and to pastors and theologians who were using the best social scientific knowledge to bring healing to those whose family members had disappeared during the war. Not infrequently, my students in these programs commented upon our return on how "American" our psychology is.

Forgotten interiority

Let me be clear: the return home was not simply romanticizing the community. As I listened to Mennonite clients, read Mennonite autobiographies, and heard Mennonite testimonies, I realized that Mennonites don't have a well-differentiated language of interiority. Given the lack of psychological understanding by our religious leaders (exhibited, for example, in the aftermath of sexual violations), it seemed to me that we needed a language that was more sensitive to internal processes. To dismiss all psychological language as reinforcing individualism is to paint the picture with too broad a brush. Indeed, what if a psychological language of the heart could be such to move us to greater marital faithfulness, increased communal commitment, and a more profound awareness of injustice?

I have therefore explored the notion that the self is multiple, believing that this notion offers a way of understanding the individual communally.[5] I asked, Could not the inner life be viewed metaphorically, as a congregation in need of pastoring? Most modern theories of the self are too hierarchical, too thin. The life of a congregation, however, is thick with diverse personalities—and so also, I began to think, is the human psyche. We are, in a sense, perambulating communities. The inner life is a representation of the many people who have shaped our lives (not just our parents). These people continue to speak to us in various ways, muted and loud, carping and gentle, sarcastic and encouraging.

Not only is the modern self plural and fragmented, the Mennonite psyche may well be divided, reflecting the sharp sectarian distinction between church and world, between ethnic clan and outside cultures. A person's worldly self and churchly self may well contend with each other. Perhaps, however, we might also come to realize God's presence in the secular self and the presence of the world in one's moral Mennonite self. I cannot but imagine that this notion of the plural self became important to me as a result of my living in Christian communities most of my life. At the same time I have found congenial spirits in the psychological tradition that lent words to my intuitions.[6]

So, then, Nicodemus was right. We are born from below, from a real people who shape the contours of our historical existences. And yet, I am far more than a scholar who affirms a cultural heritage. Jesus points to a birth that is from above. I would like to believe there is a measure of "born-again-from-above"-ness in the people who have pointed me to the life, death, and resurrection of Jesus. To be born from above qualifies not only the character of my own being, but that of my community as well.

Speaking and Listening

At the Mennonite Brethren Biblical Seminary (1984-1998), and since then at Fuller Theological Seminary, I have taught a variety of theologically integrative courses in counseling. During that time it has been interesting to observe the dialogue between theologians and psychologists. There are those who genuinely listen to one another and allow their scholarship to develop as a result of the conversation. At other times, however, the theologians look askance at the psychologists who, from their perspective, appear hopelessly empirical or obsessed with experience. For their part, the psychologists often wonder how it is possible to exegete and theologize without taking lived human experience into consideration.

In defense of the theologians and biblical scholars, I *do* believe it is possible to begin confessionally with the God of Abraham, Sarah, Mary, and Jesus, and from that starting place, to speak to twenty-first century lives. At the same time, I would contend that, more often than not, it's the psychologists who are expected to learn from theologians, not the reverse.

For students, the "integration" of theology with the social sciences usually means taking courses in the two respective disciplines, with the hope that, in the end, they will somehow bring the two disciplines together. In other words, the goal is for some form of *intellectual* integration of the two disciplines, a "Christian worldview." It will become clearer in the next section why that goal is most difficult to achieve.

I have come to the point where I view "integration" as mostly a matter of ecclesia—that is, a matter pertaining to our lives lived in the context of other believers. It is in the life of the church as a sign of God's reign that personal and professional integration really occurs. It is here that one's work is made meaningful by being blessed as an extension of the ministry of the church. As a community of accountability, our brothers and sisters can help us discern the shape of our work in the world.

Language and commitment

In this past decade, I have come to view Anabaptism and American psychology as two distinct linguistic cultures, having different histories, "Scriptures," and epistemologies. Anabaptism speaks the language of conflict and peace, the lordship of Christ, and community; psychology speaks the language of behavior, neuron, development, and therapy.

Not only is the content of the two languages different; the same word can have different meanings in the two cultures. The word *self*, for example, when placed in the center of a Anabaptist semantic network, might mean sacrifice, service, or activism. Among psychologists, the same word might be associated with esteem, assertiveness, or ego.

Given my emphasis on language, it may appear that I have bracketed the question of truth. That inference, however, is based on two faulty assumptions, both of which comprise foundational myths of modernity. The first false assumption is that one can attain a bird's-eye view from which to assess all traditions objectively; the second is that to accept one's particularity is to preclude dialogue.

I accept neither assumption. Rather, I respond by stating that I speak confessionally from within a tradition—and grant that others will speak out of their language communities, whether they are aware of it or not. More that than, I aspire both to affirm my roots and to converse creatively with other traditions—Latin shamanism, postmodern psychotherapy, neuropsychology, and Jungian dream interpretation.

Language and community

To better understand the role my Mennonite community has played relative to the scientific language in psychology, I have found the perspectives of Ludwig Wittgenstein most helpful.[7] Words, Wittgenstein argued, take on meaning with usage rather than inherently containing universal meaning. Meaning emerges from within *Lebensformen* (communal life), and the meaning of a word is related to practice.

This perspective, I believe, constitutes an affirmation of my ethnoreligious identity. The particular language I had learned as a Mennonite might well be different from other, more dominant languages, but it is nonetheless a legitimate voice in the public square. Moreover, theory apart from praxis now seems less relevant. Rather, their unity seems consistent with being a disciple of Jesus, as well as with the Mennonite conviction that following Jesus has concrete implications.

On conversation

Given the language difference, will the conversation between Mennonite psychologists and theologians be a monologue or a dialogue? To be quite honest, I am less troubled than some of my theological colleagues by the diversity of languages used to describe human life. The curse of Babel is not the diversity of languages; it is rather the hegemony of one language. The Babylonian politicians built an enclave of linguistic safety and homogeneity; as a consequence, they were cursed with confusion and separation from the cultures of the world.

When seen from this perspective, the Babel story points primarily to the fear of losing a sense of identity by being scattered, the fear of becoming restless, rootless wanderers. We become like Babel when we assume our language, theological or psychological, is the most adequate and therefore the only one that should be spoken by others. (In Judges 12, the soldiers of Gilead decapitated those Ephraimites who could not pronounce the word *Shibboleth*.)

Since learning a language is prefatory to making a contribution to and receiving the gifts of another culture, it seems to me that Anabaptist theologians and Mennonite psychologists must at least be willing to try to learn one another's language.[8] I therefore see my work as a psychologist and psychotherapist as translating Anabaptist language and convictions into psychological language.

One specific way I respond to the pluralism of languages is to fill psychological categories with the particular content of my own faith language. When theorists of the self reflect on the nature of identity, I find myself wondering, What is the mature self? For me it includes a role for voluntary self-sacrifice, for loving the enemy, etc. So I use the language of psychology, but I tend to fill it with the particular content of my faith tradition. I see this as a way of relativizing the hegemony of a wider, more public language and, at the same time, respecting the language of the land.

Non-foundationalism

To engage the different languages of psychology and Anabaptism, I have not sought a more basic language to harmonize the two. This is probably a consequence of the Anabaptist tendency toward non-foundationalism. Historically speaking, Anabaptists have not tended to build their theology on indisputable philosophical foundations; consequently, neither science, nor phenomenology, nor existentialism, nor Jungianism, nor behaviorism have served as primary languages for me. I assume such foundationalism is dead; on none of these earthly foundations could we ever hope to build up a tower to heaven. Mennonites, after all, are pilgrims—even epistemological pilgrims.

In any case, I find myself without commitment to a single psychological paradigm. While I have appreciated the concreteness of scientific behaviorism, the gentle interiority of self-psychology, the relational sensitivity of community psychology, and the mystical elements of Carl Jung, I have nonetheless resisted the temptation to adopt any of them wholeheartedly. In retrospect, I suspect my inability to find one satisfying paradigm may reflect my refusal to be overdetermined by loyalty to one perspective. I have borrowed from various approaches as I have seen fit, with the hope that the psychological insights garnered would be useful to my students, my clients, the scholarly community, and the church.

Given this non-foundationalist perspective it is not clear to me in advance where the dialogue between Anabaptism and psychology will lead me. As a result I don't find myself pursuing certain lines of conversation, even as I actively pursue others. However, if both psychology and Anabaptism are social constructions, there must always exist the possibility of surprise for each partner in the conversation.

Postmodernity and "thick" therapy

My concern with language has many implications for how I view psychotherapy. Much of Western therapy reflects the language of the Enlightenment, thereby assuming the "autonomous" individual, the universality of "human nature," and the "objectivity" of science. In the process, ethnicity is trivialized as local custom.

Following Clifford Geertz, I think of such psychological formulations as "thin."[9] They emerge from an attempt to find commonality across different communities and cultures. In contrast are "thick" descriptions of the self that emerge from the language of ethnic particularity, descriptions that are often religious in nature and communal in structure. I find myself wondering about the contours of "thick" therapy. This may be an outgrowth of my postmodern sensibilities, but it is also consistent with my Mennonite experience.

In psychotherapy the imposition of values is considered an egregious therapeutic error, an assumption I fully embrace—but in a carefully qualified way. Given my Anabaptist story of state-sponsored persecution, I fully support the notion of noncoercive therapy. My ancestors died for religious freedom, and it would therefore be inconsistent for me to use my powerful position as a therapist to inculcate my religious convictions.

In short, I cannot endorse a Constantinian approach to psychotherapy. Still, I am a person with a story—a Christian story that can be lifegiving. Clients come to therapy not simply to have their problems solved and their illnesses healed. They come seeking meaning amid their brokenness. Therapy has thus become for me a place where clients can develop a sense of hope. I affirm what is good in their lives and, when appropriate, am transparent with regard to my own story.

I believe in therapy not because it reflects the cultural ethos of individualism, is restricted to those who can afford it, or is politically aseptic. Rather, I find it preferable to violent solutions to problems. More often than we realize the issues that are brought to the consulting room are born of violence. Although the violence is often forgotten (René Girard writes that violence is that which is "hidden since the foundation of the world[10]), its effects are nonetheless palpable. Therapy may well uncover the sources of violence. The resolution of the violence is not further violence, but rather conversation—peaceable conversation. Therapy is for me a form of peacemaking.

Minding the Church

I view my scholarship as a psychologist as minding the church. I have brought to the church what I thought was useful in the discipline of psychology; conversely, I have interpreted my discipline from a churchly perspective.

As my reflections above indicate, the relationship between a scholar and a tradition is a complex one. One can offer one's skills to the religious community and/or one can translate the convictions of a small community for the larger public. But there will always be give and take between a scholar and his or her faith community. I am confident that the relationship of my scholarship to Anabaptism emerged not simply from knowing some Anabaptist "theology" but from the ethos of our Mennonite people. I therefore no longer see my integrating work as simply forcing into psychology the Anabaptist ideas I learned in seminary. Neither is it simply a matter of projecting psychological ideology onto Anabaptist theology.

I prefer to think of my relationship to the Mennonite tradition more organically, as emerging from within the nurturing life of a community of people. And I have come to realize that my ethnoreligious community has shaped my work, both consciously and unconsciously, in ways I could not have imagined. Indeed, others have sometimes recognized Anabaptist themes in my work that I had not previously seen. (A non-Mennonite seminary colleague once reviewed an address I delivered from the heart; I had not written the speech as an Anabaptist apology, but he saw as clearly Anabaptist the themes of service, lordship of Christ over culture, and commitment to faithful praxis.[11])

In all of this, I have sought to be faithful to my ethnoreligious family of origin and, at the same time, to relativize it—to be born from below and from above. At times, I have labored self-consciously as an ethnoreligious scholar. At other times, the particular life-giving story of faith intersected with the psychological in ways I cannot explain.

Notes

1. Alvin C. Dueck, *Between Jerusalem and Athens: Ethical Perspectives on Culture, Religion, and Psychotherapy* (Grand Rapids, Mich.: Baker Books, 1995).

2. For a discussion of this, see Robert N. Bellah, et al., *Habits of the Heart: Individualism and Commitment in American Life* (Berkeley, Calif.: University of California Press, 1985), 138-39.

3. Carl R. Rogers, *On Becoming a Person: A Therapist's View of Psychotherapy* (Boston: Houghton Mifflin, 1961).

4. For instance, Julian Rappaport, *Community Psychology: Values, Research, and Action* (New York: Holt, Rinehart and Winston, 1977); and Philip Rieff, *The Triumph of the Therapeutic: Uses of Faith After Freud* (New York: Harper & Row, 1966).

5. See Dueck, *Between Jerusalem and Athens*, esp. Chapter 10.

6. For example, William James, *The Principles of Psychology*, vol. 3 of *The Works of William James*, ed. Frederick H. Burkhardt, Fredson Bowers, and Ignas K. Skrupskelis (Cambridge, Mass.: Harvard University Press, 1981); and C. G. Jung, *Memories, Dreams, Reflections* (New York: Pantheon Books, 1963).

7. See Ludwig Wittgenstein, *Philosophical Investigations* (Oxford: B. Blackwell, 1953).

8. The Jews in Babylon did not expect the local residents to learn Hebrew; rather, the Jews became bilingual, learning the language of Babylon well enough to become scribes, merchants, and diplomats. See John Howard Yoder, *For the Nations: Essays Evangelical and Public* (Grand Rapids, Mich.: Eerdmans, 1977), 71.

9. Clifford Geertz, *The Interpretation of Cultures: Selected Essays* (New York: Basic Books, 1973).

10. See René Girard, *Things Hidden Since the Foundation of the World*, trans. Stephen Bann and Michael Metteer (Stanford, Calif.: Stanford University Press, 1987); and René Girard, *Violence and the Sacred* (Baltimore, Md.: Johns Hopkins University Press, 1977).

11. A spiritual director once told me that even my dreams were Anabaptist!

8: Economics

The "Anabaptist School" of Economics: Problems and Proposals

James M. Harder

WHEN HISTORIANS WRITE THEIR ACCOUNTS of the late twentieth century, a significant theme—perhaps the *most* significant theme—will be "economism." Coined only a decade ago by process theologian John B. Cobb Jr., the term *economism* has come to symbolize an increasingly dominant belief that the single most important value to modern society is economic growth. Cobb himself strongly condemns what he perceives to be the "idolatry" of economism. "It is profoundly opposed to Christianity," he argues. "A Christian must condemn a society that organizes itself for the pursuit of wealth and encourages its citizens to order their lives in this way."[1]

Despite such complaints, economism runs apace, reflected in decision making dominated by economic logic—often to the exclusion of previously cherished noneconomic values. Economism has yielded public policy that dismisses the jointly funded "public good" in favor of the individually owned "private good." Consequently, it is increasingly ceding our social future to the outcomes and needs of a competitive market economy. Some fear it has crept into the church as well.

During this triumphal era of economism, economists have often found themselves in the public spotlight. Once largely invisible academics, the comments of economists now constitute regular fare in the media. In many cases, economists are perceived to be the ultimate champions of economism, which is sometimes credited with creating unprecedented wealth and opportunity for all. That perception would be wrong, however, with respect to me. I am among a minority of economists who offer a much less sanguine appraisal. Indeed, the critique of runaway economism has largely defined my career as an academic economist seeking to serve the Anabaptist community. What's more, people's interest in this topic has presented me with opportunities and audiences not readily available to Anabaptist economists in the past.

Teaching (and Learning) Economics in East Africa

My own interest in economics—and my eventual passion for the subject—developed over time, largely in response to life experiences. While an undergraduate at Bethel College in Kansas, I was drawn to the study of both economics and history. Both disciplines provided opportunities to study issues related to people and the workings of society, and economics in particular appealed to me because of its quantitative rigor. I sensed that the insights gained from one subject helped enrich my understanding of the other. Indeed, some have claimed that economic relationships comprise the driving force of human history.

My Mennonite Central Committee assignment (1981-84) in an extremely poor section of Kenya only furthered my interest in economics. While in Kenya, I taught economics to first-generation high school students who literally walked miles from their nomadic families' encampments in the North Eastern Province desert. My students lived in contexts where their material resources were often meager, and where deaths resulting from the absence of food, water, and medical care were not uncommon.

In other words, for the first time in my life I looked directly into the faces of poverty. From that point on, I could no longer conceive economic issues only in the abstract. The bottom-line economic themes of access to and distribution of resources incarnated themselves every day in Garissa, Kenya.

So I had gone to Africa hoping to learn about and perhaps make a contribution to the broader world community. Three years later I returned home convinced of the need to better understand the economic systems that fostered the tremendous disparities in wealth I had observed. This new commitment to understanding economic systems meant facing some hard realities. For with respect to the poor people I had encountered in Kenya, individual effort and ability seemed to make little difference in their material standard of living. Such a realization forced me to admit two sad facts: (1) there were systemic variables that negatively impacted the lives of Africans; and (2) these same systems disproportionately benefited residents of the world's most powerful market economies, including me. These realizations have informed my views on the nature of economic obligation ever since, reminding me that I have economic responsibilities that extend far beyond providing for my own family.

As a result of my African experiences, I selected a graduate program in economics that would allow me to focus my studies on the economics of developing countries. It was not coincidental that this program was at the University of Notre Dame, for its openness to considering questions of economic justice was a direct consequence of the school's Roman Catholic religious commitments.

For two years, I enjoyed the opportunity to serve as a teaching assistant to Professor Denis Goulet, perhaps the world's foremost development ethicist. I completed my Ph.D. in 1990, just as many Anabaptists were gaining some awareness of the realities and consequences of the early economism of the Reagan revolution. Since then, it seems, Anabaptist church members have constantly been searching for a greater understanding of the fast-changing economic realities in which they live and in which their organizations must function. Therefore, rather than living the life of the traditional academic, who hopes to create scholarship that *might* attract an audience, I have more often found myself responding to *requests* for interpretive scholarship—especially within church circles.

Economics and the Struggle for Legitimacy Within the Church

Church-based requests for my input have come from various quarters for various reasons. Sometimes I have been asked to speculate on how changing economic forces will affect our world, our nations, our local communities, and our nuclear families.[2] I have also been asked to relate these changes more specifically to the future of our churches and our church-related institutions. For example, a recent meeting of nearly twenty Anabaptist mutual aid associations invited me to outline for them a "Map to the Twenty-First Century," a map based on my understanding of the economic challenges facing them. Similarly, mission executives at a Council of International Ministries meeting requested a keynote lecture interpreting international political economy since 1945, with the goal of helping them better understand the economic forces impacting missions programs. In 1996, I authored a paper arguing that the success and failure of church-related institutions may be driven as much by secular economic forces as by member devotion to the cause itself—and I further speculated on the impact of global economic systems changes on the funding of church institutions.[3] In addition to these national venues, more local churches than I can possibly name have invited me to speak on various themes.

This plethora of requests from within the church reflects a heightened interest in economic analysis, to be sure, but it also signifies something more profound: an increased acceptance of economic themes as legitimate topics of conversation within Anabaptist circles. Not only is it now *acceptable* to discuss economics in Anabaptist churches, many church members believe that, if the church is being faithful to its calling, it *should be* discussing economic issues. Correspondingly, the church is asking Anabaptist economists for their insights on economic issues in the same manner that it has long been asking historians for their historical analyses and theologians for their scriptural interpretations.

As other essays in this volume attest, the Anabaptist movement possesses a rich tradition of debate and analysis, often nurtured by its scholars. Yet it is clear to me that not all academic disciplines have been equally involved (or welcomed) to such debates, whether conducted at church conferences, in church periodicals, or in books published by denominational publishing houses. From my admittedly biased perspective, it has been the theologians, the philosophers, the historians, and perhaps the musicians who have most often been seated at the table for these discussions (with sociologists the most recent addition). Often left out have been the practitioners of academic disciplines traditionally perceived as being important to secular society but with scant relevance to the affairs of the institutional church, i.e., the natural sciences, the remaining disciplines in the humanities, and most of the social sciences, including economics.

Furthermore, to the extent that the church has needed the knowledge from one of these more "secular" disciplines, it has often been a practitioner from one of the church's core academic disciplines who has been asked to provide that knowledge. Thus, when reading church publications, one frequently encounters theologians speculating on biological realities and sociologists performing analyses of political and economic trends. Far less frequently does one encounter the direct analysis of a biologist, an economist, or a political scientist—even though, by virtue of their training, they may be able to offer a more informed and more nuanced consideration of the subject at hand.

These comments should not be interpreted as a critique of cross-disciplinary scholarship; indeed, I see myself as doing that sort of scholarship, and would be most frustrated if I were confined intellectually to the field of economics alone. Still, the asymmetry of the academic voices I perceive within church circles has sometimes been quite apparent (and discouraging) to me.

Understanding Supply and Demand for Economists in the Church

To illustrate the point at hand, let me offer this example. In 1990, shortly after I began teaching, I was invited to attend a conference at an Anabaptist institution of higher education. Entitled "Anabaptist-Mennonite Faith and Economics: Breaking the Silence," the conference sought to advance the understanding of how the Anabaptist-Mennonite faith had influenced the economic milieu of Anabaptist church members, and how economic life had modified their faith and practices. It was an excellent conference, but amazingly, despite the conference's announced title, less than a quarter of its twenty-one presentations were given by trained economists. The rest were rooted in other academic disciplines, overwhelmingly those I've identified as being perceived to be at the core of church academics.

As I later reflected on that reality, I did so in economic terms. Was this low ratio of economists a consequence of demand factors, or was it the result of supply factors? In other words, does the church have only passing interest in higher-level economic analysis (low demand), or are there simply few economists who are interested in minding the affairs of the church (low supply)?

While both conditions have held some currency in the past, I believe that causal factors have shifted to ensure that both demand and supply levels for *economic analyses by economists* are on the rise. On the demand side, it appears to me that Anabaptist-Mennonites are becoming increasingly convinced of the need for examining the impact of economic systems on their lives. This is true of ordinary, working church members, many of whom are less isolated from the economic mainstream than they were in the past, and who therefore have a growing awareness of the power that economic systems exert upon things they value. It is even more true of our growing number of Anabaptist business professionals, who, in the process of obtaining considerable financial success, encounter what some perceive to be "the contradiction between communal/religious and capitalist values," and who thereby develop a greater interest in understanding the economic context of such tensions.[4]

While certain sociologists (e.g., J. Winfield Fretz and Calvin Redekop) have made a good start in understanding these issues, it is significant that, even in the most comprehensive studies of contemporary Anabaptist-Mennonite life, economic analyses lacked the depth given to other subjects.[5] For example, while income and occupation were surveyed and reported, the data collectors failed to collect certain pieces of data needed to gain real insight into how Anabaptists experience the market economy and how that economy affects their households, their communities, and their congregations. More specifically, economists would have asked not just *how much* income church members had, but also how it was *derived*. Was it from the sale of one's own wage labor, or was it entrepreneurial profit? Was it rental income from property holdings, or a return on accumulated investment capital? Such information is essential if one wishes to better understand the changing economic landscape of Anabaptist-Mennonite church members, for with such data one can discern changes in the church community's concentration of wealth over time, the origin and nature of those changes, and whether being Anabaptists (or members of a particular Anabaptist group) makes a difference as compared to the broader society.

Yet even *if* the church were to express an interest in a more complete economic analysis of itself, could it call upon a sufficient *supply* of trained economists? Might this constraint be the controlling factor to explain the relatively rare voice of trained economists within the church?

There may indeed be some truth in this—but not necessarily because economists as a group don't care about the church. Certainly there have been some excellent Mennonite economists over the years who have sought to speak to church audiences through their work. Perhaps most widely recognized for their published work are Carl Kreider, now retired from Goshen College, Jim Halteman of Wheaton (Ill.) College, and Henry Rempel of the University of Manitoba. But in general, why have economists seemed few and far between within Anabaptist church circles, especially when compared to the number of academics from certain other disciplines?

Suspicion about economics

In my view, several factors combine to explain this relatively low number of trained economists. First, insofar as economics has often been characterized as focusing solely on the creation of wealth, there remains a lingering suspicion within the church about the suitability of the discipline itself. (For that matter, the same suspicion has also been known to rear its head on Anabaptist college campuses.)

This attitude is hardly confined to the church. I once attended the annual conference of the Society for International Development. At the conference, speaker after speaker offered subtle and not-so-subtle condemnations of "economists"—as if we were an undifferentiated mass of identical clones all exuding the same misguided ideologies. Finally, one of the speakers admitted that he had, in fact, minored in economics as part of his doctoral work. But he then proceeded to tell us that he had gotten "just enough of an inoculation to keep from getting the full-blown disease!"

Despite such experiences, I am convinced that, if a stereotype of economists still exists within the Anabaptist-Mennonite church, it will increasingly subside as more economists participate *as economists* in the life of the church. Moreover, such visibility will help convince our young people that the study of economics is a important means by which the broader mission of the church can be advanced.

Decline of "values-based" economics

The second supply constraint of economists in the church circles pertains to the evolution of the discipline itself. Indeed, the great economic philosophers of the past would scarcely recognize the discipline of economics as it's taught today in most of the top graduate programs. The field has largely been co-opted by a methodological approach that is strongly committed to mathematical modeling and quantifiable results and relatively disinterested in discussions of social values. Some economists, who seek to analyze economic phenomena through the eyes of a purely "objective" science, go so far as to deny the need for exploring values at all, oblivious of the truism that adherence to values of some sort is absolutely unavoidable.

Although this trend toward making economics a strictly quantifiable science may be undergoing a reversal, a budding economist who expresses interest in a "values-oriented" course of study will no doubt find an uphill path to climb. For while it is possible to find support for such an approach, it is not strongly reinforced by the discipline's internal rules of reward.

Lack of professional association within the church

Yet a third factor affecting the supply of economists serving the church is the economists' lack of organization as a group. In contrast to theologians, sociologists, historians, and others, Anabaptist economists have virtually no tradition or identity as a professional association within the church.

To be sure, a few Anabaptist economists have made significant scholarly contributions to the church by their own initiative and as scattered voices; but without a visible, professional association of Anabaptist economists, there has been no megaphone to amplify these contributions, as has been the case in the other disciplines where such groups do function. Without such a group for economists, conferences on current topics of concern are not planned, networking doesn't as readily occur, and alternative perspectives aren't exchanged and critiqued. Ultimately, the insights of economists are less likely to be available to the church.

There are hopeful signs, however, that economists within Anabaptist circles are bringing about change in this regard. In 1997, with the encouragement of Mennonite Economic Development Associates (MEDA), Henry Rempel and I organized the inaugural meeting of the Association of Mennonite Economists. The goal of this association is to provide a meaningful and rigorous forum "where professional economists who identify with a Mennonite faith can talk economics and faith—and the dialogue between the two."[6]

The most visible result to date of this group has been a co-authored statement from Mennonite Economists analyzing and supporting the

Jubilee 2000 movement in its controversial call for unconditional debt cancellation for fifty or more of the poorest countries in the world. The statement, co-authored by four members of Mennonite Economists and signed by seven others, appeared in two church periodicals, and has thereby fostered thinking and discussion on this important issue.[7]

Coming to Terms with "Religion" in Economics

While I was still in graduate school, I had the opportunity to attend a conference on the campus of a non-denominational Christian college. The conference's organizers had invited Christian economists to present papers that sought to discern the characteristics of a "biblically based" modern economic system. While various perspectives surfaced during the conference, one paper in particular sticks in my memory. This paper sought to identify a biblical mandate for an economic system based on strong individual private property rights and free-market capitalism. Most notably, the author took his Scripture references entirely from the Old Testament, especially from the Pentateuch. In so doing he put the more communal economic message of the New Testament completely aside. His justification for this approach seemed odd to my Anabaptist ways of thinking; he argued that the commandments governing economic relationships in the Pentateuch were unambiguously stated, and therefore more useful than the cryptic New Testament parables or the economic practices of early Christians.

While at the same conference, I learned something else I found quite intriguing. Though the board of the host college normally showed little interest in the college's faculty hiring decisions, it made exceptions for faculty positions in two specific disciplines: religion and economics. In those instances, the board was known to request a face-to-face interview with the final candidate—presumably to ensure a fit with the institution's values.

I left that conference having learned some important lessons about the "religion" which is often embedded within economics. I realized that, like theologians, economists operating in some church quarters might not enjoy the same academic freedoms that can usually be taken for granted by their colleagues in other disciplines.

Of course, the phenomenon of "economic correctness" can operate on Anabaptist college campuses as well, albeit with its own set of biases.

For me, the error comes not in having biases (which are unavoidable), but in refusing to acknowledge that they exist and refusing to explore the full range of perspectives on the subject.

An excellent description of the doctrinal divides within economics is provided in the book *With Liberty and Justice for Whom? The Recent Evangelical Debate over Capitalism*. In it, author Craig Gay notes that "all parties [in this debate] agree that oppression and exploitation are evil, that justice ought to be the goal of social and economic policy, that freedom is worth preserving, [and] that the problems of poverty ought to be redressed." Still, says Gay, there are significant disagreements, most notably over "the question of whether capitalism promotes or prevents the realization of the norms and values they hold in common."[8]

More specifically, the divide occurs between those on the religious left and those on the religious right. Those on the left generally hold capitalism principally responsible for many of the economic, political, cultural, and environmental evils they see in the modern world, and they are correspondingly critical of the forces they observe to be at the heart of the capitalist problem—the promotion of individual greed, wasteful economic surplus in the hands of a few, and spiritual starvation.

By comparison, those on the right see capitalism as an efficient method of producing wealth that can be used to improve the world and people's lives. Moreover, they suggest that capitalism has already provided unprecedented opportunities for the economic advancement of all classes. Immoral behavior in the market, they argue, originates with the sins of human beings who are active in the market—not with the capitalist system itself.

These different perspectives—supported on each side with favorite passages of Scripture—won't be resolved here. But I mention them because they define the ground for debate that no Christian economist can avoid, in part because so many armchair economists in the church hold passionate views on the subject. Indeed, I view participation in this debate as both a great opportunity and a significant responsibility for economists within the church.

Within Anabaptist circles over the last two decades, I have detected a significant topical shift within the church's discourse on economic themes. At one time, Anabaptists placed their greatest focus on questions dealing with *individual* responsibilities in the areas of money and vocation: Can Christians be wealthy? What constitutes acceptable

Christian stewardship of personal wealth? Can "good" Christians seek a career (and be successful) in the world of business?[9]

These questions continue to be raised, to be sure, but there is now a heightened concern over questions of *collective* responsibility for the *systemic* forces inherent in a market-driven global economy, i.e., questions about the values underlying economism. In recent years, for instance, I've received an annual phone call from an Anabaptist seminary professor who is interested in references to the best scholarship on such topics, references he then incorporates into his course syllabi.

One of my favorite quotations about economics is posted on my office door. It reflects, I think, a major reason why I find economics so interesting to pursue. It reads: "Controversies in economics persist, not because economists are necessarily less intelligent or more bad-tempered than the rest of mankind, but because the issues involved arouse strong feeling."[10]

I suspect that many pastors have concluded that economics, like politics and sex, is a topic to be handled with extreme care from the pulpit. Yet no matter how potentially dangerous, these subjects need to be addressed by a faithful church.

The "Anabaptist School" of Economics

Within the field of economics, centers of influence have emerged emphasizing different themes and approaches to the field. For example, the "Chicago School" of economics is known for insights into the importance of monetary policy. An older "Austrian School" is credited with developing an understanding of the mechanisms through which a market system efficiently allocates resources. If the Anabaptist movement has specific and perhaps unique understandings to contribute to the wider discussion of economics, what might they be? In other words, what would characterize the "Anabaptist School" of economics?

An important feature of Anabaptist life is the tradition of maintaining strong communities through the ethics of mutual accountability and mutual aid. At a minimum, this tradition has meant maintaining transparent relationships with neighbors, empathizing with them, and helping them in times of need.

When markets were primarily local, economic activity helped such social interaction, as neighbor encountered neighbor and built long-term relationships in the marketplace. In today's global marketplace, however, the economy no longer naturally reinforces healthy community dynamics in these ways. Meaningful human relationships are rarely needed to help the transactions in today's market economy. There is no need (or even an ability) to know personally a far-away producer or to have a particular interest in the producer's well-being. Indeed, the operant values in this marketplace are anonymity, indifference to others, lack of commitment, and complete autonomy—in other word, the exact opposite of traditional Anabaptist values.

The Anabaptist School of economics cannot be neutral about such trends. Limits on the way in which the market economy is allowed to operate are needed to help preserve space for strong and vibrant local economies that foster a sense of community cooperation as well as business competition.

In addition to emphasizing a strong community life, Anabaptists have traditionally (and increasingly) embraced the gospel's ethic of a preferential option for the poor—that is, a bias for helping society's most vulnerable people. How might this ethical value translate into economic principles? As a start, Anabaptist economics must look critically at the ever-expanding intrusion of market influence into public decision making. The conventional wisdom today is that the marketplace makes better decisions than government. Yet this assumption replaces democratic decision-making processes, where rich and poor have more equal votes, with market processes, where wealth alone determines strength of vote. Anabaptists, therefore, should be particularly skeptical of the accelerating privatization of what were formerly government controlled and publicly funded goods.

As many people can attest, parks, schools, bus service, recreational opportunities, and police protection are increasingly being privatized. Coupled with declining public support for income transfer programs, this trend leaves the poor to fend for themselves, priced out of access to these services.

Third, the Anabaptist School of economics cannot be silent about the ever-increasing inequality of income and wealth, both locally and globally. It must openly challenge as morally indefensible those policies that allow the wealthiest one percent of households in the United States to control 57 percent of all wealth while leaving 44 million Americans with no health insurance.[11]

Fourth, an Anabaptist School of economics would underscore an ethic of service. Of course, such an ethic flies in the face of an overwhelming market-oriented economy, where money is the only bottom line that matters. Economist Robert Kuttner has identified the problem well: "When everything is for sale, the person who volunteers time, who helps a stranger, who agrees to work for a modest wage out of commitment to the public good, who desists from littering even when no one is looking, who forgoes an opportunity to free-ride, begins to feel like a sucker."[12]

Instead of encouraging service, this money-dominated economy promotes consumerism as its highest ideal and as its dominant source of happiness. Yet there is something seriously flawed with an economy that allocates $21 billion a year for advertising to entice people to eat food they don't need, then another $32 billion for special diets to help take off the pounds that inevitably result.[13] Indeed, the Anabaptist values of service to others and careful stewardship of resources both serve as natural antidotes to runaway consumerism and should therefore be promoted by the Anabaptist School of economics.[14]

Finally, an authentically Anabaptist School of economics would be strongly experiential in nature. Taking its cues from Christ, the master teacher, Anabaptist economics would insist in action beyond the pages of textbooks. By deliberate design, it would seek to engage the real world at points where human need is greatest.

In sum, it seems clear to me that the Anabaptist community has become increasingly interested in economic issues, even during the relatively short span of my own career. Of course, Anabaptist church members have long been concerned about careful and moral stewardship of their personal financial resources. What's new in Anabaptist circles is an increased interest in understanding the economic systems through which their economic lives are linked to others in the world. What's also new, I believe, is a heightened concern that this new age of economism poses a significant threat to traditional Anabaptist social values. Anabaptist churches, together with their economists, have no alternative but to wrestle with these concerns and issues in the years ahead.

NOTES

1. John B. Cobb Jr., "The Theological Stake in Globalization," at http://www.religion-online.org/cgi-bin/relsearchd.dll/showarticle?item_id=1095.

2. I have spoken on these themes nearly annually at the North American convention of Mennonite Economic Development Associates, and I contribute regular columns to its publication, *The Marketplace*.

3. I first delivered this paper at a conference on church-related institutions, held in June 1996 at Elizabethtown College. It was later published as James M. Harder, "Church-Related Institutions: Driven By Member Commitment or By Economic Forces?" *Mennonite Quarterly Review* 71 (1997): 377-94.

4. This quotation is from Calvin W. Redekop and Benjamin W. Redekop, ed., *Entrepreneurs in the Faith Community: Profiles of Mennonites in Business* (Scottdale, Pa.: Herald Press, 1996), 15.

5. I'm referring here to J. Howard Kauffman and Leland Harder, *Anabaptists Four Centuries Later: A Profile of Five Mennonite and Brethren in Christ Denominations* (Scottdale, Pa.: Herald Press, 1975) and J. Howard Kauffman and Leo Driedger, *The Mennonite Mosaic: Identity and Modernization* (Scottdale, Pa.: Herald Press, 1991).

6. E-mail to author from Gerhard Pries, Mennonite Economic Development Associates, Winnipeg, Man., September 5, 1997.

7. Henry Rempel, et al., "Release the Poor People from the Bondage of Debt: Mennonite Economists Support Jubilee 2000," *The Marketplace*, July/August 2000, 16-19; this piece was later reprinted in the December 2000 issue of *Mennonite Life* and is available online at http://www.bethelks.edu/mennonitelife/2000dec/jubilee2000.html.

8. Craig M. Gay, *With Liberty and Justice for Whom? The Recent Evangelical Debate over Capitalism* (Grand Rapids, Mich.: Eerdmans, 1991), 166.

9. Longtime Goshen College economist Carl Kreider wrestled with these questions in *The Christian Entrepreneur* (Scottdale, Pa.: Herald Press, 1980).

10. Joan Robinson, *Introduction to the Theory of Employment* (London: Macmillan, 1964), 100.

11. Edward Chase, review of *Market Whys and Human Wherefores: Thinking About Markets, Politics and People,* by David E. Jenkins, *Challenge*, September/October 2000, 120.

12. Robert Kuttner, *Everything for Sale: The Virtues and Limits of Markets* (New York: Alfred A. Knopf, 1997), 62-63.

13. Jonathan Rowe, "The Growth Consensus Unravels," *Dollars and Sense*, July/August 1999, 17.

14. Even billionaire capitalist George Soros recognizes the dangers inherent in our market-driven society. "Unsure of what they stand for," writes Soros, "people increasingly rely on money as the criterion of value . . . . Society has lost its anchor." George Soros, "The Capitalist Threat," *The Atlantic Monthly*, February 1997, 52.

9: *Political Science*

Where's the Political Science Department?

Mark W. Charlton

Sometime ago, when I was attending a board meeting for the first time, the academic dean of a Mennonite college asked me what I did for a living. After telling him that I taught political science, he quipped, "Oh, you mean there actually *is* an academic discipline called 'political science'? I thought that was something that theologians wrote about when they wanted to be relevant." The dean was being facetious, of course, but as I've reflected on his words, I've come to realize that they contained more than a grain of truth—especially in the context of Anabaptist institutions of higher education.

Indeed, a quick scan of Anabaptist-related colleges and universities in North America reveal that, to this day, political science as a distinctive academic discipline receives only limited attention. Most of these institutions do not offer full-fledged political science majors, and while a few offer minors, most have no more than one faculty member teaching political science, usually under the umbrella of the history department.[1]

In contrast to other academic disciplines, it has been difficult (at least until very recently) to name more than a few Mennonite academics who actually "practice the discipline," i.e., hold postgraduate degrees in political science, teach in political science departments, and contribute to mainstream political science journals. While an increasing number of younger Mennonite academics are studying political science at the graduate level, it is still too early to talk about a distinctive "Anabaptist political science" the way that my Calvinist friends talk about a "Reformed political science."

It is tempting to conclude from this that holding Anabaptist convictions has largely been detrimental to seeking a career in political science. Certainly other traditions within the Christian community have done a better job of cultivating political science as an academic vocation, none more so than the Reformed tradition.

Of course, there are good reasons why the Reformed tradition has been a more fertile ground for nurturing political scientists, reasons that run even deeper than the existence of solid role models such as Abraham Kuyper and Herman Dooyeweerd. Perhaps most fundamentally, the Reformed tradition begins with a high view of the state, seeing it as part of God's order of creation. Thus, those called to public service or political office exercise as worthy a calling as those pursuing more traditional Christian vocations. Consequently, those in the Reformed tradition give much greater priority to reflection on the nature of the state and its relationship to society. This in turn calls for more attention to refining the presuppositions upon which Christians base their discussions of the state and justice. It is therefore not surprising that, in colleges and universities within the Reformed tradition, the study of political science and political philosophy assumes a much more central role.

In contrast, Anabaptists have traditionally started with a low view of the state. From this perspective, the state is perceived as an consequence of the Fall, performing the limited task of maintaining order in a fallen society. For Anabaptists, then, the redeemed community—the church—functions as the primary agent of God's work in the world. As members of this redeemed community, Christians are called to model the ethic of Christ in lives of service and peacemaking. Because the state by definition will occasionally use the sword, the Christian must avoid involvement with the state, looking instead for other avenues to live out his/her call to discipleship.

For these reasons and more, Mennonite colleges and universities have traditionally emphasized academic disciplines that prepare their students for careers of service in such fields such as teaching, nursing, or ministry. Courses in political science, while perhaps interesting, have rarely been seen as necessary in preparing students for a life of Christian service.

That Mennonite and Brethren in Christ churches have produced many excellent biblical scholars and historians should come as no surprise, given their positive emphasis on the authority of Scripture and their keen sense of God's working in history. Similarly, if one begins with a negative view of the state, including the assumption that holding political office is unbecoming of the citizens of Christ's kingdom, then few Anabaptists would choose political science as scholarly vocation. Why would anyone want to study a discipline that focuses on the nature and function of political processes when one knows from the outset that "earthly kingdoms" are unlikely to produce good fruit? Given these presuppositions, Anabaptism appears to be rocky soil indeed for the development of political science as an academic calling.

Sprouting Questions in Brethren in Christ Soil

Given this context, I am an unlikely candidate for an academic political science career. I grew up in southern Ontario in Canada's oldest Brethren in Christ congregation, founded in the late 1700s. With deep roots in the Brethren in Christ tradition, the Bertie Church of my youth emphasized a strict separation from "worldly" influences. Its members still wore the "plain dress," and its leaders discouraged voting, serving on juries, joining labor unions, and, more generally, becoming involved in activities that would unduly subject a believer to worldly influences.

During these years my grandfather, William Charlton, was pastor of the Bertie Church. As a child I would often accompany my grandfather on trips when he held revival meetings in other Ontario churches. I remember that, near the midpoint of those weeklong meetings, he would often dedicate a sermon to the subject of peace and nonresistance. In it he would recount his personal experiences as a young man who refused military conscription in World War I at a time when the Canadian government was still uncertain what to do with such people.

When my grandfather received his conscription notice, he presented himself to the authorities and informed them that his religious beliefs prohibited him from performing military service. Like the many other young conscientious objectors of his day, he was uncertain whether his stance would mean a lengthy imprisonment or perhaps even execution for treason. Fortunately for him his worst fears were not fulfilled; he was incarcerated for only a short time before the authorities decided to release him.[2]

My grandfather's stance on conscription was rooted in what he believed was a biblical understanding of the doctrine of nonresistance. As a part of this belief, my grandfather was convinced not only that the Christian should not participate in military service, but also that the Christian should not participate in any other activities directly related to government, including voting and sitting on juries.

His deep convictions on these issues—convictions he shared with his fellow church leaders—were rooted in two concerns. On a theological level, he believed that Christians should never participate in an activity that would involve wielding the sword on behalf of the state, even in an indirect or symbolic sense. On a more pragmatic level, he believed that one must be consistent in refusing any involvement in the affairs of the state, lest a perceived inconsistency be used to challenge the church's stance against military service.

This latter belief was given credence by the experience of my father, Hubert Charlton, as he was called for jury duty. After explaining to the judge the basis for his conscientious objection to jury duty, my father was dismissed from the courtroom. But before he could drive away, he was called back into the courtroom and asked by the judge whether he had ever voted. When he replied "Never," the judge was satisfied and dismissed him again. This event was interpreted as evidence that the government's recognition of our conscientious objection to military service was dependent on a consistent refusal to participate in *all forms* of political activity. As a result, I was raised in an environment in which no form of political activity, even voting, was seen as an appropriate Christian duty or responsibility.

Although I was intrigued by grandfather's experience, his stories seemed of little relevance to me as a youth. In my high school years, my intellectual struggles had more to do with the cultural boundaries and regulations imposed by the church. Whether one should wear a necktie or play a musical instrument in the church were more pressing questions than one's stance toward war and the state.

But this changed dramatically during my years as a history major at Messiah College in the late 1960s. At the height of the Vietnam War, my U.S. student colleagues were caught up in intense debates about the morality of the war and the proper Christian response. Now, for the first time, I was forced to struggle personally with some crucial questions: Can war ever be just? Should Christians participate in wars of questionable moral purpose, fought by even more questionable means? If you believe a war is unjust, then do you have a duty to voice these concerns directly to government? How do I explain my stance of "pacifist nonresistance" to that fellow Christian student whose husband has been killed in Vietnam?

As I wrestled with these issues, I discovered what I perceived as contradictions in my own denomination's approach. For while it had historically frowned on political involvement, the Brethren in Christ Church, along with other Anabaptist denominations, regularly sent delegations to Ottawa and Washington to present their cases for military exemption. In some cases the Canadians met directly with the Canadian prime minister himself. If this wasn't a form of political participation, what was?

Such realizations raised other questions in my mind. For instance, if we could speak to government on issues that affected us directly (like exemption from military duty), then why should we not speak on a broader range of issues? On what biblical basis could we take such action?

It was through wrestling with such questions that I first became interested in studying the subject of politics further. Because the options for such study at a Christian liberal arts college were limited, I decided to enroll in a summer course in international politics at the State University of New York at Buffalo. Here, finally, was an opportunity to systematically study the events unfolding in the daily news.

To Africa and Back

After college graduation my wife Lucille and I undertook a term of service with the Mennonite Central Committee (MCC). This decision was a natural outgrowth of our development as Christians. We both believed that Christians were called to live lives of service to others as demonstrated by the life of Christ. Furthermore, we felt that living in Canada (where conscription was not an issue) should not exempt us from ministry, especially while our U.S. classmates faced the choice of conscription or alternate service.

Far from stifling my interest in political science, my MCC experience in Zaire invigorated it, as I witnessed firsthand the bitter fruits of a military dictatorship. We watched as President Mobutu enacted new laws restricting Christians' freedom, a by-product of his "political religion" in which he declared himself the Supreme Guide and Savior of the

Nation. We also watched with dismay as the best intentions of Zaireans to develop their local economies and improve their standards of living were systematically thwarted by a corrupt and repressive regime. Having come of age in the 1950s and 1960s, an era when technological progress and economic prosperity appeared to bring unlimited opportunities, I now faced the hard reality that societies may in fact regress and slip into downward spirals of underdevelopment.

Perhaps more than anything, this experience convinced me that, as a Christian who wanted to bring healing to a broken world, I needed to understand better the political world around me. Thus, when we returned to Canada, I entered a master's program in political science, a program for which I wrote a thesis examining how President Mobutu used traditional and nationalist symbols to build legitimacy for his corrupt regime. My attention had thus moved away from issues of war and peace toward issues of poverty and underdevelopment in Africa.

By the time I began my Ph.D. studies in the mid-1970s, the war in Vietnam had ended and global interests were shifting to the world food crisis of 1972-74 and problems of resource scarcity. At the same time, there were growing discussions about a fundamental restructuring of international economic systems to better meet the needs of the poorest countries.

The timely publication of Ron Sider's *Rich Christians in An Age of Hunger* challenged evangelical Christians to think as carefully about issues of world hunger and economic justice as they did about questions of personal morality and piety.[3] Based on my experiences in Africa, I was increasingly drawn to issues pertaining to the relations between rich and poor countries and the impact of Western aid policies. More specifically, I began to study Canada's food aid policies and the United Nation's World Food Programme.

As most Christians would readily agree, I believe we are called by Christ to feed the hungry and clothe the naked. But as so often happens in the political realm, our good intentions frequently go awry. While giving food aid to hungry nations seems like a natural response to human need, it is often handled in ways that do more damage than good. Indeed, as critics have well established, such aid is often used to promote the political and economic interests of the donors while, at the same time, fostering a dependency that makes the recipients vulnerable to political manipulation. By using the tools of political analysis, I sought to understand how selfish motives distort the intentions of public policies, an analysis that constitutes the first step toward reforming policies to enhance justice and fairness. In all of this, I felt I was using my scholarly vocation to fulfill Christ's call to serve those in need.

Returning to Issues of Violence and Nonviolence

While I was studying food aid policy, I dealt little with *direct* questions about the relationship between my beliefs as an Anabaptist and my work as a political scientist. The influence of Anabaptism was more indirect in nature, influencing the kinds of subjects I wrote about rather than shaping the concepts and approaches that I employed as an academic.

In the early 1990s, however, I was forced to rethink this relationship between scholarship and faith as a result of the growing number of Complex Humanitarian Emergencies (CHEs) developing in countries like Somalia, Sudan, Liberia, Sierra Leone, and Zaire.

During these years the international community witnessed an increasing number of cases in which ordinary citizens faced tremendous human needs, even as their nations were being torn apart by violent civil conflict. My interests in food aid policies drew me naturally to the subject of humanitarian assistance in crisis situations, but I struggled with the issue of whether the United Nations or individual states should intervene militarily to provide such assistance. This, of course, was no abstract question. The situation that most crystallized this issue for me was the collapse of civil authority in Somalia and the emergence of famine conditions amid domestic chaos. As Somalia slid headlong into anarchy, the United Nations (led first by the United States) intervened militarily to ensure the safe distribution of food and other emergency supplies.

Understandably, events in Somalia evoked diverse reactions within the Anabaptist community. In a January 1993 article that appeared in a number of Mennonite publications, J. R. Burkholder and Ted Koontz asked how Mennonites should respond to situations in which violent chaos created widespread suffering. The authors took as their starting point the argument that, in a fallen world, government exercises a legitimate task in maintaining basic order in society, especially for the purpose of preserving life and protecting the innocent. Thus, in the view of extensive suffering in Somalia, the authors asked their readers to consider whether there might be legitimate justification for military intervention to restore order and to alleviate suffering.

"Perhaps it is time," Burkholder and Koontz argued, "to think again about some kind of dualism [by which] we would acknowledge the importance of restoring order and accept the apparent need for governments sometimes to act with force or the threat of force."[4] The authors further contended that Anabaptists do not compromise their pacifism just because they acknowledge some possible good from the military intervention in Somalia; nor must Anabaptists feel compelled to condemn such actions to be faithful to their pacifist convictions. "[T]his may be time for silence," they concluded, "a time to neither condemn nor advocate this particular use of military force."[5]

While some Mennonites expressed similar positions, others criticized Burkholder and Koontz's stance. For instance, Ed Epp and Marv Frey presented the board of the Mennonite Central Committee Canada with a paper entitled, "Away from a 'CNN Theology' of Peace." In it Epp and Frey rejected what they saw as an attempt to legitimize the use of violence, arguing instead for Anabaptists to "reject violence as a solution unconditionally."[6] They were especially unhappy with Burkholder and Koontz's counsel of silence. In a separate paper, Epp noted that this advice was "the most dangerous issue of all. . . . [T]he only justification I can see for the silence is because we fear being marginalized in our communities on this issue."[7]

This debate summarizes for me the dilemma that I faced as an Anabaptist political scientist. To accept the arguments of Epp and Frey necessitated an automatic condemnation of any coercive action taken by any government, no matter what the circumstances—a position that left little room for analysis, reflection, and nuanced argument. Yet I found the counsel of Burkholder and Koontz equally problematic. While sympathetic with their analysis of the situation, their advice that Mennonites remain silent undercut the possible contributions that an Anabaptist political scientist might make to discussions of international policy involving the use of force.

I was thus caught on the horns of the dilemma. If I did not instinctively condemn the actions in Somalia, was I merely justifying military violence and betraying my heritage? But if I chose the more traditional Mennonite stance of remaining quiet, wouldn't I be surrendering my vocation as a political scientist?

In working out a response to this dilemma, I found the writings of Walter Wink and Glen Stassen very useful, particularly their call to move beyond the just war/pacifist stalemate. In grappling with how to respond to the struggle against apartheid in South Africa, Walter Wink suggested the need to focus on the development of violence-reduction criteria. In other words, we need to ask many of the same questions posed by traditional just-war criteria. Wink insists that his approach is not a dualistic vision of God and Caesar in two separate realms. Rather he portrays it as two concentric circles, Caesar's being the smaller circle and God's being the larger. "The church's task," notes Wink, "is to maintain relentless pressure from that larger circle of God on the smaller circle of Caesar."[8]

In building on this idea, I have attempted to apply the following principles:[9] First, war (and the use of violence in any form) is a reflection of humankind's fallen state and is outside the will of God. All violence is therefore sub-Christian and must be acknowledged as such. The church must be unambiguously committed to nonviolence and the search for alternative methods of conflict resolution.

Second, in a fallen world in which God's redemption is not wholly complete, there is a legitimate role for some form of government to use force on occasion to preserve the basic order of society and make possible the achievement of higher values. Such force has only a limited purpose and can never be justified by any appeal to myths of redemptive violence, holy crusade, or just war in which the kingdom of God is advanced by the "Christian" use of force.

And third, when governments use force in such circumstances, we should to seek to identify those ways in which the level of violence and suffering can be reduced from a position of principled nonviolence.

In light of these principles, I believe there are two important sets of questions to ask as a political scientist. The first set, in essence, entails many of the same questions posed by traditional just-war criteria. But these questions are not asked to justify or Christianize the actions. Instead, they are used, as Wink suggests, as violence-reduction criteria to determine whether the actions undertaken will lead to an increase or decrease in the level of violence and suffering being experienced.

The second set of questions reflects what Glen Stassen has called "just peacemaking" criteria.[10] These questions recognize the insufficiency of asking only whether one policy will lead to lesser violence than another. We should also be asking whether a given policy contributes to a just resolution of a conflict. In other words, we must ask how we can move beyond a mere absence (or reduction) of violence toward a set of new relationships that are based on principles of justice.

These approaches have had a significant impact on my work as a political scientist. In the case of armed humanitarian intervention, I have argued that we should choose neither to remain silent nor to automatically condemn all such actions. Rather, in our commitment to principled nonviolence, we should be willing to analyze each case and speak to possible ways of dealing with the difficult dilemmas facing us as members of a global community. This may mean that we occasionally take positions that are not entirely "purist" in nature.

The works of Wink and Stassen have also influenced me in the way I've addressed other issues since the Somalia crisis. For example, I have analyzed and written about the ethical dilemmas of using economic sanctions as an instrument of foreign policy.

Economic sanctions have had great appeal to North Americans (especially Christians) because they appear to be a nonviolent alternative to military action. As we have learned, however, the use of comprehensive economic sanctions against nations such as Haiti and Iraq can indeed inflict great harm and suffering upon those whom we claim to be helping. As a result, I have both criticized as misdirected some recent attempts to "humanize" economic sanctions and have suggested ways that violence reduction and just peacemaking criteria should shape our policies toward those sanctions.[11] In working through such issues, I have come to the conclusion that Anabaptism, with its call to principled nonviolence and constructive peacemaking, is an important resource rather than a hindrance to my work as a political scientist.

Where *Is* the Political Science Department?

As we embark on a new century, how do I *now* feel about the possibility of a distinctive Anabaptist political science? To answer this question we must first revisit the point I made earlier about the relative absence of political science majors at most Mennonite universities and colleges. A closer look will reveal that, while downplaying political science as an academic discipline, many Anabaptist-related schools have developed programs in peace and conflict studies, mediation, and development studies. Most of these programs have an important service component, some requiring their students to do a full year of overseas service.

This speaks to an important element that distinguishes Anabaptist approaches to public policy issues from other traditions. In a recent volume on Christian higher education, editor Richard Hughes cites a Mennonite scholar as telling him that the Reformed approach to higher education is more "cerebral," seeking to "transform living by thinking," whereas the Anabaptist approach "transforms thinking by living and by one's commitment to a radically Christocentric lifestyle."[12]

I similarly suggest that Anabaptist reflections on public policy issues do not generally derive from abstract notions of justice or reasoning from philosophical presuppositions. Rather, Anabaptists have tended to address policy issues from the context of their global service experiences with MCC and similar organizations. As Anabaptists subsequently reflected on these experiences (and sought to share their learnings), they developed service-oriented programs in conflict resolution and development studies, programs addressing such issues as hunger, conflict, underdevelopment, and injustice through a problem-solving approach. In sum, Anabaptists have been less concerned with "developing the discipline" as an academic enterprise than with using the lessons derived from practical experience to minister to the needs of a hurting world.

As a result, Mennonites have tended to address issues of public policy in a broader, more interdisciplinary fashion. This approach has yielded many positive dividends. In Canada, for example, the work of Mennonite researcher Ernie Regehr has had a significant impact on the evolution of Canada's recent foreign policy emphasis on the concept of "human security." Similarly, the work of Mennonites in developing the Victim Offender Reconciliation Program as a concrete embodiment of Christ's ethic of reconciliation has gained a significant hearing within the circles of the criminal justice system.

There is a downside to this, however. Churches in the Anabaptist tradition have done best at addressing issues related to peacemaking and feeding the hungry. They have not, however, developed a coherent political philosophy that helps them address in any systematic way such public policy issues as the environment, abortion, homosexuality, genetic engineering, and reproductive technology.

Many of these public policy issues—the kinds of issues that church members face in their everyday lives—are rife with ambiguities that complicate even the most careful analysis. Without a coherent political philosophy to guide our thought, it will be increasingly difficult for Anabaptists to address such issues with clarity. It is my hope that, in attempting to provide that voice, Anabaptists will increasingly see political science as an academic discipline worth taking seriously.

NOTES

1. Messiah College stands out as an exception here, with a Department of Politics and three tenure-track political scientists.

2. The details of my grandfather's life can be found in Lucille Charlton, "I Was a Stranger: The Story of William Charlton," *Brethren in Christ History and Life* 12 (1989): 3-49.

3. Ronald J. Sider, *Rich Christians in an Age of Hunger: A Biblical Study* (Downers Grove, Ill.: InterVarsity Press, 1977).

4. J. R. Burkholder and Ted Koontz, "When Armed Force is Used to Make Relief Work Possible," *Gospel Herald,* January 12, 1993, 6.

5. Ibid., 7.

6. Ed Epp and Marv Frey, "Away from a 'CNN Theology' of Peace," Winnipeg, Man.: Mennonite Central Committee Canada, March 1993.

7. Ed Epp, "Military Intervention in Somalia: A Case Study and Background Material," Winnipeg, Man.: Mennonite Central Committee Canada, January 1993, 6.

8. Walter Wink, *Engaging the Powers: Discernment and Resistance in a World of Domination* (Minneapolis, Minn.: Fortress Press, 1992), 227.

9. The following principles are drawn from my article "Pursuing Human Justice in a Society of States: The Ethical Dilemmas of Armed Humanitarian Intervention," *Conrad Grebel Review* 12 (1994): 1-20.

10. Glen H. Stassen, *Just Peacemaking: Transforming Initiatives for Justice and Peace* (Louisville, Ky.: Westminster/John Knox Press, 1992).

11. See Mark W. Charlton, Heidi Rolland Unruh, and Keith J. Pavlischek, *Justice and Economic Statecraft: The Ethics of International Economic Sanctions* (Wynnewood, Pa.: Crossroads Monograph Series on Faith and Public Policy, 1998); and Mark W. Charlton, "Humanizing Economic Sanctions: A Misplaced Agenda?" presented at the Canadian Political Science Meetings, Sherbrooke, Quebec, in June 1999.

12. Richard T. Hughes, "Introduction," in *Models for Christian Higher Education: Strategies for Success in the Twenty-First Century*, ed. Richard T. Hughes and William B. Adrian (Grand Rapids, Mich: Eerdmans, 1997), 6. The quotations are from Hughes; he does not quote the Mennonite scholar verbatim, nor does he identify the person by name.

10: Education
___

Education as the Practice of Faith

Polly Ann Brown

*F*OR MANY YEARS I SEARCHED FOR A WAY TO CONNECT faith and learning, a search that was largely motivated by my educational work with high school students and adults in a Mennonite community. I became a part of their lives, participated in their struggles to learn—and, to my dismay, saw how the use of certain educational practices hindered their learning. In the process, I began to think about how the biblical call for justice and compassion could influence the work of educators.

In the academy, I had learned about sound educational practices that were compatible with key themes of an Anabaptist faith, e.g., community, mutuality, justice, peace, and service. Indeed, these themes comprise the dynamic threads of an exemplary education. And so, by combining certain educational theories and methods and the central themes of an Anabaptist faith, I worked to create a faith-and-learning model.

When others learned about my work, they invited me to present my model to various audiences. But it soon became clear to me that the essence of a faith-based education could not be summarized in written language and presented via monologue. Indeed, the link between faith and learning is not primarily about ideas; rather, it is about people, their relationships, and the human longing to hear, respond, and be known.

Looking back, I see that my life and work as an educator were born, not from disembodied ideas, but from encounters with teachers, students, and parents. They were born from my desire to hear and respond to some, and from my resistance to hear others (i.e., my need to prove I was right). Some of the encounters were marked by trust, reciprocity, and dialogue. Others were marked by a need for healing and reconciliation. And so I can only point to a way of educating by telling this story and inviting response.

Beginnings

In 1975, my husband, our four sons, and I returned to the United States after three years in Ethiopia, where my husband had been practicing medicine under the auspices of the United Presbyterian Church. Upon our return, we settled in a largely Mennonite community. We were somewhat familiar with Mennonites. We knew that they were pacifists; we also had a sense that when people were in trouble—outsiders as well as insiders—they would be there to help. As a friend whose town had been damaged by floodwaters put it, "The Mennonites were the first ones here."

We enrolled our sons in Mennonite schools and soon were invited to a Sunday morning worship service in a no-frills, centuries-old meetinghouse with wooden benches and hat racks. To be courteous, we planned to attend one Sunday and then return to our Presbyterian church. On that Sunday, however, the pastor and his wife invited us to dinner the following Sunday, an invitation which meant a return Sunday morning visit. This became the pattern for enough Sundays to make us wonder whether we would ever return to the Presbyterian church.

About that time, our youngest son fractured his skull and spent a week in the hospital. The Mennonites were the first ones there—with cards, flowers, gifts, words of support, and meals delivered to our home. In February 1976, one year after we had moved into the community, my husband and I joined our new friends' Mennonite church.

The community quickly became the context for my educational work. Almost immediately I began to teach reading and writing to a few adolescents, working out of my home. In 1980, I undertook literacy studies in the Graduate School of Education at the University of Pennsylvania and, three years later, became the reading specialist at the local Mennonite high school.

Many of my students there had been labeled "learning disabled." All were described as "poor" readers, had fared badly on conventional tests, and had generally been unsuccessful in school from the beginning. As I got to know the students, however, I quickly saw that they were more capable and their experiences richer than test scores or labels indicated. Nor did labels and test scores offer practical guidance; they did not help me know how I could help the students. I needed to understand the students' potential and limitations more fully.

The search for useful information on my students became the focus of my dissertation research. In the belief that learning is affected by people's relationships within particular social settings, I explored (among other things) how attitudes and practices associated with literacy and learning in students' families and in their community impacted their learning.[1]

By the time I completed my dissertation in 1987, I was clear about two things. First, I recognized there were conflicts and tensions in the community surrounding literacy and learning, conflicts related to the desire to remain faithful to traditional beliefs, on the one hand, and the attraction to modern cultural trends, on the other. More specifically, there was a tendency to separate physical and mental activity and to divide people into two categories, those referred to as "workers" and those called "thinkers."

Second, I had come to oppose the use of (or at least the consequences of) educational practices such as tracking, labeling, and certain kinds of tests. These means for ranking and sorting students appeared, from my perspective, to further polarize the community. Moreover, these practices ignored family history and cultural contexts, insuring that individual students would sometimes be misunderstood.

For example, one of my students, born and raised on a farm, had not had experiences with print (story reading, for instance) similar to those of her kindergarten peers. By the end of second grade, school officials in her public school had labeled her "learning disabled." Another of my students had been placed in the low reading group in her public school second-grade class, because she could not answer questions about fairy tales or nursery rhymes on a standardized test. What school officials had neglected to consider, however, was the fact that, in her home, books that were "made up" instead of "built on truth" were not permitted.

A Search for Justice

In opposing such labeling, I believed I was on the side of justice. Dividing a community of learners into those called "gifted" and "disabled" on the basis of test scores seemed to me both unfair and unbiblical. Thankfully, colleagues in the school where I worked were raising similar concerns, often in response to their faith commitments. "Labels are for the birds," one teacher told me. "I don't like to stereotype. . . . I guess that's my faith consciousness."

In my dissertation I quoted our school administrator, who favored heterogeneous grouping. "Both from our practical experience and from a congregational orientation," he said, "we should all be learners together." I also quoted the guidance counselor, who contended "there are just too many factors in being human to give [standardized tests] much credit."

Other activities at the school reinforced my thinking. At an in-service program in the fall of 1983, we heard from Orville Yoder of the Mennonite Board of Education and discussed his document, "Anabaptist Ideals and Mennonite Schools: In Search of Congruence." Yoder emphasized cooperation over competition, assessment of progress toward goals rather than comparative status, and "bringing people together rather than isolating them from each other." In all of this I began to see how the Anabaptist faith story might help people to imagine an alternative to predominant educational models and practices.

In the course of these years I freely expressed my opinions about educational matters to those who seemed to agree with me. When I was with people who disagreed with me, I voiced my views passionately and generally ignored their arguments and concerns. In fact, I tended to distance myself from such persons. When I was invited to chair a committee whose task it was to create an educational philosophy statement for the three Franconia Conference Mennonite schools, I believed I had created a process that would incorporate wide-ranging voices into the statement—and yet, as I now recognize, there was nothing in the final draft that I could not embrace. While it crossed my mind at the time that I had steered the process toward my own educational preferences, I certainly didn't dwell on that possibility.

In any case, finding ways to strengthen links between faith and learning became my passion, and the academy served as a rich resource. I was intrigued by the harmony between Anabaptist themes and insights from emerging educational perspectives, and I listened closely to the dialogue between educational scholarship and religious faith—a dialogue that offered both ideas and language for building a faith-based education.[2]

For instance, some scholars were suggesting that knowing was "relational" and pointed to the need for "collaboration" and creating "communities of learners."[3] Others contended there were "multiple intelligences" (a view compatible with the New Testament view of "many gifts"), while still others argued that "narrative" offered the key to understanding and remembering.[4] (I even found a book entitled *Teaching as Story Telling*, not a new idea to those who recall that Jesus frequently answered questions by telling stories.[5])

On a more concrete level, I discovered that teachers were using writing workshops and interactive mathematics programs to promote quality learning in groups of learners whose histories were diverse.[6] What's more, "service learning" had become one of Pennsylvania's "State Standards," and significant connections were being made between liberation theology and a "pedagogy of hope."[7] Increasingly, educational scholars were suggesting that equity was a precondition for excellence; they were also suggesting that preparing students "for life" demanded that students learn how to collaborate with persons of varying interests, abilities, and histories.[8]

These and other educational trends only confirmed my faith-based sensitivities, none more so than the growing tendency to challenge the medical model of education, a model that demanded finding "pathologies" in students who experienced learning difficulties. Over the years, these pathologies have included "learning disabilities," "minimal brain dysfunctions," "hyperactivity," and since 1980, "Attention Deficit Disorder" (ADD) or "Attention Deficit Disorder with Hyperactivity" (ADHD).[9]

I learned that, even with the increase in use of the medical model, almost all special education scholars agreed that neurologically based learning difficulties were rare. These scholars suggested that school failure resulted not from *student* disabilities, but rather from ineffective, highly disorganized bureaucratic *institutions* that were simply incapable of dealing with diversity.[10] That the medical view of learning (or the diagnostic-prescriptive model) tended to ignore the family and cultural pieces of students' lives only exacerbated that problem.

In addition to finding educational themes running parallel to my faith commitments, I would sometimes find "secular" educational literature making overt expressions of faith. One researcher, a winner of the MacArthur Award, began her book with a New Testament verse (2 Cor. 10:12) and an expression of gratitude to those who had invited her to preach in their churches.[11] One of the leading journals in my field, *Harvard Educational Review*, included an affirming review of a book on how to foster religious knowledge.[12] And in a discussion about liberatory education in the same periodical, Paulo Freire's honest expressions of his faith were most evident.[13]

Looking Within

Having learned of these links between educational scholarship and religious faith, I worked to create an "Integrated Faith and Learning Model," which I presented at a Mennonite educators' conference in fall 1999. Shortly afterwards my world turned upside-down (or was it right-side-up?) when my mentor asked me a question that profoundly reoriented my thinking.

We were discussing my ideas for integrating faith and learning and about the need to reject the use of the diagnostic-prescriptive model of learning. She affirmed my desire for dialogue and my general willingness to live with dilemmas. Then she encouraged me to think about how those desires might apply to my own learning model. "So what would you say are the benefits of the other model, the one that opposes yours?" she asked.[14] To my chagrin, I had no answer to her question.

Over the course of the next week, I reviewed my model closely. I had condensed it into a one-page document, neat and succinct. This one-page summary specified goals, learning principles, ways of relating to others, learning experiences, evaluation methods, and a bibliography of "compatible principles and practices."

The model (which I still affirm) pointed to a relational ethic that is life-giving and just. In it I began with the theological assumption that "everyone is created in the likeness of God, is of inestimable worth, and deserves to be confirmed in his or her uniqueness." From there I suggested ways for teachers to use *everyone's* gifts to benefit the *whole* learning community, and I emphasized the need for a commitment to "genuine dialogue." In sum, the model called for a biblical mode of address and response that "reverberates back to Adam . . . when he is asked, 'Where art thou?'"[15] Or, to place it in a New Testament context, it reflected a commitment to the "rustic face-to-face model of social relations" that Jesus demonstrated.[16]

Given those commitments, the model advocated open, honest communication that refuses to gloss over differences for the sake of easy compromise. While operating by such a model may include head-butting and tugs of war, the model rejected the idea that there is merit in only one side. So while it called persons to hold their ground and speak their truths in love, it also called for affirming the other and for stretching to see merit in the other's side.

As I let the model's words sink in, I began to see the contradictions between the principles I had outlined and the way I related to others. The model advocated dialogue; I often presented my ideas through monologue. The model stressed the need for transformation; yet I was maintaining the status quo by retreating from potential conflict. Reflecting the words of Paul, the model pointed to a knowing that is partial, that sees through "a glass dimly"; it therefore advocated an open and tentative stance. I, however, clung to my views as if they were Truth with a capital T. Indeed, I had adopted an either-or mindset, however subtly expressed; one side (my side) was right and the other was wrong. While claiming that we should look for learners' gifts, I viewed those who opposed me in terms of deficits.

Finally, the model stressed that every context is informed by justice dynamics. And yet, while pursuing justice in a larger arena, I had overlooked the need for justice in my way of relating to the persons in front of me. I had forgotten that there can be no justice without compassion, no compassion without justice. While embracing a faith that required radical reconciliation to God and neighbors, I had allowed my "intellectual" endeavors to become barriers.

Recognizing this gap between my theory and my practice was a painful realization. Still, I recognized it as an opportunity. Now, perhaps, I could *really* begin the work of placing my educational perspective and my faith into conversation. I would begin by looking back, by reconsidering the stories I had gathered during my study of the Mennonite community.

As I began to do so, I discovered that I had instinctively responded to the various splits in the community by taking sides. Perhaps this time around I would find a better way to respond. Perhaps this time I would see ways to bring healing.

"Pious Ignorance" and "A Thirst to Know"

When I first began my study of the Mennonite community, years ago, I was presented with a literacy artifact, a collection of journal excerpts written by a bibliophile in 1889. In the journal, the man recalled how, as a child and against the will of his father, he had developed a love of books and learning, a "thirst to know":

> I bought books and they were attached to my heart . . . I had such a thirst to know. . . . Father was opposed to learning. . . . [H]e made it a point of conscience to bring me up in pious ignorance. . . . I did most of my reading at night by stolen time . . . until I was found out. . . . Such a scolding I got. . . . [Father] said he did all he could to bring me up as he thought he should. . . . what the final end would be God only knew. . . . [S]o he washed his hands in innocence, like Pilate.[17]

"A thirst to know" and "pious ignorance." These two phrases poignantly evoked what I was noticing in the community where I worked. Other expressions (expressions I was both hearing and using) likewise reflected the ongoing community conflict, for they referred to people as belonging to one of two distinct groups: the "intellectuals" and "the anti-intellectuals"; "those who value the life of the mind" and "those who prefer to work with their hands"; "the academically oriented" and "the practically minded"; "the educated" and "the uneducated"; "the work-study student" and "the college-bound student"; "those who value education" and "those who do not value education."

While I was somewhat ambivalent about these dualistic ways of categorizing people, I realized that, for the most part, I had accepted these distinctions uncritically. And when I began to look for ways this community conflict had played itself out in my students' lives, I discovered that I had fallen into the trap of viewing some of my students as "anti-intellectual."

For instance, one of my high school students had said to me, "I like to work with my hands, not my mind." As part of his work, Scott (not his real name) read and used information from many different kinds of texts, including engine repair manuals. In school, he demonstrated that he was an active and confident reader as he engaged poetry, short stories, John Steinbeck's *The Pearl*, *New Yorker* articles, and many other texts. Moreover, he seemed genuinely interested in what he referred to as "real reading" during what he called "a break in the day." And yet, Scott would sometimes say that "school has nothing for me." At the end of his sophomore year, Scott quit school—and, to my discredit, I thought of him as one more of our number who opposed "intellectual" pursuits.

I also looked at ways the community dichotomies created tensions in individuals well into their adult lives. A middle-aged friend, Sarah (again, not her real name), decided to go to college and asked me to help with the reading, writing, and study that were now required of her. In our work together, it quickly became obvious to me that she was still beholden to the voice of her deceased father. Growing up on a farm, Sarah had been allowed to read after the supper dishes were done, but her father told her that reading during daylight hours (when there was work to be done) was "laziness." Later, Sarah had wanted to go to college and had even enrolled, but her father told her that "girls don't need a college education," for "if they get married the money spent will be wasted."

Sarah did eventually marry, and after her children were grown, she decided to attend a private, Christian college. "I want to prove to myself that I'm not dumb," she told me, adding, "I have always felt that people who don't go to college do not have the same value as those who do. . . . The question, 'Where did you go to college?' made me feel inferior."

Sarah worked hard to succeed in college. Because she had little experience with the kinds of reading and writing required for college work, she took a speed-reading and study skills course, attended a writing workshop, and worked with tutors. She was determined to get A's, and she believed that doing so meant knowing almost everything that was said in class. She therefore taped class lectures, transcribed them into handwriting, and then studied the transcripts along with assigned readings in preparation for class discussions, exams, and writing assignments.

Despite this hard work, however, remembered voices hindered Sarah's learning and the corresponding development of her *own* voice. More specifically, messages she had received while growing up—messages that discouraged academic pursuits, "impractical" reading, and critical thinking—negatively impacted her college work.

For instance, when Sarah was invited to put the author's message into her own words, she expressed frustration to me and said that she had been told not to "change people's words." When asked if she agreed with a particular professor's or author's point of view, Sarah responded, "I was taught not to express my own opinion or to question [authority figures]. . . . The church and the home told you what and how to think. . . . Now when someone asks me 'What do *you* think?' I don't know how to begin."

In addition, Sarah struggled to integrate the new information she learned at college with various voices from her past. At college, Sarah heard that God could be understood in male *and* female terms, that persons ought to love and care for themselves, and that women and men should be granted equal rights. Looking up from her transcribed lecture notes one afternoon, she said to me, "I was made to feel that women were second-class citizens . . . that they were to submit to men." Sarah was also becoming aware of such issues as the inherent bias in standardized tests against African-American students (and also against members of her community).

But this new learning was not easy. Indeed, Sarah's fear of forsaking her traditional beliefs, when coupled with her desire to open herself to new ideas, created a tremendous dissonance. Once, in tears, she complained to me, "It's like there's no good or bad, no right or wrong anymore."

Sarah received the A's she sought and even an A+, grades that were based both on her hard work and her response to extra credit opportunities. At the end of our work together, she reported, "My schoolwork makes me feel good. . . . When I go out and people talk about things, I'll think 'Oh! I heard that somewhere before,' and I can enter into a conversation . . . , but it's hard work just to enter into a conversation. . . . All this reading, writing, and studying, and I haven't cleaned the house in weeks."

What I've Learned as a Mennonite Educator

Today I look for the way these tensions and conflicts play out in my own life. The pathway between faith and learning was not to be found "out there"; I needed to look within and see how I was divided into an intellectual self and a faith-and-justice self. The struggle to integrate these two pieces has helped me see things in the stories that I did not see the first time around.

Conflicts as resources

For instance, I have come to see that both the father who wanted to raise his son in "pious ignorance" and the son who had "a thirst to know" were seekers of truth. Different though they were, both demonstrated real forms of devotion and knowing. I've also come to see that, to varying degrees, all human performance is both physical and mental.[18] I helped to extend Scott's learning by introducing literature that went beyond the "practically relevant." Yet I missed the opportunity to help him see that there are no nonintellectual or non-thinking manual laborers. Farmers, mechanics, brain surgeons, homemakers, theoretical physicists, computer engineers, piano tuners, backhoe drivers, accountants, and landscape managers all represent differences in their forms of knowledge and in the degrees to which their activities are both bodily and conceptual. I missed the opportunity to help Scott see the difference between (a) learning carpentry for the sake of earning a living and (b) learning carpentry for the sake of acquiring the skill of thinking with one's hands and tools.[19]

Of course, conflicts over various sorts of learning were not new to the Mennonite Church in the late twentieth century. Major differences over literacy and formal education had contributed to a church split as early as 1847.[20] At that time, one church family became two, and not until a century and a half later (1995), following years of face-to-face dialogue, did representatives from the two separate Mennonite denominations vote to reunite.

Reuniting a divided church has not been easy, nor is it *going to be* easy. Concerns linger, as does the awareness that tough organizational and theological issues still need to be addressed. And yet reparation and reconciliation had been wrought out of the grace of residual trust—and through the risky, hard work of genuine dialogue. Conflicts have become resources. I have only begun to consider the implications of this kind of work for students, their families, and educators.

The significance of family loyalties

Looking back I also see more clearly the significance and power of family dynamics in my students' lives (and in my own). According to

New Testament scholar Walter Wink, family is "the most profoundly soul-shaping institution in human society."[21] I would agree. Family is the place where pain and alienation are most intensely known; it is also the place where God's grace, healing, and redemption can be incarnated most radically. As I've already noted, a student's so-called failure is most often related to an institution's inability to deal with diversity, and family context is no doubt the most significant context informing the "diversity" with which schools must contend. Family ties, for good and for ill, powerfully affect students' school achievement.

Returning more specifically to the stories above, we see various family contexts influencing students' learning. We see a father caught between loyalty to his own father's ways and loyalty to his son, who was embracing new ways of learning. We see a young man caught between his parents' work ethic and his teachers' aims. And we see a woman whose ties to her father meant struggling for the freedom to critique others' ideas, even while she was bound to near-perfect standards for performance. It didn't matter whether it was course work or cleaning the kitchen floor: Sarah needed her work to be perfect.

I sense similar struggles in myself. I carried into the academy pieces of my own family legacy (pieces to which I am still bound, at least to some extent). For instance, I still feel the need to please others, to comply with the rules, to demonstrate "scholarship," and to do things "right." When the going got tough during my doctoral program, I considered bowing out. My father's words of encouragement, "You can do it!" meant to me, "You *must* do it!" and so, out of loyalty to him, I persevered. There was both gain in that decision and a price to be paid. Loyalty to my father surfaced in other ways—for instance, in the way I felt caught between professors who urged me to write in academic language and my father who asked, "Polly Ann, when are you going to write for the man on the street?"

Many educators acknowledge that lurking beneath students' decisions about ways of relating—whether to engage or not, comply or not, act out or not—are loyalty conflicts rooted in family life. In collaboration with others, I have only begun to seek a way for teachers, parents, and students to ensure that family pieces will be integrated into the life of the school.

The need for connection and healing

This, I believe, is the place where faith and learning come together: it is found in the daily struggle of teachers, parents, and students to hear and to be known, in the human longing to connect. The longing to connect drives young children to accomplish the most extraordinary learning achievement of their lifetimes. In the first three years of life, driven by their need to communicate, children all over the world learn human languages, systems of remarkable complexity, without much instruction and without much effort. Linguists refer to children as linguistic geniuses, and the source of their genius is nothing less than the longing to engage others. That, indeed, is the very essence of learning, and I'm pleased to say that I have seen the lives of children and young people transformed by teachers who embrace as a rich resource children's relentless drive to be known, to know others, and to know their worlds.

Some teachers believe it is even possible to penetrate the resistance to learning built up over years of difficult life experience, and to thereby rekindle a person's innate passion for learning. Boston University professor Elizabeth "Ma" Barker is one such teacher.

In 1972, Barker started a prison education program that now offers both bachelor's and master's degrees. By reciting poetry, by inviting speakers such as Nobel Prize-winning biochemist George Wald and historian Howard Zinn, and by various others means, Barker endeavors to convince her students that a liberal arts degree is well worth the work. And her program has succeeded. Among her former students are a tunnel worker, an aspiring novelist, a criminal defense lawyer, a director of a job training program for homeless people, and an associate editor of the Pacific News Service.[22]

Granted, most stories about educational initiatives are not that dramatic, but such should be our hope and our vision. The core of an Anabaptist faith, as I understand it, is that faith *is* practice. I therefore envision schools and classrooms where knowledge will be pursued not as an end in itself but as a means to heal a broken world, broken relationships, and broken selves.[23] In such classrooms the history of civilization will be linked to our relationship to the ecosystem and our responsibility to use natural resources wisely; the study of democracy will lead to discussions about racial strife and the need for social justice; and the Bible will be studied for the purpose of knowing how our lives are to be lived in response to a loving God and in relationship to others.[24]

Conclusion

For much of my adult life I focused on getting my doctrine right. I thought I had it wrapped up in an airtight system. Then I met the Mennonites. They served us meals and helped us clean and move into our new house. They taught us how to play Dutch Blitz, how to make bread-and-butter pickles, and how to freeze corn and applesauce. Together we stood by our son's hospital bed and prayed. From Mennonite friends, I learned that faith, at bedrock level, is about loving God and neighbor.

In my work, I believed education could be transformed if only we would find the right theories, use the best practices, and pull the right lever in the voting booth. And then I worked side-by-side with Mennonite educators and participated in the lives of Mennonite students and their families. And I learned that a faith-infused education is primarily about a way of relating to others that is mutual, just, and rooted in trust. It is about the embodiment of a relational ethic and the living union of teachers, parents, students, and subjects. It is about educators who seek to bring healing to a broken world by extending the practice of faith into the life of their classrooms.

Notes

I would like to thank Barbara Krasner, John K. Stoner, and my husband, Ken, for their careful reading and helpful suggestions as I revised this chapter. As noted in the text, the names of students have been changed to protect their privacy.

1. Polly Ann Walker Brown, "Toward a Dynamic Assessment Model for Understanding Literacy Learning Difficulties of Adolescents: Case Studies in a Mennonite High School" (Ph.D. diss., University of Pennsylvania, 1987). My study drew on theories summarized in David Bloome and Judith Green, "Directions in the Sociolinguistic Study of Reading," in *Handbook of Reading Research*, ed. P. David Pearson, et al. (New York: Longman, 1984), 395-421.

2. Moving between so-called "secular" and "sacred" spheres, I found Paul Tillich's distinction between that which is Christian in *substance* and that which is Christian in *name* very helpful. See, for instance, Paul Tillich, *Christianity and the Encounter of the World Religions* (New York: Columbia University Press, 1963).

3. For the relational aspects of knowing, see Michael Polanyi, *Personal Knowledge: Towards a Post-Critical Philosophy* (Chicago: University of Chicago Press, 1962), 300-21; and Jerry H. Gill, *On Knowing God* (Philadelphia: Westminster Press, 1981), 141-52. For emphases on collaboration, see Jeannie Oakes and Karen Hunter Quartz, ed., *Creating New Educational Communities* (Chicago: National Society for the Study of Education, 1995).

4. For multiple intelligences, see Howard Gardner, *Multiple Intelligences: The Theory in Practice* (New York: BasicBooks, 1993). For the importance of narrative,

see Diane Gillespie, *The Mind's We: Contextualism in Cognitive Psychology* (Carbondale, Ill.: Southern Illinois University Press, 1992).

5. Kieran Egan, *Teaching as Story Telling: An Alternative Approach to Teaching and Curriculum in the Elementary School* (Chicago: University of Chicago Press, 1986).

6. See Nancie Atwell, *In the Middle: New Understandings about Writing, Reading, and Learning*, 2nd. ed. (Portsmouth, N.H.: Boynton/Cook, 1998); and Dan M. Fendal and Diane Rosek, with Lynne Alper and Sherry Fraser, *Interactive Mathematics Program* (Berkeley, Calif.: Key Curriculum Press, 1999).

7. For ideas about service learning, see Joan Schine, ed., *Service Learning* (Chicago: National Society for the Study of Education, 1997). For issues related to liberatory pedagogy, see Daniel S. Schipani, *Religious Education Encounters Liberation Theology* (Birmingham, Ala.: Religious Education Press, 1998); and Paulo Freire, *Pedagogy of Hope: Reliving Pedagogy of the Oppressed* (New York: Continuum, 1994).

8. Thomas Skrtic, "The Special Education Paradox: Equity as the Way to Excellence," in *Special Education at the Century's End*, ed. Thomas Hehir and Thomas Latus (Cambridge, Mass.: Harvard Educational Review, 1992), 203-75.

9. Since 1990 the numbers of children and adults diagnosed with ADD has risen from about 900,000 to five million, a rise accompanied by a 700 percent increase in the amount of Ritalin produced. See Lawrence H. Diller, *Running on Ritalin: A Physician Reflects on Children, Society, and Performance in a Pill* (New York: Bantam Books, 1998).

10. See Skrtic, "The Special Education Paradox."

11. Shirley Brice Heath, *Ways with Words: Language, Life, and Work in Communities and Classrooms* (Cambridge: Cambridge University Press, 1983), xi-xiii.

12. Arthur J. Schwartz, review of *Godly Play: A Way of Religious Education*, by Jerome W. Berryman, *Harvard Educational Review* 63 (1993): 125-26.

13. Paulo Freire and Donald P. Macedo, "A Dialogue: Culture, Language, and Race," *Harvard Educational Review* 65 (1995): 377-402.

14. Personal conversation with Barbara R. Krasner, Ph.D.

15. Barbara R. Krasner and Austin J. Joyce, *Trust, Truth, and Relationships: Healing Interventions in Contextual Therapy* (New York: Brunner/Mazel, 1995), 4.

16. John Howard Yoder, *The Politics of Jesus* (Grand Rapids, Mich.: Eerdmans, 1972), 16.

17. Excerpts from "The Autobiographic Reflections of a Mennonite Bibliophile," June 13, 1889. The excerpts were given to me by John L. Ruth, Harleysville, Pa.

18. See Polanyi, *Personal Knowledge*, 58-60, 321-23.

19. Mortimer Adler, *Reforming Education: The Opening of the American Mind* (New York: Macmillan, 1988), 283.

20. John L. Ruth, *Maintaining the Right Fellowship* (Scottdale, Pa.: Herald Press, 1984), 272, 539.

21. Walter Wink, *Engaging the Powers: Discernment and Resistance in a World of Domination* (Minneapolis, Minn.: Fortress Press, 1992), 120.

22. Farah Stockman, "Ex-Inmates Owe Success to 'Ma': Say Teacher Gave Dignity, Direction," *Boston Globe*, March 9, 2001.

23. Parker J. Palmer, *To Know as We are Known: Education as a Spiritual Journey* (San Francisco: HarperCollins, 1993), 8.

24. In other words, these classrooms will help students avoid the quandary illustrated in the Broadway play *Copenhagen*, in which two quantum physicists return to life and discuss what they would have done differently. During their lives the physicists did not reflect sufficiently on how their science, which led to the creation and use of the atom bomb, might harm people. The play ends with one of the scientists musing that, instead of focusing on quantum physics, he and his colleagues should have been pursuing quantum ethics.

11: Old Testament

Anabaptists and the Old Testament: Two Peas in Different Pods

Terry L. Brensinger

I REMEMBER WITH GREAT CLARITY AN EXPERIENCE I HAD during my first visit to Israel in 1980. I was taking a class on Judaism taught by a feisty and charismatic Jewish professor. At some point during the semester, we discussed the book of Leviticus. Aware that there were a number of Christians in the class, the professor seized the moment and vented his frustration. "I don't care what you Christians do with Leviticus," he shouted while pounding the podium, "but do *something* with it!"

I share much of this same sentiment with respect to the *entire* Old Testament. I want people, particularly Anabaptists, to do something with the Old Testament, and I would hope that my work as a scholar might help them in that process.

Discovering an Interest: Anabaptism and Historical Studies

From the moment I became a Christian, I wanted to enter some type of full-time ministry. As a result, I enrolled at Messiah College as a religion major—that seemed like the logical field in which to begin. Having attended a United Methodist church, I was totally unaware of the theological tradition of the college, and to be honest, I never really looked into it. The fact that Messiah was a Christian college satisfied the level of my inquiry at that time. Little did I know how profoundly the decision to attend Messiah would influence the rest of my life.

At Messiah College, I underwent a dramatic conversion—to the love of history. I dabbled temporarily in the behavioral sciences, but I never found them quite to my liking. Then, as part of the general education curriculum, I came under the tutelage of historian E. Morris Sider.

During my years in high school, history ranked among my least favorite subjects. In my mind, studying history involved little more than memorizing dates, names, and places, all of which had no apparent relevance to me. While listening to Professor Sider, however, that perception began to change. Now I was introduced to sweeping ideas that stood behind the various dates, names, and places, and I sensed for the first time the remarkable connections between the past and the present.

Furthermore, in Sider I saw firsthand a life of devotion and learning. Here was a highly educated man who served the Lord, gave himself to the church, and wrote articles and books. After meeting with him and Carlton Wittlinger, another historian, I eagerly added history to my ongoing religion major. Along with this newfound love of history came a growing appreciation for the Anabaptist tradition. Both Sider and my academic advisor, Martin Schrag, were deeply committed Anabaptists, and their views on various subjects often challenged the ideas that I held. Particularly disquieting to me were their understanding of the nature of the church and their all-embracing theology of peace.

Although I had been raised in a loving Christian home, I had not previously conceived of the visible church as a distinct and separate "kingdom" within the world. For me, the church was little more than a place where individual Christians gathered weekly to sing and pray. Likewise, my father served as a tank sergeant in World War II, and I grew up intrigued by his uniform, German lugers, and other military paraphernalia. My dad, in all fairness, is a gentle and gracious man, and he neither spoke about his experiences in the army nor encouraged any type of violent behavior. The point, however, is that I never seriously encountered pacifism and nonresistance—they remained alien concepts. While I hardly grasped the many nuances of Schrag's and Sider's positions at this time (and by no means accepted them painlessly), I now began the process of careful investigation.

This process reached its culmination, at least at the undergraduate level, during my senior year, when I completed a semester-long independent study of Anabaptist history and thought. The study, completed under the direction of Schrag and Sider, resulted in a paper fifty pages in length. In it I traced the historical events that led to the rift between Zwingli and the early Anabaptists, and I also examined Anabaptist views on selected theological issues.

Increasingly, I sensed an emerging affinity with this tradition and its emphases on radical discipleship, service, community, and peace. In my heart and mind, these convictions and beliefs best captured the essence of the Christian faith as I had come to experience it.

At this point in my life, however, I had little idea of where this would lead. I assumed that I would attend seminary—again, it seemed like the next logical step—but, beyond that, I did not know. While I never ruled out pastoral ministry, I sensed a mounting desire to pursue scholarship and teaching as my life's work. This sense arose in large part due to the mentoring of my professors, who repeatedly challenged me to consider further academic work, scholarship, and teaching.

Confirming a Passion:
Anabaptism and Old Testament Scholarship

Since both Sider and Schrag were historians, I imagined that my journey might lead me to pursue church history as my own area of academic specialization. Before long, however, I realized that my primary interests lay elsewhere.

This realization came to me during my first year at Asbury Theological Seminary, in 1978. I enrolled in Introductory Hebrew, an experience that nearly leveled me. Working at a pace more rapid and intense than any I had previously known, I maneuvered my way through this strange and "backward" language, hoping simply to survive. Much to my surprise, this hope to survive soon gave way to a sense of calling. I now began to recognize Old Testament studies as my academic and vocational home.

In retrospect, several factors undoubtedly led to this recognition. First, my interest in history meshed well with the study of the Old Testament which, to a large extent, is a historical discipline. Second, my innate curiosity found a happy outlet in reading and interpreting ancient texts and archaeological artifacts. I had always enjoyed roaming through unknown places and searching out curious items (I could spend considerable time reading tombstones in local cemeteries); the Old Testament presented an endless array of places, people, and stories to explore. Third, my desire to be in full-time ministry fit nicely as well.

My Hebrew professor at Asbury, a man of profound learning and spirituality, was deeply involved in training ministers as well as serving the church and academy through preaching, teaching, research, and writing. As I observed his life, I realized that serious scholarship and ministry were not mutually exclusive. The fact that the wider church appeared to me to be rather illiterate with respect to the Old Testament only reinforced my desire to continue in this direction. The further fact that the Anabaptist world in general and the Brethren in Christ Church in particular had few Old Testament scholars—even today there is only one other Brethren in Christ person with a Ph.D. in Old Testament and two more (both former students of mine) on the way—sealed the decision to enter graduate school.

Here, more than ever, I began to see the confluence of my Old Testament studies and the Anabaptist theological tradition. Various ideas and themes that I typically associated with the New Testament—grace, obedience, and community—leaped from the ancient pages of the Old Testament like never before, leading me further along my theological journey. In fact, a friend of mine and I actually came to embrace a more comprehensive theology of peace while studying ancient Israel's war narratives and prophetic texts in graduate school. Since that time, I have devoted much of my life to exploring these texts and sharing my discoveries with others.

Meeting a Need: The Problem of the Old Testament

During its best moments, the church has viewed the Old Testament as an important part of sacred Scripture. It was, after all, the Bible that Jesus and his disciples read. While there have occasionally been dissenting groups, including the Marcionites, who removed the Old Testament from the Bible, the overwhelming majority of Jesus' followers have always affirmed the foundational nature of the Old Testament and its continuation, not abandonment, in the New Testament.

For many of us Anabaptists, however, the Old Testament has long presented something of a problem. Given the apparent discrepancies between the Old Testament and the teachings of Jesus, particularly with respect to war and other ethical issues, we often either downplay the Old Testament or ignore it altogether. As Ben Ollenburger has pointed out, the early Anabaptists did this because they lacked the theological sophistication to refute their opponents' arguments based on Old Testament passages. To preserve their commitment to Christ *and* the Old Testament, these early Anabaptists deliberately lessened the force of the Old Testament and made the New Testament normative.[1]

Today, we in the Anabaptist world find ourselves in a much different situation. Thus, rather than either avoiding the Old Testament or downplaying its significance, it is time for contemporary Anabaptists to examine its pages and explore its teachings *rightly*.

Exploring the Questions:
From Interpretation to Application

Nearly sixteen years have passed since I completed my Ph.D. in Old Testament studies. Since then, I have taught a range of courses, preached scores of sermons, and written numerous articles (and a few books) on a wide range of Old Testament subjects and passages. While it is difficult for me to condense the issues and topics I have covered during those years, it is nonetheless clear to me that a few critical questions continue to drive my work.

Understanding the Old Testament world

First, I continue to ask, "How can I better understand the world and culture in which the Old Testament developed and took shape?" Although such a question is commonly asked among scholars in my academic discipline, its importance is not nearly as self-evident among everyday readers. For some readers, the connection between cultural setting and text is foreign and therefore remains untouched. For others, including many of us in the Anabaptist world, our self-conscious attempts to read the Bible "at face value" negate the need for historical and cultural analysis and sometimes ignore the interpretive process as a whole.

In so doing, we betray a wrongheaded conviction that the Bible was written *to us*, in *our* language and *our* cultural categories. Quite to the contrary, studying the Old Testament approximates taking an extended cross-cultural trip. In the same way that contemporary literary materials from other cultures are better understood in the context of that culture, so too can the Old Testament be read more faithfully when the ancient context is carefully explored.

This task, of course, is made more difficult precisely because the Old Testament is a collection of *ancient* texts. Readers cannot travel to the same culture in which the events of the Old Testament transpired like they might, for example, if they were studying a contemporary African novel. Nevertheless, the centrality of this first question ("How can I understand the cultures of the Old Testament?") has led me to live for three years in various places in the Middle East, study several of the languages spoken by Israel's neighbors in antiquity, and even earn a master's degree in Near Eastern archaeology. Through these various efforts, the historical and cultural context of the Old Testament has come into clearer focus and, as a result, the texts have taken on new meaning.

Learning from the complexity of the Old Testament

A second and related question that I regularly ask is, "How can I more fully appreciate and learn from the complexity and diversity of the Old Testament?" In my various attempts to enter the ancient world, I have increasingly realized that the Old Testament is a wonderful collection of materials that were written by many people over a long period of time. These materials include songs, poems, archival records, historical narratives, and many other types of literature. Furthermore, they developed in a countless number of situations, and were written by a great variety of people, not all of whom always thought the same way about everything. Rather than constituting a simple and straightforward narrative, as many readers assume, the Old Testament consists of countless different texts that are often in conversation with each other.

The complexity and diversity in the Old Testament result at times in an exciting and fruitful tension; this presents scholars like me with rich interpretive opportunities. As an Anabaptist, I have probably sensed this complexity and diversity most directly with respect to issues of war and nonviolence. For casual readers, the frequency with which wars appear in certain Old Testament books suggests that violent resolution of conflict in general and military confrontation in particular are both necessary and appropriate, even for the people of God. God, after all, commanded the Israelites to fight and assisted them in their various military campaigns.

A more careful and thoughtful study of the Old Testament, however, reveals dissenting voices that, in my mind, point to an emerging alternative to war and violence. Such voices, once again, first came to my attention in graduate school, where they played an instrumental role in my own journey toward a theology of peace. I wrestled rigorously with these same voices when, in the mid-1990s, I wrote the commentary on *Judges* for the Believers Church Bible Commentary series.[2]

To summarize some of my conclusions, I see at least three significant ideas unfolding in the Old Testament that, taken together, provide a foundation for an Old Testament theology of peace:

1. The war narratives in books such as Joshua and Judges depict military campaigns in what seems to me to be a comical fashion. Israel's troops are reduced or irrelevant, and God alone brings about the victory. This theme of reduction, so important in the Old Testament, plays virtually no role in the war narratives of Israel's neighbors.

2. In Deuteronomy, Samuel, and Kings, the power of Israel's monarchs is greatly restricted, and various kings are severely criticized for relying upon military might (see, for instance, Deut. 17:14-20; 2 Sam. 24; and 1 Kings 10:26-29 and 11:1-13).

3. In the prophetic literature, hints appear of a time when peace will reign and war and violence cease (Isa. 2:1-5; 9:6-7; 11:1-9; Mic. 4:6-7; Jer. 23:5-8; Zech. 9:9-10). And in Isaiah's vision, at least, God's people are called to begin modeling that peace in the present world (Isa. 2:5).

Rather than consistently condoning or even encouraging warfare, the Old Testament subtly critiques it, pointing the way to imaginative alternatives. If we Anabaptists begin to take the Old Testament more seriously and enter the conversation on this and other significant matters—the role of the community, holiness, social justice, and so on—we will no doubt encounter new and challenging texts that stretch and enrich our theological convictions.

Applying the Old Testament to contemporary life

Third, I continue to struggle with issues of contemporary application and relevance. I recall a point during my seminary days when, after sensing a call to do further graduate work, I made a covenant of sorts with the Lord that I would wed serious scholarship and ministry, rather than divorce them. Such a covenant took on increasing importance as I completed my doctoral program. As I looked around the academy, I felt that a disproportionate amount of attention was being given to observing and interpreting texts, to the near total neglect of applying them in appropriate ways. Historical-critical approaches to Scripture, as helpful as they can be, often failed to nurture my soul or alter my lifestyle.

Fortunately, I soon realized that I was not alone in responding this way. Two experiences stand out that reinforced in my mind the need to pay careful attention to matters of application and relevance. First, I heard Bruce Waltke, an evangelical Old Testament scholar from Vancouver's Regent College, present a paper titled "Hermeneutics and the Spiritual Life."[3] Second, I read *Life Journey and the Old Testament*, written by Conrad L'Heureux, a Harvard-trained Catholic scholar at Washington, D.C.'s Catholic University.[4] Both of these men had struggled with frustrations similar to mine, and both were seeking fresh and creative ways to breathe life into a sometimes barren land.

Now, after carefully interpreting the biblical texts, I repeatedly ask two related questions: (1) "How can I make these ancient texts more accessible to people in the modern world?" and (2) "How can I foster a greater appreciation for the value of the Old Testament as sacred Scripture among Christians in general and among Anabaptists in particular?" In addressing these two questions, I regularly include reflective exercises in my classes, take students on service projects that directly relate to course material (we volunteered in homeless shelters while studying Amos and Hosea last semester), and include in all of my sermons a call for some type of meaningful response. I not only want people to better understand these sometimes perplexing passages; I want them to appreciate them and *grow spiritually* as a result of reading them.

Finding a Home: The Academy or the Church?

Given these issues that continually occupy my mind, my life as an Anabaptist Old Testament scholar has thus far been challenging and deeply rewarding. Opportunities to work within the academy as well as the church have been plentiful, and subjects to explore never seem to run out. Yet the life of a scholar who is committed both to academic excellence and to Christian piety also includes frustrations. While I cannot speak for those in other fields of study, I suspect that some of these frustrations are accentuated for those of us in explicitly religious disciplines.

Frustrations within the academy

In my professional context, most biblical scholars and theologians used to reside in church-related colleges and seminaries. In recent years, more scholars have moved to positions in public (and therefore more pluralistic and secularized) institutions, and the locus of the discipline has shifted with them. At the same time, related professional societies have increasingly emphasized nonsectarian examinations of the Bible.

While such a shift has perhaps brought with it certain benefits, including insights and methodologies from a wider range of disciplines, it has done so at a high price. One notices, for example, an ever-escalating "hermeneutic of suspicion" in which scholars raise more problems with the biblical text than they offer constructive suggestions. Similarly, the agenda at professional meetings and the array of articles in professional journals include what, to me at least, seems like an increasing mass of scholarly minutia with little if any theological content. Over and over again, we ask "When was this text written?" or "Did a certain prophet *really* say this?" To be sure, these are at times crucial matters and should therefore not be totally avoided. However, one senses an alarming refusal among scholars to ask a question that we Anabaptists have long emphasized, namely, "What does this text require of me?"

I suppose this frustration in my professional context parallels what I had already grown uncomfortable with in graduate school—a perceived separation of scholarship and faith. This is not to say that the vast majority of Old Testament scholars are people of little or no faith. No doubt many of them are deeply committed to the things of Christ. Rather, it is to suggest that the onslaught of secularized scholarship has made my professional context one in which faith issues are rarely placed on the table for consideration. Such concerns are swiftly swept away, leaving some of us with a sense of spiritual displacement.

Frustrations within the church

As might be expected, the frustrations that Old Testament scholars like myself feel within our church contexts differ radically from the frustrations we experience in the academy—though the feeling is no less intense. If in my professional context I mourn the disinterest in faith issues, in the church I at times mourn the disinterest in academic or theological issues. This frustration typically grows out of two recurring responses or attitudes among various people.

First, there are some within the church who demonstrate a noticeable disregard for (or even distrust of) education, particularly education of a religious variety. For such people, everyone is an "expert" in religious education, and everyone is therefore equally qualified to offer interpretive comments concerning biblical texts and other spiritual matters. Often, these same people do not want to be bothered by new information or ideas. As Jerome Murphy-O'Conner has aptly stated, "the prudence of reason has little chance against the certitude of piety."[5]

Admittedly, Anabaptists through the years have rightly emphasized the role of the community of faith in reading and interpreting the Bible. The congregational process of interpretation, as Walter Klaassen has pointed out, "is designed to save Christians from the tyranny of the specialized knowledge and equipment of the scholar."[6] Yet emphasizing the value of the community does not demand the dismissal of individual gifts and training. Instead, the community provides a suitable context for the exercising of such gifts, even with respect to interpreting and teaching the Bible. In failing to recognize this, the church relegates its scholars to the fringes, often without realizing it.

In addition to this disregard for education, there are others in the church, including many leaders, who elevate practice and "success" over theory and spirituality. The church is far more than a "think tank," of course, and it is assigned the task of living out the gospel in the contemporary world. In doing so, the church needs to develop strategies and plans to help it in performing this task more effectively. This is as it should be.

Tensions often arise, however, between strategy and theory—or perhaps better stated, between practice and theology. While practitioners seek to provide more effective plans, scholars want to reflect carefully and think theologically. In reality, we desperately need each other. What often results when we get together, however, is a sense of mounting frustration and a perceived need to defend our particular orientation. "I'm proud to be a scholar and an educator," I sometimes want to shout, all the while rehashing my own practical experiences so as not to be labeled a heartless intellectual.

Contemporary examples of this tension are numerous. I might simply cite the matters of church growth and worship style as cases in point. Given the church's mandate to evangelize the lost and disciple new converts, countless new strategies have emerged to stimulate growth. While affirming the need for cultural sensitivity, effective strategies, and good planning, I fear that such strategies often circumvent crucial biblical teachings and thereby run the risk of compromising a biblical understanding of the church in favor of evangelistic expediency. Yet when I raise certain questions and criticize certain methods, I may be accused of being "too academic" or uninterested in the everyday work of the church.

Such criticism might at times be deserved. Perhaps my commitment to a careful and thoughtful interpretation of Scripture does leave me overly skeptical of strategies so popular in the North American church these days. On most occasions, however, I seek genuinely to safeguard important biblical teachings against the mad rush of contemporary effectiveness. I want to emphasize the importance of building a visible and obedient church like that envisioned in both the Old and New Testaments. I must affirm the prophetic call to pursue peace and justice, not just the spiritualized salvation of individual souls. Further, I will not sacrifice the depth and richness of Israel's worship to make everyone happy and comfortable.

In short, I do not simply want to *grow* a church, but to develop and nurture a biblical church that, in addition to carrying out its evangelical mandate, preserves the essence of the Christian gospel. In a day when materialism and individualism rip at the very fiber of our Anabaptist heritage, I want to ask, "How might we build a church that is culturally relevant yet true to our core theological convictions?" Such questions, however, may very well threaten the practitioners among us.

Where do I belong?

As a result of such tensions in both my professional and church contexts, the central frustration that I experience is essentially one of finding a place. For people like me who want desperately to bridge the gap between the academy and the church, there exists at times a sort of spatial uncertainty—do I belong here or there? The frustration that emerges from this uncertainty is not easily dismissed, and it requires regular consideration and conversation. Even then, I frequently question my role in the academy and the church, as well as the amount of time and effort that I contribute to each.

In response to this ongoing frustration of finding a place, I attempt to maintain at least some involvement in both my academic and church contexts. With respect to the academy, I regularly attend professional meetings and periodically present papers and write articles or books primarily intended for an academic audience. I never do so, however, apart from my faith commitments and my Anabaptist orientation. For example, in my most recent scholarly article, entitled "Compliance, Dissonance and Amazement in Daniel 3," I carefully explored how the narrator employed various literary techniques to underscore the importance of remaining faithful to God, even in the face of foreign and oppressive forces. In so doing, I sought to combine serious academic research with significant faith issues. My own view is that, rather than avoiding professional contexts, scholars like me ought to participate in academically sound and theologically profound ways.

While seeking to remain active in the academy, however, I have contributed more time and energy to the life of the church, both locally and beyond. These contributions include teaching Sunday school and chairing the worship commission in my local congregation, preaching regularly in many places, teaching a course entitled "The Theology of the Church" for those seeking ministerial credentials with the Brethren in Christ Church, and writing for various church publications. In each of these activities, I always try to present the best of my scholarly pursuits in readily accessible ways. I generally preach sermons from the Old Testament, for example, and I continually look for meaningful ways to call attention to our Anabaptist heritage.

Some might interpret my scholarly work as exhibiting an imbalance that favors the church over the academy. If that is indeed the case, my bias stems from two key factors. First, I deeply enjoy regular ministerial outlets—ministry is simply a fundamental part of my personality. Even when wrestling with the most sophisticated academic questions, I find myself wondering how I might use the resulting ideas to help the church in doing its work. Second, I believe that the church is, in fact, the primary community in which the Bible is to be read. This conviction, coupled with the church's continuing unfamiliarity with the Old Testament (as well as the previously mentioned shortage of Anabaptist scholars in my field), suggests to me that my involvements in the church are crucial and more immediately needed.

Given all of the challenges, joys, and frustrations that go along with being an Old Testament scholar in the Anabaptist tradition, I can scarcely find the words to underscore my ongoing passion for what I do.

Studying and teaching the Old Testament provide not only a source of personal satisfaction but also a channel through which I can meaningfully contribute to both the academy and the church. In light of the spiritual emptiness often characterizing the academy and the unawareness of the Old Testament so prevalent in many churches, the task of bridging the gap between them will no doubt remain important to me for years to come.

NOTES

1. See Ben C. Ollenburger, "The Hermeneutics of Obedience," in *Essays on Biblical Interpretation: Anabaptist-Mennonite Perspectives*, ed. Willard M. Swartley (Elkhart, Ind.: Institute of Mennonite Studies, 1984), 57-59.

2. Terry L. Brensinger, *Judges* (Scottdale, Pa.: Herald Press, 1999).

3. This presentation has since been published in *Crux* 28 (March 1987): 5-10.

4. Conrad E. L'Heureux, *Life Journey and the Old Testament* (New York: Paulist Press, 1986).

5. Jerome Murphy-O'Conner, *The Holy Land: An Oxford Archaeological Guide*, 4th ed. (Oxford: Oxford University Press, 1998), 141.

6. Walter Klaassen, "Anabaptist Hermeneutics: Presuppositions, Principles and Practice," in Swartley, *Essays on Biblical Interpretation*, 10.

12: New Testament

Keeping Faith: New Testament Scholarship and the Church

Mary H. Schertz

AMID PLANNING THIS ARTICLE, MY LIFE changed radically. From northern Indiana to central Minnesota may not seem to be much of a shift. From a few lakes and lots of cornfields to a few cornfields and lots of lakes, perhaps. But from a Mennonite seminary to an ecumenical institute on the edge of a Benedictine monastery—well, that is something of a leap. From chapel three times a week to the liturgy of the hours. From chairs in a semicircle to choir stalls. From hymns to canticles. From preachers in suits, men and women, to black-robed monks. From Mennonite politics and gossip, to, well, Catholic politics and gossip. (I guess some things are the same everywhere!)

What Makes Me an Anabaptist Scholar?

Back in my Mennonite world, I was pretty sure that I knew what an Anabaptist scholar was and why it mattered. Here, I am not nearly so sure. What really sets me apart from my colleagues at the institute—nine other scholars from all sorts of religious traditions who are here, as am I, to write and read and replenish their spirits?

All of a sudden, the qualities of Anabaptist life and faith that I appreciate the most do not seem particularly Anabaptist. Community? The Benedictines have much to teach us about community. Indeed, their blend of communal spirit and respect for privacy is a lesson in humility and tolerance. The importance of peace and justice? All the scholars I have met here at the institute, as well as the monks and other staff members, also care deeply about these issues. Some of them are pacifists.

Perhaps the way we read the Bible. But my colleagues are all interested in my project on the gospel of Luke—and there's a Baptist in the group. If anybody knows the Bible, it's the Baptists. Besides, I know in my heart that there is no uniquely Anabaptist way of reading the Bible. We not only read it in widely differing fashions, but we fight a lot about how we read it.

Maybe the Sermon on the Mount. When one of the computer experts makes a joke about my suing him, I say I can't, I'm a Mennonite. He likes that. But our attention to the Sermon seems to be waning and, at any rate, it may be a fairly narrow band of practical difference after all.

So what does it mean to be an Anabaptist scholar here at the ecumenical institute—or anywhere else, for that matter? That I'm the one who sings too loud and too fast and doesn't pause long enough between the lines of the hymns? Or perhaps I could bring borscht and zwieback to the next institute potluck. (The other scholars probably do not know that the biggest group of Mennonites is actually African or that I do not even come from the strand of Mennonites that grew up with borscht and zwieback.)

In short, I conclude, there is very little of real significance setting me apart from the other scholars at the institute. I have my traditions, some of which I honor and some of which I critically and carefully discard. But so do each of my new friends. Perhaps the point of this exercise is not so much to say that Anabaptist scholars are different from all other scholars in significant ways. Perhaps the point is to say that all scholars are particular, that all have their traditions from which they speak and to which they relate in various ways. Perhaps the point is to articulate how it is that I speak from, for, and to the Anabaptist tradition as a scholar.

An Incidental Journey

To find myself here at a Benedictine abbey is, in truth, only slightly more strange than finding myself in the Sermon on the Mount Chapel at an Anabaptist seminary—or in its classrooms, committee rooms, or offices. Certainly for the first thirty years of my life this idea of being a seminary professor of New Testament was not in my mind at all. My journey as an academic started out quite incidentally, or so it seems from the perspective of these many steps into it.

A single impulse propelled me into seminary studies, and another propelled me into doctoral studies. I was at a particularly fumbling point of life, having come to the conclusion that one cannot really earn a living by teaching in a daycare center for low-income kids, even though that work may be the most important in the world. But one day, crossing the Illinois River in Peoria on the way home from work, I remembered that one of my best memories from college was tracing the theme of Sonja as a Christ figure in *Crime and Punishment*. While this reflection was the first time I acknowledged the pull of theological studies on my life, I nevertheless managed to recognize it as a subterranean but powerful stream in my personality.

I entered seminary with no more sense of call or vocation than that single impulse. What I told people was that I might go into pastoral counseling. Twenty years ago Mennonite women didn't say that they wanted to be pastors even if they knew that they did (which I did not). And certainly pastoral counseling was more easily understood than talking about Sonja as a Christ figure and what that meant to me.

At any rate, I entered seminary with little interest in the Bible. First, I thought I knew it. Second, I thought it wasn't kind to women. Third, I was pretty sure that I did not want to study Greek or Hebrew, not having had especially great experiences with languages earlier in life. But I soon found, somewhat to my dismay, that I did not really have a choice, and so I set out to plod my way through Hebrew—only to fall in love with the biblical languages. Although it was hard work, it was also like play—like doing a crossword puzzle or figuring out "who done it."

Translating texts became not only my tangible, concrete, daily discipline, but also a source of empowerment and vitality. To be able to figure out the Bible for myself brought me face to face with God—there is no other accurate way to describe it. It also brought me face to face with the realization that I had a lot to learn—about the Bible, about life, and about God—which I suppose was the beginning of some faint wisdom.

Though I was not aware of it then, this time of my life may have been my most "pure" academic experience. I had no particular vocational goals formulated. I had no pastoral aspirations. I had no idea whether or how I would ever use the skills I was developing and from which I was deriving so much pleasure.

So it was with some surprise, amusement, and a huge gulp that a second impulse propelled me on to doctoral work in biblical studies. I was pulling on my coat and hat one snowy day in the student lounge, waiting for the car pool to collect itself. Millard Lind, my Hebrew professor, was there drinking coffee. He had witnessed both my reluctance to learn Hebrew and my conversion to its joys. With a glint in his eye, he suggested to me that day, quite casually, that I might give graduate studies in Bible some thought. Until that minute, study at that level had never, ever entered my mind as something I might do with my life. But after that minute, it was an idea that I simply could not dismiss—jarring, unlikely, and remote as the possibility seemed.

And so two steps of the journey were taken, seemingly incidentally, or at least quite casually. There was no voice from heaven. A memory that bloomed into a tiny inner conviction brought me to seminary, and the simple words of a gentle, Old Testament professor took me from there to graduate school.

Of course, incidental is not accidental. God *was* leading. But the journey was neither easy nor simple. Much took place between these impulses, these broad strokes. There were internal questions and important external affirmations from people in addition to Millard. There were decisions to make and obstacles to overcome. But it happened, one form filled out at a time, one assignment completed at a time, and finally, one job offer considered at a time. Four years after I graduated from the Associated Mennonite Biblical Seminary (AMBS), I was back in Elkhart, Indiana, as a junior faculty member.

Teaching at an Anabaptist seminary has been at the same time nurturing for my scholarship and death on it. It has been nurturing in that there is a large, active, and exciting Bible department. After talking to other biblical scholars in other settings, I do not take this wealth for granted. I have colleagues with whom to work, brainstorm ideas, read papers, discuss projects, and share bibliographies. Nevertheless, teaching at the seminary has presented difficulties in getting to scholarly work. There are a million and one ways to distract ourselves from scholarship and, as a result, not as much of that scholarly interaction takes place as we might wish.

I want to be quite careful at this point not to blame the institution, even though the institution may be partly responsible. There are many highly productive scholars at AMBS, scholars who write and edit books on top of their teaching loads and administrative assignments. It can be done, and there are rewards for doing so. The administrators and colleagues there are genuinely supportive and enthusiastic about scholarly efforts.

The problem is that there is lots of pressure to fulfill teaching and administrative responsibilities and very little pressure to do scholarly work. I keep thinking that if it were as difficult to excuse myself for not writing some days as it is to explain my not attending a Strategic Planning Council meeting—well, my life, not to mention my scholarly production, would be quite different.

But that begs the question. Scholarship is, by definition, an internal discipline, and while our institutions could do some things to help nurture the hard work of thinking, institutional practice cannot make scholarship happen.

Of course, one of the most important ways that institutions such as AMBS *do* foster scholarship is by granting sabbaticals. Time to get out of the usual routine is important, and so is getting out of one's ordinary context. Worshiping with the Benedictines is extraordinarily helpful for gaining a new perspective on my usual milieu. For despite my discoveries that Anabaptists do not have a corner on community, how I am Anabaptist in my thinking and practice—how I belong to my tradition and how it belongs to me—is becoming much clearer here in the Minnesota woods with the abbey bells ringing the hours across the lake.

A Severe Belonging

However theologically incorrect this statement might sound, being an *Anabaptist* scholar is almost *not* a choice, since I have been a Mennonite all my life. I do, of course, understand that faith is not ethnicity, that it involves conversion, and that one chooses to be a part of the body of Christ rather than being born into it. Nevertheless, that I have been a Mennonite all my life is also a true statement. I have a Baptist friend who says she is Baptist-born and Baptist-bred and when she dies, she will be Baptist-dead. Whatever the theological problems with that statement, it is also true for me as an Anabaptist.

My belonging is not a question. Periodically at AMBS we are asked to evaluate how we, or others on the faculty, "fit." I am always slightly amused because the true answer is that I fit like a hand in a glove. These are my people. I have to listen to them because they are part of me. They have to listen to me because I am one of them. Whether I continue to teach where I am, or find myself somewhere else doing something very different, that relationship will always be there, and it will always be real.

Not only am I personally quite certain that I belong to this tradition, I happen to be a New Testament scholar in a tradition that talks about a hermeneutic community, that values the New Testament as a guide to ethics, that proclaims itself to be a biblical people. One would think that with all those factors in place—to feel thoroughly Anabaptist, to be teaching in a Mennonite seminary, to be teaching *New Testament* in a Mennonite seminary no less—I would have few questions about how my scholarship is useful for the church. That would be wrong.

For many years now, the phrase *a severe belonging* has been the most accurate way I can find to describe my reality as a scholar in my tradition. The hand in glove often feels more like sandpaper on sandpaper than it does like velvet on skin. The irritation did not begin with my scholarship, but becoming a scholar certainly did nothing to ease the irritation. In my experience, what might seem like a natural fit is far from easy.

Part of that uneasiness is circumstantial, a result of my embeddedness in a particular historical situation. I began my scholarship at a time when women were not accepted as leaders and ministers in the church. I chose New Testament studies at least partly because these were the texts that, at the time, were being used most actively for and against women's ministries in the church. While understandings of the Genesis accounts, both traditional and nontraditional, lay powerfully in the backgrounds of these articulations, the explicit arguments and rationalizations of positions were being made from New Testament texts. I felt that it was important to study these texts and become a voice that spoke to these issues. I felt that it was important to explore the texts about women and feminist approaches to them as important avenues of research and reflection. In addition, I tried to integrate these studies with a Mennonite theology of peace and justice.

There is no question but that I came into scholarship as an advocate for Mennonite women and their ministries. Given the existence of that agenda, I suppose that some uneasiness between my Anabaptist tradition and me was inevitable. I do not think, however, that the rub of prophetic edges comprised the source of that uneasiness. Rather, the source of the irritation had more to do with the tension between "the hermeneutic community" and "biblical scholarship." And as I reflect on that tension, I see two fundamental factors that continue to foster it. One is a kind of laziness, and the other is a noble egalitarianism.

"Don't Lose Your Faith!"

When I talk about laziness, I want to be clear about two things. Most important, I am not blaming or pointing fingers. I am describing *us,* not *them* or *you.* This foible is one in which I participate fully. Second, I am talking about laziness in a very specialized sense. I am not, in any way, accusing myself or Anabaptist people of being lazy in any of the normal ways we think about laziness—far from it!

Anabaptists have normally been hardworking and determined people—our farms, our quilts, and our service records all attest to this fact. My students at AMBS are by and large also hardworking and determined. Often they do *more* work than I ask, and often they do far *better* work than I insist.

Still, we Anabaptists have entertained a notable intellectual laziness. In myself and in others, yes, even in some of the brightest and most hardworking students, I sometimes encounter a kind of blockage, an intellectual waffling, an unwillingness to think something through to its implications, a reluctance to follow a thought no matter where it might lead. I sometimes miss, in Mennonite settings, a sense of excitement about the intellectual adventure, the joy of learning, an enthusiasm for exploring ideas, a playfulness of the mind. It is not that I never see this special quality. I just wish that it would be more abundant, more frequent, and more widespread.

The components of this lack of joy include fear, false humility, and perhaps even arrogance. With respect to fear, some of us may be afraid of losing our faith. (When I went to seminary, I was warned by some people in my conference not to "lose my faith" out there in Elkhart.) For some, however, fear is much less a problem than humility. We may simply be afraid to excel, as if that very fact might separate us from our community in some manner. Or perhaps we are afraid that others will think that we are proud of our accomplishments. And sometimes, I have reluctantly concluded, it is a kind of arrogance—a fear that we can out-think God or go intellectually where God is not.

All of this is quite inappropriate theologically. If we believe that we are created in the image of God, then our intellect is part of the gift of life. Even more broadly, if we believe that God is omniscient and omnipresent as well as omnipotent, then there really is nowhere we can go (even in our minds) where God is not.

Sometimes in my prayers at the beginning of the class period, I pray for the courage to seek excellence in thought. At other times I pray for freedom from the false humility and pride that keeps us fearful of our God-given minds. Even as I know this tendency in myself, I am committed as both a scholar and, perhaps even more importantly, as a teacher to doing what I can to lift this psychological and sociological burden. It is so unnecessary and so antithetical to the joy of discovery for which God gave us such fine minds.

The Hermeneutic Community Has No Clothes!

In addition to what I feel is a rather distressing lack of joy in the intellectual enterprise, another factor in the scratchy fit of a New Testament scholar in the Anabaptist world has to do with the hermeneutic community and a rather noble but somewhat misguided egalitarianism.

Two recent books by Anabaptist scholars have assumed that there is indeed a lively and active hermeneutic community in Anabaptist circles that can be traced to the sixteenth century. Stuart Murray's *Biblical Interpretation in the Anabaptist Tradition* describes a "congregational hermeneutic" which, although practiced in different ways, effectively distinguished the radical reformers from both state-sanctioned interpretation, on the one hand, and the individualism of Spiritualist interpretation on the other hand.[1]

This setting for interpretation was established early and explicitly. The first Anabaptist congregational order, *The Swiss Order*, was based on the rule of Paul as outlined in 1 Corinthians 14:26-29. It stated, "When brothers and sisters are together, they shall take up something to read together. The one to whom God has given the best understanding shall explain it, the others should be still and listen."[2]

In *Obedience, Suspicion and the Gospel of Mark*, Lydia Neufeld Harder notes that the practices rooted in the sixteenth century faced pressures in the first half of the twentieth century from the fundamentalist movement, on one hand, and historical-critical methods of biblical study on the other. According to Neufeld Harder, Anabaptist scholars of that era chose a "third option," an interpretive stance that emphasized the values of biblical ethics and obedience (discipleship) as a prerequisite to understanding.[3] This choice effectively meant that the truest forms of interpretation could only be done by believers in the context of fellow believers. The church community was reaffirmed as the locus of authoritative interpretation.

In this view, obedience and knowing are intertwined in a somewhat circular fashion. Obedience opens the mind to the revelatory Word, but the Spirit of God makes this Word powerful and alive, lighting a spark to the obedience that makes knowing possible.

The story of how this tradition was handed down to subsequent generations of Anabaptist believers is a complex and diverse one. But for the purposes of this essay, we may simply note that what has been passed down to the present generation is an "enfranchisement of all believers as interpreters."[4] Whereas, as I noted earlier, the enfranchisement of all believers as interpreters sounds wonderfully and nobly egalitarian, it has had some ill effects on the hermeneutic community. One is the disenfranchisement of biblical scholars. Many of us must overcome a kind of suspicion if we are to be heard in the church at all. But there has been a much more serious consequence of this enfranchisement than the silencing of scholars, most of whom have ample opportunity to be heard in other ways and places. A practical outcome of this enfranchisement is that very little serious reading of the Bible actually happens among all these interpreters in the church.

It is much too simplistic, I am sure, to suggest that the reason behind this lack of Bible study is that "if everyone can do it, nobody does it." Increasingly, however, our Anabaptist people are becoming less biblically literate. We spend less and less time with the text in our worship services. We have fewer opportunities to read, study, and discuss Scripture at the congregational level, whether in smaller or larger groups. Except on controversial issues, where we tend to throw texts at each other, little serious reading of texts goes on in our communities. At AMBS, we have had to lower our expectations considerably in what we can expect incoming students to know about the Bible.

In short, we have a hermeneutic community, but it is largely an *inactive* community. We have a noble intention to engage every believer in discerning the Word from the word, but seldom does it happen. We have committed ourselves to hear all the voices in the congregation and choose our interpretive wisdom from among them. But seldom do we hear enough points of view to have something from which to choose. The hermeneutic community is largely silent. In that sense, it is like the famous emperor: it has no clothes.

Why the Church Needs Us and Why We Need the Church

The entity that neither Neufeld Harder nor Murray addresses directly is the texts themselves and their integrity. In his last chapter, Murray discusses the relationship between scholars and lay people with respect to biblical interpretation. In comparing Anabaptist hermeneutics and liberation hermeneutics, for instance, he talks about a common distrust of a "scholarly monopoly" on interpretation.[5] He goes on to say that both the Anabaptist movement and the liberation movement have emphasized application over intellectual interpretation and opposed the notion of "academic detachment."[6]

Murray also mentions, almost in passing, that Anabaptists have never managed to integrate biblical scholarship into its hermeneutic, "to the detriment of the ongoing movement."[7] Nor, I would add, have the biblical scholars of the Anabaptist movement ever been integrated into the hermeneutic community—even though we have produced a relatively large number of such scholars and even though many of these scholars have been skilled interpreters who have received recognition in the wider world.

This lack of integration has effectively meant that the case for the text, i.e., the argument for *hearing the text*, has too seldom been given vigorous attention in the congregation. That the biblical texts have too often had no advocate in the congregation is one of the reasons that the hermeneutical community has been less active than it could be. This, I believe, is where biblical scholars can be particularly helpful to the church, and it provides a reason for all of us—congregations and biblical scholars—to work hard to integrate scholarship and scholars into the hermeneutic community.

In the hermeneutic community, we need people with divided loyalties. We need people who have both a loyalty to the community and a loyalty, just as powerful, to the texts themselves.

My call as a New Testament scholar is really twofold. It is a call to interpret the Bible in, with, and for the church, whether that means the particular congregation of which I am a member or the church at large. It is a call to work in the moment of a sermon that will be forgotten in another week, as well as in writing an exegetical piece that may outlive me and go where I cannot. I take this part of my call very seriously. It means that, as I read and study texts, I also read the writings of my people—from the news items in the *Mennonite Weekly Review* to the various confessions of faith and conference proceedings. It means that, as I read and study texts, I participate regularly in worship, conference activities, and assemblies of the wider church. It means that, as I read and study texts, I listen actively and intently to my friends, my family, my students, and the people in my congregation (and in the congregations in which I am a guest). I strive to make connections, to see ways in which the work I am doing is illuminated by these various issues, events, and personalities known as "the church."

But the other part of the call is just as important. It is a call to read the texts for their own sake. It is a call to read odd texts, difficult texts, texts for which the church has never had much use, simply because they are part of the biblical canon. It is a call to ponder how the different parts of Scripture fit together—or do not fit together. It is a call to evaluate the best I can which readings of the texts are better than other readings. It is a call to say what readings cannot possibly be valid. It is a call to study for the sake of study, to indulge the joy of learning, the excitement of discovery, to follow a thought to see where it leads me. It is a call to be the best scholar that I can be.

Far be it from me to say that keeping the needs of the hermeneutic community and the demands of scholarship in balance is easy. Far be it from me to say that any of us can possibly keep faith with both commitments without help from others in the church and other scholars. Far be it from me to suggest that we scholars succeed more than we fail to honor these loyalties.

But that is the vision—a vision for an active and engaged hermeneutical community that profits from the work of scholars without reneging on its own responsibility to discern. Indeed, that is the vision—a vision for an active and engaged community of scholars who care about the church as well as the texts they serve.

NOTES

1. Stuart Murray, *Biblical Interpretation in the Anabaptist Tradition* (Kitchener, Ont.: Pandora Press, 2000), 157-85.
2. Quoted in Ibid., 161.
3. Lydia Neufeld Harder, *Obedience, Suspicion and the Gospel of Mark: A Mennonite-Feminist Exploration of Biblical Authority* (Waterloo, Ont.: Wilfrid Laurier University Press, 1998), 26.
4. Murray, 226.
5. Ibid., 229.
6. Ibid., 230.
7. Ibid., 243.

13: Theology

Naming Myself a Theological Scholar in the Anabaptist Tradition

Lydia Neufeld Harder

WHEN MEETING WITH PROSPECTIVE GRADUATE STUDENTS in theology, I often warn them about the risks of standing in this particular scholarly space. From the perspective of a critical analyst standing on the boundary between church and world—that is, from the perspective of a trained theologian—the disjunctions and contradictions with respect to our language about God can sometimes seem overwhelming.

At the same time, I cannot help but share with these students my enthusiasm for studying theology. Where else do the discourses of church and world meet so overtly in a dialogue about the mystery of life? What other subject matter is so inclusive of every aspect of experience, both personal and communal? Though long displaced as the "queen of the sciences" in the university, theology remains in the church an integral element of discourse as we listen to the voice of God and testify to that experience. Who would not welcome the privilege of being part of such a constructive and necessary enterprise?

Still, it is the contradictions that first come to my mind. Indeed, as I reflect on my scholarly journey, I realize that it has been the tensions and contradictions in both life and God-talk that first drew me into the formal study of theology. It has been my search for wholeness and unity that has encouraged me to ask ultimate questions and seek universal truth. My journey into theological studies can best be described by focusing on some of the choices I have made as I struggled with polarities and dualities that often seemed beyond reconciliation.

Theological Questions: Theoretical and Practical

Since childhood I had noticed that the teaching of the church and the actual life of church members did not always correspond. My natural response to this disjunction between theory and practice, between knowing and doing, was to name practice as the real problem; indeed, it was relatively easy to label persons "hypocrites" because their walk did not match their talk. When I became more sensitive to the contradictions in my own life, I resolved to try harder to live out what I had been taught.

For me this unity of knowing and doing was "discipleship." My Anabaptist forebears had died because they too believed in this focus on practicing the faith. The quotation of Hans Denck was deeply ingrained in my consciousness: "No [one] can know Christ unless he [or she] follows after him in life"[1]

It wasn't until my second year in Bible college that I began to reflect more seriously on "knowing," the second aspect of this duality. How could I be sure that the knowledge that I was being taught was true?

I had enjoyed my first year of college, thriving on the social life of the community and the rigorous biblical study. Gradually, however, my experiences gave rise to theological questions that could no longer be satisfied by simple answers. My home church was embroiled in a conflict that involved my family and friends. As I watched the congregation play out its power struggles, and as I listened to the name-calling and rejection of persons whom I had considered sincere Christians, I recalled the images of the church that I had just studied. The church was the "body of Christ," the "temple of the Holy Spirit," the "family of God." Honesty demanded that I face the contradiction between the ideal and the real, the theory and the practice.

I consequently began to ask questions that had to do with the very source of my faith. Could I still name this group of people as "church" if there was so much inconsistency between word and deed? If God could not be found in this congregation, would I be able to find God anywhere else? If the church was suspect, what about my own life? To what reality did all our language about God and God's people actually refer?

Even the Bible became suspect for me. After all, I had been learning that it was written by ordinary people and authorized by the church through a long, difficult political process.

These questions focused in a crisis of faith for me the very semester that I had registered for several courses on Paul's epistles. It was these doubts and questions that enabled me to see the realism in Paul's letters (especially in 1 Corinthians), as he struggled with the problems and challenges faced by early Christians. I noted that the sinfulness of the congregation was not hidden or camouflaged in these letters. Yet Paul still dared to name this community the "body of Christ." Where did he find that faith? As I wrestled with these issues, the God of grace who accepts people wherever they are met me in the reality of life. I realized that only God could transform my home congregation into the people of God, the Bible into the Word of God, and me into a Christian.

A subtle change was beginning to happen in my theological beliefs. I started to appreciate that the reconciliation between theory and practice in our God-talk could only come about when God was actively transforming both human theory and human practice. Instead of relying on statements of belief, giving them ultimate authority, I began to trust the God who is beyond human systems of thought. This God encouraged me to explore the contradictions and tensions in our human belief systems in order that I could hear the Word of God anew.

I began to realize that "knowing the will of God" is not self-evident, but rather comes through a process of listening and waiting for the divine voice while exercising our God-given aptitudes and skills. Though raising questions would sometimes create strong objections and fears within the church, I determined not to be afraid to explore the language we used about God. After all, even our most lofty language can never be equated with God.

Gradually I became convinced that the "practice" of critical scholarly work could be helpful to the church in discerning the difference between human idols and the true God. But I also realized that accompanying that practice must be a faith in the presence of the Holy Spirit who could use our limited theological language to witness to the good news of the gospel. These convictions gave me the courage to enter the field of theology with a strong sense of personal calling from God.

A Scholarly Identity: Freedom and Responsibility

After a number of years of elementary school teaching and homemaking, I began to consider graduate studies in the field of theology. When I sought the advice of a Mennonite professor (and former teacher of mine), he encouraged me to begin taking some theological courses—this despite the fact that I was already in my early forties. Despite this encouragement, however, his next words presented me with major decisions, even as they created an identity crisis that occupied me for many years. He suggested that I was lucky that I could study theology "just for fun," implying that my work would not lead to an academic vocation, let alone a calling to serve the church. Rather, it would be a hobby.

I felt crushed and humiliated. Had I succumbed to that greatest of all sins—pride—by wanting to engage in a scholarly vocation? In the Anabaptist tradition, especially in the writings of Menno Simons, there exists a strong suspicion of the "learned ones" who do not have a calling from God.² More generally, there seems to be an underlying fear that scholarly activity will rely solely on human knowledge and that it will thereby lead to false teachings, pride, and the wrong use of power. After all, it was the educated theologians and preachers who persecuted the early Anabaptists! With these things in mind, I began to understand the reluctance of many Mennonite scholars to refer to themselves as "theologians" or "scholars," preferring instead the label "teachers."

Of course, my self-doubts were only exacerbated by being a woman. How could I, a woman, presume to have a calling from God to practice theology (a calling that would take me into the public sphere) when service in the domestic area was already my vocation as a female disciple? As I reflected upon the painful conversation with my mentor, I realized that he had accepted an implicit division between males and females, a division that assumed male responsibility for the church's leadership while restricting female responsibility to less prominent forms of churchly service, e.g., nurturing "personal faith" and "service."

This division was further confirmed for me a few years later, at a Mennonite theological conference to which I was invited. By the late 1980s there had been much ferment in the larger society and church about the need for women's voices in public conversations. At this meeting, however, only three of the one hundred delegates were women.

In light of these experiences, I began to search the Anabaptist-Mennonite tradition to understand the roots of the situation. As I did so, I discovered the struggle between various trajectories within the tradition, and even within the Bible itself. Again it was helpful to name these trajectories as *human* attempts to speak about the will of God, while realizing anew that God often speaks through the marginal voices and minority traditions. On a more personal note, I learned I could not escape the calling of God by bowing to dominant views. Instead, I was directly responsible to God for my theological work.

Thus, after a long struggle to own my interests, abilities, and calling, I (secretly) named myself an Anabaptist-Mennonite theologian. A retreat with Katie Funk Wiebe, a Mennonite writer who told of a similar struggle to name herself an author, encouraged me to accept both the privilege and the responsibility that this naming entailed. What freed me from the attempt to be "god-like" was again the acknowledgment that all theological research was a human enterprise. At the same time, naming theology a human endeavor affirmed for me the conviction that women shared completely in the human task of responsible discourse about God.

A Scholarly Language: Public and Communal

I had almost finished my master's degree in theology at a small Catholic seminary when I was asked to give my first theological paper at a Mennonite conference. True to Anabaptist convictions, the participants at that conference were made up of pastors, scholars, and lay persons. I had read extensively and rewritten my paper many times, using the latest theories on hermeneutics and authority to illuminate my ideas. At the same time, I had reflected on the biblical resources in an effort to correlate my ideas with the Scriptures. Afterwards, a number of people remarked that my paper had been helpful.

What I remember most, however, was a critical remark made by someone from my home congregation. He asserted that he had understood nothing of what I had said. Why could I not use straightforward language that could be understood by everyone? Had I forgotten my roots in the congregation?

It is no accident that, in my research since that day, I have focused on the notion of the interpretive body, or "hermeneutic community."[3] According to John Howard Yoder, who invoked that term almost twenty years ago, the early Anabaptists insisted that biblical interpretation was best done in hermeneutic communities that were committed to structuring their communal life and practice according to their understanding of the text.[4] In other words, it was within a church congregation (not a scholarly gathering) that the best biblical interpretation took place, because the members of the congregation were actively involved in discerning God's will in their lives.

Practically speaking, of course, theological conversation in the Anabaptist tradition has usually been limited to persons of the same sex, ethnic identity, and social class. But the notion of a "hermeneutic community" has nonetheless meant that the role and authority of the theological scholar in congregational life has been ambiguous—an ambiguity that is particularly evident in discussions about the kind of language that scholars should use and the kind of accountability that scholars should have to the church.

In response to such discussions, I have found helpful Walter Brueggemann's imagery of a "wall" that separates the community of faith from the larger society.[5] Brueggemann suggests that people of faith, particularly theologians, must learn to be bilingual, speaking different languages in their different conversations. Their primary theological conversations will take place "behind the wall," with other members of their faith community. Here they will use a communal language, a language shaped by the conviction that God is alive and active in the world.

But the wall is more than a boundary that keeps the world out; it is a meeting place where people with different perspectives on reality gather. People of faith must therefore carry on conversations that take place "on the wall," conversations that will need to be conducted in a "foreign" tongue. Indeed, because these public conversations are frequently constructed around outsiders' dominant perceptions of reality, they will often use a language that assumes a different view of the world from the insiders' view.

Sometimes these meetings on the wall will be friendly, creating new insights for both insiders and outsiders. Sometimes, however, these meetings will be controversial or even hostile.

Whatever the climate, conversations on the wall carry with them inherent dangers and tensions. While they may be tempted to do so, the faithful who stand on the wall dare not ally themselves with the powerful in society, who assert that their language is the only universal language and the only grounds for negotiation. At the same time, because this conversation at the wall is a *public* conversation, the faithful dare not monopolize their sense of truth. The best the faithful can do in this regard is to thoughtfully translate the convictions of the church into a foreign tongue and thereby propose alternative views of reality to those on the other side of the wall.

Of course, even this carries dangers and temptations. Too often those in the church will consider this translating work marginal, even heretical. On the other hand, those involved in the translating process (including theologians) can all too easily forget the more primary language of the faith community and instead bow to the absolute claims of the public view.

I have often become aware of the bilingual nature of theological language, as well as the temptations that come to those standing on the wall. I have realized that I cannot collapse the two languages (the communal and the foreign) into one language without giving up the integrity of my own calling. I therefore stand on the wall, sometimes speaking a foreign language, sometimes speaking in my own primary tongue, but always attempting to witness to the truth wherever it is found.

A Scholarly Method: Suspicion and Obedience

One of the first choices that must be made when one begins doctoral studies in theology is to decide among the distinct departments within the larger school of theology. Since Anabaptists have not been able to imagine theology without a serious study of the Bible, I had assumed that I would enter the biblical studies department.

The director of the program affirmed my choice—until I said that I was interested in the contemporary meaning of the Bible. He quickly informed me that I could not do that in the biblical studies department, because that department concentrated on the historical meaning of the texts. I was therefore told to register in the systematic theology department, where I soon discovered that the basic division between departments also discouraged any connection between the practice of reading the Bible and contemporary theological reflection. In none of my theology classes was the Bible ever used directly or recommended as reading material. My greatest conflict with one of my committee members had to do with her objection to my wish to explore particular biblical texts as I worked on my thesis. That would be "crossing disciplines," she said, and I therefore would not have adequate tools for that task. Moreover, she assumed that my interest in using the Bible as a resource was merely a naive fideistic strategy rather than a rational-critical approach to theological method.

I began to realize that theological scholarship is complicated not only because it is human discourse about the divine. It is also complex because each of the different interpretive communities roots its language in its own authoritative presuppositions, convictions, and methodological approaches.

How does a theological scholar negotiate her way between the contrasting claims of university and church? Can one be detached and objective, as is often demanded by the university, and still be committed to faith perspectives as required by the church? Alternatively, can one do scholarship for the church and not succumb to merely justifying the church and its interests and actions?

It was within these tensions that I began to hammer out my own methodological approach to theology and particularly to the Bible.[6] My rootedness in the Anabaptist tradition, long suspicious of "the world," encouraged me to ask critical questions about the function of departmental boundaries in the university.

Gradually I noticed that one central function of these boundaries was the protection of the interests of scholars in each discipline. This realization gave me the courage to explore a variety of disciplinary approaches to theology despite the objections of my advisory committee. In this process I gained new tools and perspectives from which to analyze my own theological tradition. For example, philosophical studies opened my eyes to the importance of language that can connect past and present, thus making the past active in the present; biblical studies illuminated the truth claims within historical texts, claims that continue to challenge present understandings; sociological studies described the relationship between particular social-political contexts and theological language in both past and present; and systematic theology helped me to understand the networks of beliefs developed over time.

One significant result of this approach was that I became increasingly suspicious when the church justified its beliefs by appealing to biblical proof texts. I had long suspected that Christians feared a critical look at their cherished beliefs because they might not hold up to inspection, and scholarly methods helped me distance myself from my own theological tradition in order that I might assess its claims more critically. This in turn led me to an intensive study of the book of Mark, with a particular focus on the pre-understandings that I myself had been bringing to the text.

It was during this study that I first noticed the difficulty that the disciples had in "hearing" the divine Word in the words of the Jesus, a deafness that was rooted in their political aspirations and strivings.[7] I realized anew that revelation cannot be guaranteed by our appeal to being disciples (the "people of God") or by our insistence that we are the ones who are simply obeying the Bible. Instead, our focus must be on opening our ears by becoming self-critical to hear anew God's self-disclosure. In sum, suspicion of others' claims must always stand side by side with the suspicion of our own superficial claims to truth.

The theological methodology that has emerged for me therefore refuses to accept the polarity commonly assumed by scholars—a polarity that places critical thinking and religious commitment, human endeavor and divine revelation, at opposite ends of scholarship. Both objectivism, with its scholarly detachment, and biased scholarship, with its assumption of the relativity of all truth, are rejected. Instead our prior commitments and interests must be identified to open ourselves to methodological distancing and critical accountability.

Accountability to more than one community encourages self-conscious choices between various claims to truth while, at the same time, opening up a space to listen again to God's disruptive Word. This critical discernment rests on the ultimate faith that the Creator God was active in the particularity of Jesus and continues to be actively present within human history through the Spirit.

A Scholar's Ethic: Power and Vulnerability

It was during my graduate studies that I began to realize that methods stressing logical coherence and rational justification were not enough to legitimate a claim to truth. Indeed, I realized that the constructive task of exegeting the Bible, of finding language to speak of God and the world, is an *ethical* practice and therefore needs also to be judged by its use within particular contexts.

Correspondingly, I began to struggle with the way biblical language such as "servanthood" and the "way of the cross" had been used within the Mennonite church to justify the marginalization of women and the silencing of victims of sexual abuse.[8] At the same time, I became aware of how society at large had legitimated its treatment of First Nations people by using Christian theological language. My reading of liberation theologians further sensitized me to the political dimensions of language use. And I recognized that, as an Anabaptist, I too was part of a minority theological tradition that had been trivialized throughout much of recent history. I therefore began to turn my attention to issues of authority and power, focusing especially on the power of biblical language as it is used to speak of the divine.

Indeed, as long as theological language is considered only theoretical, it does not have much power to heal or hurt. Only when we begin to understand that language use is a praxis—that is, a combination of theory and practice—can we begin to speak of the power of our scholarly work.[9] Moreover, only when we see communication (listening, speaking, writing, and teaching) as central to our churchly task can we understand the need for ethical criteria for those actions.

Having made those recognitions, and desiring such ethical criteria for my own scholarly activity, I looked to the Anabaptist tradition for assistance. Ethics, nonviolence, and peacemaking have always been considered central to Anabaptism, but I discovered that modern-day Anabaptists wrestled more with business decisions, political processes, and personal ethics than with ethics for the idea-oriented professions.

What the Anabaptist tradition did provide, however, was the Bible—more specifically the Bible as a model for a communication salvific for people throughout the centuries As I explored this text more thoroughly, I discovered a Bible that is vulnerable to misinterpretation because it was formed within human history, a Bible that nevertheless has integrity because it included the voices of many different kinds of people.

I found within the Bible a conversation (and sometimes even a struggle) between traditions that allowed no one tradition to be supreme, since only God was to be worshiped. For example, the Torah tradition of Moses was often challenged and renewed by the prophetic tradition. The wisdom tradition, which included much knowledge from outside of Israel, was challenged by the exodus tradition, which speaks of a unique experience of salvation and election. And the messianic tradition of a warrior king was challenged by the Messiah Jesus, who came in peace and reconciliation.

This shape of the biblical canon, replete with its many voices and perspectives, created a new set of questions for my own theological work. Who was included and who was excluded in the scholarly discourse in which I participated? Were certain people's writings excluded because of race, color, gender, or political commitments? A quick survey of the books on my shelves testified to a rather limited conversation.

In my reflections I began to focus more and more on the area of dialogue, asking questions of power and authority. What does it mean to listen to the voice of the marginal and powerless? How can theologians speak authentically about their own discoveries and convictions while being open to the views of the "other."

Reflecting on the Anabaptist tradition with its ethic of justice, nonviolence, and peace has been helpful to me. More and more I have realized that being vulnerable and open to critical dialogue comes first of all with a strong sense of God's active role in the whole world—even beyond the church. I do not need to resort to weapons of destructive words nor appeal to divine justification if I can acknowledge that the knowledge of God is always beyond all of us.

I do not need to defend God, if God will ultimately be the one who reveals truth and destroys falsehood. I can open myself to the dialogue of others because I believe that God loved the world and offers everyone revelation and salvation. I do not need to feel threatened by those with whom I differ; rather, I can be both discerning and open to the words of others. I must therefore acknowledge the power of my words while remaining vulnerable, opening myself to a broad group of critical conversation partners.

Theology's Focus: Process and Truth

In 1987 I was asked to be on the Faith and Life Committee of the Mennonite World Conference. During the three years leading up to the celebration in Winnipeg, Manitoba, a small group of representatives from the broader Mennonite world tried to hammer out a confession of faith that would provide the language for a public act of commitment during the final worship service.

Because we came from radically different contexts, and because we wanted the statement to have integrity, we became very sensitive to the kind of process that we needed to engage in. We attempted to draw many different people into the process, to work at the power issues that were involved, and to look at the different theological approaches that were natural for different groups of people.

While I continue to affirm that sort of careful process, I must also acknowledge my final, post-conference reflection: regardless of the process, the powerful words of the confession mean nothing if they are not true. If God is not active in our history, it really doesn't matter that we have worked out a wonderfully freeing process of theological reasoning. Process must be connected to convictions that have substance.

This has been one of my growing insights. The process of theoretical work is a political process and must have integrity. However, theology is finally of value if God's real presence among us is discerned and named.

This implies some substantive naming of Truth. Yet no naming of God can adequately describe the God beyond names. I have therefore found it helpful to use the term *truth claims* to stress the fact that, when I am convinced of an aspect of truth, it begins to make its claims on my life. I cannot go back to what I have known before without losing my sense of integrity. My worldview begins to shift to include this new insight, and with this shift comes the urge to communicate what I believe to be true.

But which language shall I use to express my limited sense of who God is and what is true? Traditionally Anabaptists have rejected philosophical, symbolic, and more doctrinal language in favor of concrete biblical language (e.g., "following Jesus"). At the same time we have been influenced by the various streams of theological thinking around us, particularly those that stress literal interpretations of Scripture and the factually oriented language of science and technology. Will our traditional approach to theological language be rich enough to mediate experiences of the transcendent God in this age? Or are there new images, concepts, and metaphors that can speak truthfully in our day?

Recently I have begun to move into the more intuitive language of symbol and image in my public speaking. This overtly multivalent language tends to open us to dialogue and challenges us to rethink our convictions and re-imagine our visions for the future.[10]

Instead of using language that communicates supremacy and absolute authority, I search for simple but rich terms that will witness to something larger than the words themselves. Thus, for example, in speaking about the Bible's power, I do not begin with talk of inspiration and revelation. Instead, I use the image of the Bible as our "home." This encourages exploration of the "family" narrative and the various discussions that arise from interpretations of that common story. It also allows us to acknowledge the dysfunctional aspects of how that home has functioned in our lives.[11] At the same time, confessing the Bible as home points to how our very identity as Christians is totally dependent on the one to whom the Bible points with its rich imagery and narrative.

As a "biblical people," Anabaptist-Mennonites have been tempted to focus on factual language to draw boundaries around God. In the process we have sometimes created a God too small to worship. Focusing on the richness of language by multiple witnesses is a new way to point to God, who is beyond our human limitations, even the limits of our theological language. And it is to that God of Truth that all theological language must point.

The Scholarly Agenda: Individual and Communal

The phone call from Mennonite Central Committee (MCC) seemed innocent enough. Would our fledgling institution consider hosting some Muslim exchange students from Iran? The complications of arranging a doctoral program for Islamic students at the Toronto School of Theology, with its Christian commitments and its university affiliation, did not immediately strike me. Instead, I became excited about the opportunity to be involved in interreligious dialogue as part of MCC's larger peacemaking effort. After all, I was aware of how often interreligious conflict was at the root of war.

Soon I realized that a theoretical understanding of dialogue does not always include an awareness of the time and energy needed to insure authentic conversations with those of different cultures and religions. This realization was driven home again this past year, when my husband and I were asked to visit Iran. There we spent several weeks in a totally Muslim environment.

I had not counted on this kind of intensive encounter. In fact, my scholarly research had been going in a different direction, focusing most directly on my own heritage of faith. I had been quite content to stay within a more comfortable Christian (albeit university) context. The new theme of interfaith dialogue felt somewhat intrusive.

This experience raised important questions for me. How do I choose my specific research projects? What motivates me in my choices? How do I discern which projects to spend time on?

I realize that often my own interests and curiosity—my questions and suspicions as well as my past experiences—dictate my choice of subject. Sometimes the larger church community assigns a topic to me. Usually financial remuneration has not been the largest factor, though I have realized that it is tempting to work in those areas for which research grants are more easily available.

I have learned to say yes to certain assignments within my area of expertise and no to others. Sometimes, however, I am drawn into an unexpected area, as in the cases above. It is then that I need to discern whether this is a call to me to move beyond my own comfort zone. Usually this is a time for self-reflection and reprioritizing my work.

At times I have even called together a group of people from the church to help me in this decision making. If my research is to be of use and relevant to the larger church and society, I must also pay attention not only to my own interests but to what the needs of the community are.

I have discovered that my endurance during the slow, sometimes agonizing work of research is proportional to the degree to which the personal and the communal agendas come together. This means that I must maintain contact with both the church and the university to choose projects that will be relevant as well as interesting.

Choosing a Third Way

Naming myself a theologian in the Anabaptist tradition has been a long and gradual process. The tensions that invariably arise when the words *scholar* and *Anabaptist Christian* are placed side by side have no doubt nourished some of my most fruitful and satisfying scholarly work. At the same time, I have discovered that being accountable to both the church and the scholarly community is exceedingly difficult. Again and again I am faced with crucial ethical and faith decisions arising out of these commitments.

Having experienced the reality that neither the church nor the scholarly community fully understands or supports me in this work, I have often been tempted to align myself with one or the other to dissolve the tensions. Yet the place on the "wall" is the place to which I am called. Here I can work out a third way beyond the polarities and dualisms that ask me to reject either the world that God created or the church that is called to witness to God's salvation.

It is here on the wall that I feel I can be most open to God's revealing presence. Indeed, it is through my work as a theologian that I most freely and joyfully witness to the God that I have come to know.

NOTES

1. Denck's observation has been quoted many places, including John H. Yoder, "The Hermeneutics of the Anabaptists," in *Essays on Biblical Interpretation: Anabaptist-Mennonite Perspectives*, ed. Willard M. Swartley (Elkhart, Ind.: Institute of Mennonite Studies, 1984), 27.

2. See Menno Simons, *The Complete Writings of Menno Simons*, trans. Leonard Verduin (Scottdale, Pa.: Herald Press, 1956), 605.

3. I explored this notion in "Hermeneutic Community: A Study of the Contemporary Relevance of an Anabaptist-Mennonite Approach to Biblical Interpretation" (master's thesis, Newman Theological College, 1984).

4. Yoder, "The Hermeneutics of the Anabaptists," 21-22.

5. See Walter Brueggemann, *Interpretation and Obedience: From Faithful Reading to Faithful Living* (Minneapolis, Minn.: Fortress Press, 1991), 41-69.

6. I elaborate on this approach in my book *Obedience, Suspicion and the Gospel of Mark: A Mennonite-Feminist Exploration of Biblical Authority* (Waterloo, Ont.: Wilfrid Laurier University Press, 1998), esp. 1-24.

7. Ibid., 104-15.

8. See for instance my response to Mary H. Schertz, in *Peace Theology and Violence Against Women*, ed. Elizabeth G. Yoder (Elkhart, Ind.: Institute of Mennonite Studies, 1992), 25-28.

9. See Lydia Harder, "Biblical Interpretation: A Praxis of Discipleship," *Conrad Grebel Review* 10 (1992): 17-32.

10. Lydia Neufeld Harder, "Postmodern Suspicion and Imagination: Therapy for Mennonite Hermeneutic Communities," *Mennonite Quarterly Review* 71 (1997): 267-83.

11. See my use of this image in *Peace Theology and Violence Against Women*, 25-26.

14: Christian Ministries

The Academy Is No Friend of the Church (But Does the Church Really *Deserve* a Friend?)

J. E. McDermond

I SPENT CONSIDERABLE TIME PONDERING THIS ESSAY. I teach Christian ministries; is that a "scholarly" undertaking? I read widely in the areas of history and literature, and while these disciplines provide useful tools for my work, I am certainly not a scholar in these areas. (In fact, my graduate training was in biblical studies, but I don't often teach in that discipline either.)

Early in the process of formulating this essay, I had a vague notion of what I wanted to write; but the central idea was fuzzy, indeed, so fuzzy that it was impossible to articulate it in any coherent fashion. My thoughts began to gel only after receiving an e-mail message from a recent graduate.

Jesse (not his real name) was wrestling with a number of questions that he lumped under the larger heading of "struggling with Christianity." Initially, he was not entirely clear as to his view of God. Even when he concluded that God comprised an element of his worldview and ethical system, he found himself puzzled by a further question: What was he to make of Jesus as the savior of the world?

Jesse acknowledged he had been positively influenced by college professors who held to a universalistic view of religion and negatively influenced by church leaders who, in his opinion, unflinchingly advocated flawed teachings. Ultimately, he admitted, "I hate going to church. . . ."

I found this e-mail disturbing, for two reasons. First, it reminded me, again, that the academy is no friend to the church. In its purest form, and seemingly in some self-avowed Christian forms, the academy's goals undercut much for which the church strives. As Duke University professor William Willimon writes, the university often works hand-in-glove with our larger culture to push people toward an individualistic and detached pursuit of reality and truth.[1] The church, on the other hand, calls us to accept a communal approach to understanding revealed and inherited truth.

The other disturbing element of Jesse's note was this: the church often gets it wrong. We do not think. We do not give the individual freedom to question and doubt. We know the truth; our tendency is to want to live forever on the strength of inherited understandings of what it means to be faithful to a holy and revealed God. The meaning of the revelation is seen as unchanging. Thus it is the believer's task to accept it—even if the message does not square with reality. The academy, on the other hand, gives students (and faculty) freedom to explore the world, then commit themselves to the truth they find.

While I would challenge the notion that we must choose between the academy and the church (i.e., embrace one approach as right and dismiss the other as wrong), I would also question the assumption that church and the academy can easily exist as equal influences for the Anabaptist scholar. If we Anabaptists still take "two-kingdom theology" seriously, we ought to consider the real possibility that the church, while far from perfect, is closer to the kingdom of God than is the academy. We ought also consider the fact that the academy, while certainly not demonic, often undercuts the efforts of the church to embody the kingdom of God on earth.

In sum, while we can and should use the academy's scholarship in service to the church—sometimes illuminating its faith and practice and at other times confronting its tendency toward blind acceptance of tradition—I would argue that our first allegiance as Anabaptist scholars must be to the church.

Having said that, I must confess that my (sometimes checkered) experiences with both the church and the academy inform my views on these matters. And so I'll begin by recounting a few of those experiences.

Introduced to the Joyful and Painful World of the Academy

My introduction to the academy occurred midway through my sophomore year at Messiah College. Having treated my first year of college as if it were "Camp Messiah," I registered for a class entitled "The Nature of the Holy Life." The course's agenda consisted of visiting three seminaries from three different theological traditions, with the purpose of studying these institutions' understanding of "holiness."

To be perfectly honest, the course's greatest appeal to me resided in the fact that it was a road trip, as opposed to an opportunity to visit three graduate schools. But despite my less than admirable motives, the week spent at Associated Mennonite Biblical Seminary (AMBS) changed my life.

In the course of that week we spent most of our time with J. C. Wenger and Gertrude Roten. They lectured on the Anabaptist understanding of holiness and 1 John, respectively, and assigned what seemed to be incredible amounts of collateral reading. I still recall their passion for the subject material they were covering. It was as if I was a cartoon character and the light bulb suddenly went on above my head: studying could be engaging and rewarding.

But the real trigger was the Wednesday evening session we had with John Howard Yoder. I cannot recall what the subject was; I just remember that I was mesmerized by this man. His presentation was clear and engaging—even for an unfocused college sophomore like me. And what amazed me even more was that some of the seminary students attended this lecture *voluntarily*!

I knew I wanted to attend seminary. What's more, I wanted to attend this seminary. And that was interesting because I had not grown up Mennonite, and I was only now, two full years after my conversion, exploring the possibility of joining the Brethren in Christ Church. Imagine my shock when I learned that a B average was required for admission to AMBS. I had work to do. And so for two and a half years I studied, raising my less than stellar grade-point average to an acceptable level for admission.

I would describe my final years at Messiah as spent in the narthex to the house I wanted to enter. Although I was a Bible major, none of my major courses were taught by biblical scholars. Rather, the men who taught these classes had primarily been trained as church historians and pastors. (At that time, the mid-1970s, people in our denomination knew church history and pastoral ministry were "safer" disciplines than biblical studies.) So while I found the biblical text engaging, I suspected I was missing something.

The text presented challenges which could not be easily resolved, and my classes did little to help. As I struggled through these problems, I wrote papers that raised concerns on the part of certain profs. I recall one paper, in particular, on the authorship and dating of Ecclesiastes. It came back to me with a note commending me for a well-written paper—despite the grave errors of my "liberal" conclusions.

As I look back upon it now, my conclusions were not exactly earth-shaking. Nor had I drawn upon scholarship to its fullest extent, mainly because I had not been taught how to do this. I did not even know who the groundbreaking biblical scholars were.

As I further reflect on my undergraduate education and my subsequent transition to seminary, I recall that some well-intentioned individuals would have had me remain uninformed. I remember my local bishop meeting with me to discourage me from attending AMBS, because of that institution's openness to scholarship—more specifically, its historical-critical approach to studying the biblical text. The seminary's commitment to this methodology was a significant contributing factor to his belief that the seminary would not do a very good job of preparing me for ministry—or at least for ministry in the way our denomination deemed appropriate.

This was an issue that did not go away. During my third year at AMBS, there was another meeting between the seminary's Brethren in Christ students and Brethren in Christ church leaders. Once again the agenda revolved around the "dangerousness" of the seminary's openness to scholarship. To their credit (I'll now admit), these church leaders knew that the academy was often no friend to the church; to their discredit, they were largely attempting to defend indefensible territory against the wrong enemy. But in my immaturity, I overestimated their narrow-mindedness and chose to ignore their attempts to help me be more reflective about the road I was traveling.

The main reason I discounted their advice was that I had met Howard Charles, a New Testament professor at the seminary. During my first semester I took a required course entitled "Introduction to the

New Testament," which Howard taught. It was unlike any other Bible course I had ever taken. As my introduction to both ancient history and to the historical-critical method, it opened up for me doors to whole new worlds.

I hung on Howard's every word. Through his presentations and his own engagement with the secondary texts, he radically changed my understanding of the word *study*. With his help I met an entirely new group of people, albeit only through their writings: Hans Conzelmann, Rudolf Bultmann, C. H. Dodd, Raymond Brown, James D. G. Dunn, and many others.

I simply could not acquire enough of their views. In fact, my Friday routine often included a late afternoon nap, supper, studying in the library until closing time, then reading in my room until 5:00 or 6:00 a.m. I knew I wanted to be a scholar like one of them.

If I had been wiser, I would have set as my goal being a scholar like Howard. While he knew the views of famous scholars, his writings were not directed at them or at the academy. Instead, Howard spent his entire scholarly life taking the more worthy insights of the academy's studies and making relevant connections to the life of God's people. He is perhaps best known for his writings for the Mennonite Publishing House's Sunday school materials, and through that medium he helped many lay people better understand the world in which the biblical text was written. By intelligently bridging the chronological and cultural gaps between our time and those ancient worlds, he established a frame upon which many people wove a more informed faith.

Yet instead of modeling my scholarship after Howard's, I left seminary thinking that Rudolf Bultmann and the Gospel of Matthew were of relatively equal value. In doing so, I embraced the academy's ideal of holding the biblical text (and most other subjects) at arm's length and analyzing it dispassionately and in minute detail. It was therefore not without cause that a good brother bishop went out of his way to lovingly warn me of the dangers of my plans to undertake biblical studies at a "secular" university in Europe.

At the time I had forgotten that the Bible belonged to the church long before it was taken up by the academy, and I was very confused as to the biblical text's role in the believing scholar's life. Armed with these naive ideals I went to Europe to study New Testament at a leading university. Fortunately, disaster was awaiting me there.

To be sure, there were many excellent benefits from being at this university. The library resources were absolutely superb. My adviser was a first-rate New Testament scholar and a wonderful Christian, and his reputation as a scholar and person sympathetic to evangelicals drew excellent budding scholars from around the world. In fact, we postgraduates were repeatedly told this university's theology department was one of the few intentionally Christian theology departments in the country. We were not told about the deep tensions that existed between the junior and senior faculty members, but we all learned soon enough.

On the day of my oral examination, I was informed that my dissertation would not be accepted for a doctorate. Instead I was "awarded" an M.Litt., the second highest degree conferred by the university. Later my adviser explained that I was a casualty of departmental politics. (I subsequently learned that I was fortunate; another doctoral candidate was initially turned away without any degree.) Shortly thereafter the department went through a significant shake-up. The senior members remained, and the junior members either retired or located other positions. It was a hard lesson to learn, and it took me many years to come to terms with this event. Looking back, however, I see this as a pivotal moment when my thinking about scholarship began to shift in other directions.

I was, and still am, baffled how we can honestly want to read Scripture without wanting it to grab hold of our lives, shake us, and mold us into new beings. That's a large part, if not the core, of what the biblical text is about: it is "useful for teaching, for reproof, for correction, and for training in righteousness, so that everyone who belongs to God may be proficient, equipped for every good work" (2 Tim. 3:16-17). As Thomas Merton notes,

> any serious reading of the Bible means personal involvement in it, not simply mental agreement with abstract propositions. And involvement is dangerous, because it lays one open to unforeseen conclusions. . . . We all instinctively know that it is dangerous to become involved in the Bible. The book judges us, or seems to judge us, on terms to which at first we could not possibly agree.[2]

The Bible is not a textual frog to be dissected. It is one of God's tools for cutting the cancerous tumors from and healing the lives of those who would be followers of Jesus.

Developing a Scholarly Faith

My journey toward developing a "scholarly faith" gained added impetus during the 1992-1993 academic year—a year which, not coincidentally, brought me significant healing from my academic disaster of five years earlier.[3] Messiah College had seconded me to Daystar University College (DUC) in Nairobi, Kenya. The year at Daystar provided me with many eye-opening experiences, though I was perhaps most affected by the way in which my African students approached their Christian lives.

In some cases, as with the Sudanese students, faith was literally a matter of life and death; to be a believer was a dangerous and courageous undertaking. For many other students, and even for some faculty members, financial disaster was never far away. Still, these Africans exhibited a quiet confidence in God. Although DUC certainly had its share of problems, the degree to which my students and colleagues made God a priority in their lives provided a startling contrast to the Christian world from which I had come. That year's experiences forced me to rethink many things, most importantly, the issue of Christian "spirituality."

Surprisingly, it was also this environment that renewed my willingness and desire to be involved in scholarly endeavors. Between 1987 and 1992 I had rather successfully avoided libraries and never entertained the possibility of doing any kind of research again; but this year in Africa forced me to revisit that stance.

The academic year began with a DUC faculty retreat and, in the course of the first day's meeting, an intense argument erupted over the issue of "modesty" and what the university could expect from its students. As an uninformed observer I listened to the various points and counterpoints. To my amazement only passing reference was made to any biblical models that could be brought to bear on this subject. A lunchtime conversation with a Kenyan colleague revealed this subject was a widespread issue in most Kenyan Christian circles, and not just a passing discussion for DUC. I suggested that my colleague write a paper and submit it to an African journal. He countered that I should do it myself.

Much to my surprise I found myself at Hekima College, the local Jesuit seminary. I can still visualize its amazingly well-stocked theological library. The more time I spent there thumbing through the card catalog, locating books and journal articles and comparing viewpoints, the more it came back to me: there is great joy in studying. But a newly added factor intensified this sense of fulfillment. My study was to be directed toward helping people better understand Scripture as they endeavored to be faithful in their walks of discipleship.

I returned from Kenya with a renewed interest in scholarship and a new direction. The solution to my checkered academic experience was not to abandon the academy and swear off the life of study the academy tries to foster. Rather, I finally came around to realizing the essential value of a life like Howard Charles's. I am called to stand between the academy and the church, on the fringes of both circles, listening to questions, seeking answers, and attempting to communicate divine truth for the good of the faith community.

This newfound goal was reinforced in 1994, when a colleague who was responsible for teaching the majority of Messiah's Christian ministry courses retired. Before we inaugurated a search for his successor, I asked my department colleagues if they saw any wisdom in reallocating my teaching load from biblical studies to Christian ministry. Since that time I have used my formal training in biblical studies to inform the various Christian ministry classes I teach, such as "Homiletics," "Christian Spirituality," "Worship," and "Nature and Mission of the Church."

My Role as a Person with Scholarly Faith

Given this self-understanding and the close proximity of my academic discipline(s) to the life of the church, I view my primary task as teaching young men and women preparing for the ministry. As I perform that task, I do so with a scholarly faith, my ultimate hope being that my students (the church's future ministers) will likewise become skilled at incorporating the academy's useful elements into the life of the church.

Having said that, I readily admit that my secondary agenda is to write for and speak to *the church at large* with that same scholarly faith. Not only is this undertaking an important model for my students, it is needed by the church, for we live in times when the church can no longer rely on traditional modes and methods of operation. Indeed, one particular cultural development has reinforced my desire to teach and write for the church: the emerging post-Christian nature of Western civilization. While I have much work to do to hone my thinking on this topic, one thing is certain: "Both Christian mission and modern culture, widely regarded as antagonists, are in crisis."[4]

Generally speaking the church in the West, including North America, no longer holds the privileged position it held in the past. Some European countries are talking of "disestablishing" their state churches and, as we well know, the church's influence in many Western European countries has already dropped to an almost negligible level.

Whether we like it or not, many segments of North American society are following the same trend. While rarely established in a legal sense, the churches in the United States have nonetheless had a considerable influence on American society. But this widespread influence seems to be narrowing. While some people continue to think of United States culture as "Christian" (and will likely continue to do so), an increasing number of people recognize the religious diversity of U. S. society and therefore hesitate to use this label. The question, then, is, What is the church's role in a society that no longer views itself as Christian?

This is a great opportunity for Anabaptist scholars and congregations. As other Christian groups struggle to understand themselves in this post-Christendom environment, we Anabaptists can attest to a long history of practicing our faith in contexts where we didn't have influence and didn't much seek it. In other words, we have something to offer our fellow Christians, who are entering this territory anew.

Of course, we, like they, will need to think "outside of the box." And as we do, I hope we will realize we have more in common with our Lutheran and Baptist neighbors than we do with the larger society, a realization that will provide a good starting point for exploring our common commitments as well as our theological differences.

In part, it is my task as a person of scholarly faith to begin that exploration and share these ideas with the church. One example will suffice here.

Some years ago I became convinced that in the coming new order of post-Christendom, Christians of various backgrounds will need to worship together, thus removing the focus from themselves and their preferences and refocusing on the Lord and Savior of the world. In response to that growing conviction I wrote a short article entitled "A Plea for Liturgy." I later developed the main theme into a larger essay entitled "Common Ground: An Appeal for Brethren in Christ Openness to an Ecumenical Spirit of Worship," which has been submitted to another journal.⁵ I can't say the ideas espoused in these articles are taking root in the Brethren in Christ Church, but I think I'm being faithful to my calling by raising the issue.

I readily admit I am occasionally frustrated in such a role. I would like to think I am a fairly normal person, and most normal people do not enjoy being ignored or vilified. And yet I suspect that, within our Mennonite and Brethren in Christ circles, people of scholarly faith are often viewed as threats, and are thus ignored and sometimes even vilified. Change is difficult, even if it is necessary.

Still, I hold out hope that the church can recognize the benefits of making changes that are based upon careful reflection. While no doubt threatening, such changes, I believe, are actually safer than changes precipitated by shifting cultural mores or desires for self-aggrandizement—both of which seem to be common in our current North American context.

Much as I would like to avoid this imagery, I think the scholar's role within Anabaptism may best be described as prophetic. In times of crisis God has called prophets who analyze the context in which the people of God find themselves. The prophet's task is to articulate clearly the alternatives that lie before the faithful, and he or she is further called by God to advocate the most faithful path for believers to take.

Ironically, the academy—no friend to the church—has trained us well to analyze, articulate, and advocate. I therefore believe that God is calling us, or at least me, to use these skills for the benefit of the church. Fortunately for me (in contrast to many of the scholars contributing to this volume), my discipline is at least superficially valued by the church. And two of its subdisciplines in particular— preaching and spiritual formation—provide me with wonderful opportunities to speak prophetically to the church.

I realize preaching has fallen into disrepute in many Christian circles, and frankly I think that is most unfortunate. But it is also understandable. For too long sermons have fallen into one of two categories: well-organized, argumentative essays about propositional truth or poorly organized, passionate defenses of tradition. Neither option is very useful in the post-Christian world, a world in which more and more people want to *experience* God, but also want to be able to *understand* those experiences. Good preaching assumes God still speaks through the Bible, the sacred text of the church. The preacher's challenge is to hear and speak the gospel in new ways, enabling the church to hear it again, for the first time.

Here is where the academy can provide tools to help us achieve our goals, but we must recall they are only tools dedicated to a greater task: helping the church remain faithful to God. I like the way Stephen Farris approaches the tool of biblical studies. In an essay rather critical of the academy's attempt to elevate its tools over the Bible, Farris concludes,

> The role of biblical studies . . . is to teach the wrestler preacher a few new holds. Which holds are the most useful? In the end it hardly matters what holds are used as long as it is the God of Israel and of our Lord Jesus Christ with whom we wrestle. Any method of interpretation will suffice as long as it is God to whom we are listening in these texts.[6]

Ultimately, scholar preachers, armed with their best "moves and holds," are pitted against the King of the universe. The mat is the Bible. If we are wrestling the right Person, and not the mat, the outcome is virtually guaranteed: the scholar preacher will concede to God. But having wrestled, he or she will have something of value to talk about on Sunday morning. And then it will be the gathered faithful's turn to begin wrestling.

When I prepare sermons, whether printed or preached, I always want to go about the process in this way. On the one hand, I don't merely want to report on my own inner longings and share a few good ideas I thought up in the course of the week; on the other hand, I certainly am not going to give the congregation a summary of how the latest critical tool assesses a given text. I will have used that tool, of course, but only as a means for achieving my ultimate end: a sermon that allows the people of God to hear the divine voice that comes into our chaotic world and speaks of grace, justice, and hope. Only then will we have any idea of where we can and must be transformed into the likeness of Christ Jesus.

This note of transformation leads me to my final point. I would hope that I might make some lasting contribution to the ongoing work of spiritual formation within the life of the church. This, of course, is a very broad area, for it includes such subtopics as the spiritual disciplines, theology and spirituality, psychology and spirituality, and more. But the one area that I would most like to influence the church is in its approach to spiritual role models—in particular, the persons it highlights as role models.

In many circles in which I travel, there seems to be an ironic juxtaposing of spiritual malaise and yearning. I suspect the irony is a result of seriously misguided and overly rigid approaches to theology and church traditions. For significant progress to be made in this area we will have to shift from a law-based faith to a grace-based faith. We will need to exchange our primary goal of intimacy with one another for the primary goal of intimacy with God, which then fosters spiritual intimacy with other believers.

Perhaps most threatening of all, we will need to learn from the spiritual journeys of believers residing in other Christian traditions and eras. Only by becoming the best *Christians* we can be will we become the best *Anabaptists* we can. And by becoming the best Anabaptist Christians we can be, we will encourage others to be the best Lutheran Christians, Catholic Christians, Methodist Christians, and/or charismatic Christians they can be. Our post-Christian culture will eventually force us to work together, and I believe my role as a Christian with scholarly faith is to encourage us to begin the task voluntarily before our hands are forced.

There is no doubt that God gave Anabaptists specific spiritual ancestors, and we must continue to value their wisdom and insights on the spiritual life. But God also gave us Thomas Merton, Dorothy Day, Evelyn Underhill, Hannah Whitall Smith, Martin Luther, Teresa of Ávila, Thomas à Kempis, John Chrysostom, and a whole host of others.

It strikes me as essentially unwise to reject God's good gifts in favor of venerated traditions, even one I value as highly as the Anabaptist tradition. Traditions have value only as they help us live faithfully. The more fully we understand the Christian spiritual life, the more faithfully we can live it. And because that life is more than any one individual or group's understanding, we must be prepared to learn humbly at the feet of those who have gone before us—even if they sat at different communion tables from ours.

Through the past two thousand years, many people have attempted to live faithful lives as followers of Jesus. We need to broaden our horizons and seek out their wise counsel as we also seek to become more like Christ.

Conclusion

In this essay I have suggested that my primary calling as an Anabaptist with scholarly faith is to help the church become more faithful in its pilgrimage. But to do that I have willingly moved to the church's fringe, assuming something of a critical and prophetic role.

At the same time, I have moved toward another institution that has never claimed to be a friend to the church. The academy has provided me with tools, ideas, and freedom, all of which are very useful in my attempt to move that seemingly immovable object called the church. At the same time, I am keenly aware that the academy claims more from me than it deserves. It often encourages me to pursue that which is mundane and transient compared to what the church knows and seeks to know better.

And so I am torn. Both the academy and the church possess laudable attributes and elements, and both have incredible weaknesses.

Still, I dance the dance, and sometimes I even enjoy it. Indeed, if I were pressed to conclude this essay with an image of the Anabaptist scholar's role, I think it would be this. The Anabaptist scholar takes one favorite partner to a dance, and spends most of the evening with that person. But there is another intriguing dance partner with whom the Anabaptist scholar dances. That partner teaches the scholar a few new steps, which are in turn shared with the original partner—not for the sake of gaining respect, gratitude, or love, but with the simple hope that the first partner would thereby be enabled to move more gracefully in the world that God created.

Notes

1. William H. Willimon and Stanley Hauerwas, *Preaching to Strangers* (Louisville, Ky.: Westminster/John Knox Press, 1992), 32.

2. Thomas Merton, *Opening the Bible* (Collegeville, Minn.: The Liturgical Press, 1970), 43.

3. See the opening essay to this volume, in which David Weaver-Zercher cites Douglas and Rhonda Jacobsen's definition of scholarly faith: "faith [itself] subjected to the kind of disciplined reflection and creative thinking that characterizes all scholarship." According to the Jacobsens, this sort of Christian scholarship assumes the Christian community as its primary audience.

4. So write Alan Neely, H. Wayne Pipkin, and Wilbert R. Shenk in the series preface to Douglas John Hall, *The End of Christendom and the Future of Christianity* (Valley Forge, Pa.: Trinity Press International, 1997), vii. In addition to Hall's text (and

the other books in the Christian Mission and Modern Culture series), one may also wish to read Rodney Clapp, *A Peculiar People: The Church as Culture in a Post-Christian Society* (Downers Grove, Ill.: InterVarsity Press, 1996) and Michael Riddell, *Threshold of the Future: Reforming the Church in the Post-Christian West* (London: SPCK, 1998).

5. Jay E. McDermond, "A Plea for Liturgy," *Shalom! A Journal for the Practice of Reconciliation* 16, no. 4 (Fall 1996): 5-6. See also Walter Klaassen, *Biblical and Theological Bases for Worship in the Believers' Church* (Newton, Kan.: Faith and Life Press, 1978); Eleanor Kreider, *Communion Shapes Character* (Scottdale, Pa.: Herald Press, 1997); Marlene Kropf, "The Trinity as a Template for Worship," in *Anabaptist Visions For the New Millennium: A Search for Identity*, ed. Dale Schrag and James Juhnke (Kitchener, Ont.: Pandora Press, 2000), 145-51; and John D. Rempel, *The Lord's Supper in Anabaptism: A Study in the Christology of Balthasar Hubmaier, Pilgram Marpeck, and Dirk Philips* (Scottdale, Pa.: Herald Press, 1993).

6. Stephen Farris, "Limping Away with a Blessing: Biblical Studies and Preaching at the End of the Second Millennium," *Interpretation* 51 (1997): 367.

15: Response

Minding the Scholars: A View from the Pew

Harriet Sider Bicksler

AS I ANTICIPATED WRITING THIS CHAPTER, my Sunday school class began a study of petitionary prayer and how God works in the world. Our resource for the study was *Providence and Prayer,* a book in which seminary professor Terrance Tiessen analyzes ten different ways of understanding petitionary prayer.[1] More than once, I was struck by how our class was a laboratory for this volume's topic: the intersection of scholarship and the church. As I listened to and participated in our class discussion, I found myself alternately frustrated and stimulated.

I was frustrated because, at times, it seemed we were engaging in meaningless—albeit interesting—intellectual discourse of the proverbial "how many angels can dance on the head of a pin" variety. I need concrete answers to complex questions. I need an *affective* rather than an intellectual and academic discussion of prayer. I don't need a lot of philosophizing involving abstract concepts that are meaningful mostly to people who spend their lives studying such things. At the time of the class, I was struggling with a very specific issue about which I did not (and still don't) know how to pray. Many times the class stretched my tolerance for heavy doses of scholarship when there were real-life issues intruding on my mind and heart.

On the other hand, I was stimulated by discussions that forced me to think critically about my faith in God and how I approach prayer. Once again, in this Sunday school class filled with a mixture of college administrators, professors, and community folks like myself (and taught primarily by one of the professors), I found that the critical approach helped me understand better why I believe and act as I do.

This Sunday school class is just one place where my world intersects with the academic community. I have lived near Messiah College and attended the "college church" for forty years. I have friends and church colleagues who are professors and scholars at the college. I am secretary of the church board and pastoral search committee that selected one of the scholar-contributors to this volume to be our new senior pastor.

In my professional life, I am employed by the Pennsylvania State University, working as a publications specialist at a training institute that provides continuing education to children's mental health workers. Penn State is known for its major contributions to research and scholarship in various fields, but our work at the institute, while benefiting greatly from our association with the university, also pushes academicians and scholars to connect their work with the everyday experiences and concerns of children and families.

In my extracurricular life, I edit *Shalom!*, a quarterly Brethren in Christ publication on peace and social concerns, and I serve as chair of the board of Mennonite Central Committee U.S. and on the executive committee of the binational board of MCC. In both capacities, I frequently need to approach complex issues in ways that will help not only in understanding them better but also in sifting through the many different viewpoints that sincere Christians bring to those issues. In all these cases, I have appreciated the contributions and perspectives of persons in the academic community.

First Impressions

My first impression as I read the essays was how I connected personally with the authors' stories and resonated with the issues they have encountered in their scholarly careers. On a very practical level, and without trying very hard, I immediately noted examples of how this particular set of scholars contributes to church life—both at an individual and a corporate level.

One particular point of connection for me (and no doubt for other readers) came in the accounts of the scholars' journeys from their more isolated home communities to the academy, where they typically found whole new worlds to explore. For people like me, coming from homes where education was valued and reading was encouraged, formal academic endeavors provided an added resource—namely, a broader context in which to think about things in which we were already interested. For many of us, this resource helped to stimulate both our minds and our souls, the result being more mature Christian faiths. Even persons who have journeyed to the academic world from settings where education is suspect have frequently discovered that Christian faith can remain intact and, in fact, mature when examined carefully. These scholars helped recall the wonderful (though sometimes painful) possibilities of that journey.

In addition to resonating with that general transition from home to the academy, many Anabaptist Christians over a certain age can also relate to the feelings of tension between the utilitarian and the artistic that poet Jeff Gundy and some of the others describe. This tension is more than a historical fact; it is contemporary and ongoing, as Christians continue to wrestle with how to relate to the secular society and its cultural components (politics, economics, education, books, music, television, movies, art, and so on). Christian scholars who immerse themselves in such subjects, and even earn their living by studying them, make the important point that faith is not automatically undermined by exposure to the outside world. More than that, they remind us that secular people and institutions (and cultural and artistic expressions) frequently possess great insight into the nature of God, the world, and humanity.

Significantly, at least one account debunked the idea that a rural conservative upbringing is antithetical to doing this sort of scholarship. As I read Caleb Miller's account of his Beachy Amish father's appreciation for reason, which was one factor influencing him to pursue philosophy, I thought of the stereotypical attitudes that some more progressive thinkers have toward conservative people. Miller proves that one does not need to repudiate one's background to pursue scholarship; in fact, Miller suggests that his scholarly pursuits actually sent him back to his roots and some of the ideas and beliefs he grew up with.

Others, of course, emphasized insights they initially learned far from home. Perhaps because of my connection to the work of Mennonite Central Committee (MCC), I was struck by the way that overseas experiences directly influenced the academic interests of several scholars. For instance, Mark Charlton's MCC work in the former Zaire served as a catalyst for his studies in political science, and Jim Harder's interest in economics intensified as a result of his MCC experience in Africa.

Charlton's and Harder's research efforts continue to be important to MCC, as the agency considers its role in international aid policy, its attitude toward humanitarian military interventions and economic sanctions, and the impact of systemic forces on the economies of the Two-Thirds World countries in which it works. Harder and his wife (who is also an academic) spent time during their sabbaticals in 1999 evaluating MCC programs in Asia, and other scholars over the years have contributed their professional skills to similar evaluation and research.

Similarly, Lydia Neufeld Harder's participation in a Muslim exchange venture continues to inform her scholarship. Her commitment to engage in interfaith dialogue and examine the language we use about God is important to MCC's ongoing collaboration with Muslim people to meet human needs in the strife-torn Middle East. For example, MCC has joined with the Red Crescent Society (the Muslim equivalent of the American Red Cross) and the Middle East Council of Churches to address needs of children and families in Iraq who suffer due to the policies of Western "Christian" countries like the United States and Canada, and to minister to refugees fleeing Afghanistan during the bombing that followed the September 11, 2001, attacks on the United States

MCC's collaborative role with non-Christians in the Middle East and elsewhere has sometimes been criticized by people in the church constituency. Neufeld Harder's respectful attitude toward people of other faiths, guided by her understandings about the nature of God, is a helpful affirmation of MCC's instincts in this regard.

A final way the endeavors of these scholars have intersected with church life (and my own) is in making scholarship accessible. In the late 1970s, when my commitments to peace and social justice were being shaped and solidified, a book that had a profound influence on me was Donald Kraybill's *The Upside-Down Kingdom*,[2] which opened my mind to new understandings of Jesus' life and teachings. Lights went on in my head as I read Kraybill's interpretation of the meaning of Jesus' temptations, which I had never heard explained in ways that made such sense.

Few books before or since have had as much influence on my thinking as a Christian. This book is just one example of the significant influence that serious scholarship presented in a popular and easily understood format can have on ordinary people in the pew.

Common Themes

I turn now to several themes that recurred throughout the essays. Perhaps there is a strong convergence of themes because of the common context in which each is writing—that is, their relationship as scholars to the church and especially the Anabaptist church. Or perhaps any group of Christian scholars would identify many of the same themes in their consideration of how their scholarly lives "mind the church." I suspect, however, that this particular group of themes may be somewhat more specific to Anabaptists.

Perhaps the most common theme was the tension between individualism and community, a tension that often becomes apparent in the scholar's own work. New Testament scholar Mary Schertz characterizes this tension as a "severe belonging," noting that, despite being thoroughly Anabaptist in every way, her continuing desire to explore certain questions has set her at odds with other Anabaptists. In a similar manner, Lydia Neufeld Harder confesses the difficulty of being accountable to both the church and the scholarly community, concluding that her place is on the "wall" between the two. Such tensions between the individual and the collective have constituted the very essence of sociologist Donald Kraybill's work; his Amish-related scholarship explores the problem of how individual rights are appropriately balanced with collective concerns without suffocating the individual.

Of course, the tensions between individualism and community are not unique to scholars, but are simply a fact of modern life. Still, it may well be that scholars feel them all the more, since scholarship is by practice (if not by definition) a largely individualistic endeavor.[3]

In that regard, it is not particularly surprising that a second theme among these scholars is the sense that their work is often misunderstood, sometimes even mistrusted, by their fellow church members. In the case of some—for example, Jim Harder's economics and Mark Charlton's political science—their disciplines' relevance to the church is sometimes questioned. For although money and politics are widely discussed in our culture, Anabaptists have often found these topics so threatening that scholars who devote their lives to their study can easily feel relegated to the fringes.

Even with theological and biblical studies, however, the scholars in this volume perceive a fear on the part of church members that the study of these fields will weaken rather than strengthen faith. Furthermore, as several scholars point out, the sacred tenet of Anabaptism regarding the priesthood of all believers sometimes results in the disenfranchisement of biblical scholars. Bluntly put, since everyone is free to read and interpret Scripture for him- or herself, who needs the scholar who has spent a lifetime examining and understanding the biblical texts?

A prominent third theme, and one that may contribute to this churchly mistrust of its scholars, is the call to embrace (or at least live with) contradiction and ambiguity. For example, poet Jeff Gundy quotes F. Scott Fitzgerald's statement that "intelligence is the ability to hold two opposed ideas in the mind at the same time," and he recounts his own experience of dissonance in being a Mennonite poet and an intellectual in a tradition "long suspicious of book learning." Other writers, who similarly acknowledge the contradictions and polarities of life, illustrate the fundamental truth that the more one knows and understands, the more there is to know and still not fully understand.

Scholars can do the church a great service by helping us embrace the emotional discomfort that comes from living with partial knowledge and shades of gray, and by helping move to some tentative resolutions of those ambiguities. Too often Christians opt for easy answers and either/or thinking rather than doing the hard work of forging coherent beliefs from diverse and seemingly contradictory ideas.

Turning finally to considerations of style, these essays illustrate the power of story. I have to admit that part of me dreaded reading all the essays because I was afraid they would be difficult to read—or at least boring to anyone who wasn't interested in the discipline at hand. I've tried to read enough scholarly writing over the years to know I often don't like it! These stories drew me in, however, as stories almost always do, and I was fascinated by autobiographical accounts to which I could relate personally, from which I could learn to know these people I was responding to, and which made human the sometimes abstract world of scholarship.

What the Church Needs From Its Scholars

The common themes I've identified begin to point to ways that scholars can "mind" the church—using that term in the sense of "devoting intellect and creativity to the service of the church" (see David Weaver-Zercher's introduction). As a result of living on the edge of Messiah College all these years, I have frequently reflected on the sometimes uneasy relationship between academia and the church. When considering how Messiah College and the Brethren in Christ Church ought to relate to one another, for example, it seems clear that the relationship should be mutually beneficial. To put it simply, the church needs scholars to help it sort through the complexities of the world, to provide careful analyses of issues and events, and to serve as mentors to thoughtful and committed people who will become church leaders. For its part, academia needs the church to ground it in the nitty-gritty of real life, to provide a laboratory in which to test ideas and put them into action, and to nurture genuine and heartfelt Christian faith.

What the church does not need from its scholars is academic pretentiousness, arrogance, and elitism. For example, at a recent seminar attended by Christian scholars and laypersons, most of the presenters held no more than bachelor's degrees. The subject under consideration was a controversial one that has been researched and analyzed by both scholars and nonscholars alike, and that has engendered strong emotions over the course of many years.

Given the subject's significance, it was essential for the participants to get beyond "definitional work" and begin to address the issues that affect people's lives on an everyday basis. Yet some of the academics in attendance seemed stuck on definitions, and they soon grew frustrated at what they perceived to be unsophisticated analyses. Worse, some of the academics seemed to be using their disagreements with the approach as a way to avoid the real issues.

In their defense, I understand the scholars' desire for intellectual integrity and careful thought; certainly I too am frustrated by sloppy thinking. But it seemed to me that, in this case, much of the good being taught was lost because of scholars' unwillingness to admit that less academically sophisticated people might have something worthwhile to offer.

To be honest, I don't sense much of that arrogance and elitism on the part of scholars in this book. Instead I sense the kind of humility that allows them to learn from others, knowing full well that, despite their many years of study, there is still much to learn even from less educated people. I also sense among them a genuine desire to be connected to the church, to use their considerable gifts in their chosen disciplines to help the church.

What might that mean? And how might the kind of scholarship represented in this book do that? Based on my own life in the church, and the kind of issues I think the church faces, let me suggest several ways.

Assist the church with worship and growth issues

My congregation, like many others these days, has dealt with issues of worship style and what a church must do to reach new people from the surrounding community. In contrast to other congregations in our area, our worship style has tended to be relatively formal, and we have often felt pressure to meet the needs of a changing culture. Susan Biesecker-Mast's work in rhetoric, which focuses on how human beings persuade one another by what they say and how they say it, has significant implications for how Anabaptists do outreach and, more specifically, for how Anabaptists should use evangelistic methods that are different from those of the megachurches.

In a related way, when Old Testament scholar Terry Brensinger discusses the tension between practice and theology in the church, he too is arguing for thoughtful reflection on doing church in ways that are true to our theological convictions—and don't just give in to the current church growth fad. In a slightly different manner, Jay McDermond pleads for liturgy as a way to refocus attention in worship on God rather than on self-fulfillment, and he calls for openness to learning from believers from other Christian traditions and eras.

Rather than pass off these ideas as the well-meaning but irrelevant meanderings of scholarly minds, the church would do well to include them in the mix of factors that are considered when changes are made. Too often such changes are made without reflection. The scholars among us can help us think critically about what we're doing.

Assist with biblical interpretation

The emphasis of several authors on the importance of a "hermeneutic community" also has implications for the church. As the church wrestles with such controversial issues as abortion, homosexuality, war and peace, and the role of women in church and society, the Bible is increasingly under attack or being used as a club by one side to try to beat the other side into submission. I deeply appreciate the desire of scholars like Mary Schertz to participate with the church community in reading and interpreting the Bible together. I am distressed, however, by her assertion that "very little serious reading of the Bible actually happens among all these interpreters in the church," except when we throw proof texts at each other. If she and the others are right that many laypeople are uneducated when it comes to biblical history, language, and methods of interpretation (not to mention basic biblical knowledge), we desperately need the scholars in the church to help us as we "rightly divide the word of truth."

I would like to offer one caveat, however; I would hope that the biblical scholars among us would not overestimate this shortcoming on the part of ordinary church members. Indeed, my experience has been that, while people may be unsophisticated or literal in their biblical interpretations, they are certainly serious and sincere. Furthermore, many people who would not consider themselves "scholars" (or be considered scholars) have nonetheless devoted themselves to serious Bible reading and study.

I remember a conversation I once had with a pastor who argued that, since I was not seminary-trained and had not studied the Bible in the original languages like he had, I couldn't possibly know that the Bible did not in fact support women in leadership. He refused to accept as legitimate the reality that I had read numerous books by scholars who *had* studied the Bible in the original languages and had come to the opposite conclusion from his.

My point, then, is not to dismiss the importance of scholarly work, but rather to insist that people who are not scholars can thoughtfully study and speak to issues *even though it is not their professional work to do so*. I suspect there are many laypeople in the church who would like to be given credit for being serious, thoughtful, and committed to an honest and consistent faith. I would also hope that people and congregations in places that don't have direct access to scholarly folk aren't automatically assumed to be at some kind of disadvantage.

To be clear, I am not implying that I think the scholars in this book are making such assumptions. Moreover, I would be the first to acknowledge that there is validity to these scholars' concerns about biblical illiteracy and sloppy thinking in our churches. Still, I believe this concern is sometimes leveled too broadly, thereby trivializing the intellectual contributions of those of us in the hermeneutic community who aren't professionally trained scholars.

Bring social science insights

The economists, political scientists, sociologists, educators, philosophers, and writers among us must also participate in the hermeneutic community, even if their particular expertise is not biblical studies or theology. Jim Harder suggests this when he writes about how an Anabaptist economist can help the church think about economic values that are different from standard "market" values.

I've often thought that Christians ought to question why economists always measure economic strength by new housing starts and automobile sales, so I would welcome discussion of alternative measures more consistent with our values. As globalization becomes more of a factor in international economic relationships, and hence in relationships between churches in North America and other parts of the world, Anabaptist economists like Harder have much to contribute.

Similarly, Mark Charlton's efforts at understanding the science of politics holds potential for helping the church forge a coherent political philosophy that is based on the whole of the Bible and not just a selection of proof texts. Such a philosophy might be helpful for all Christians, but it would be particularly helpful for those of us who live in participatory democracies. In the United States, for example, politicians have considered assigning more funding (and more responsibility) for social programs to faith-based organizations and agencies. What insights might Anabaptist political scientists offer as the church considers whether it is good to accept government funding for things we have traditionally done because of faith commitments and not because we were being paid to do them?

The way we provide Christian education in the church (e.g., in adult and children's Sunday school, youth groups, small groups) also bears examination by such scholars as Polly Ann Brown, who approach the educative process critically and deliberately. Brown's emphasis on the convergence of Anabaptist faith themes with contemporary educational theories is a useful perspective for all those who want to know how to do Christian education, and indeed, for any Christian who is involved in any kind of education, public or private, Christian or secular.

Unfortunately, the standard North American approach to education is often deficit-based rather than strength-based; it focuses on inabilities and failures instead of the strengths that each person brings to the process. I have felt this for a long time as I have watched my son (now a young adult) struggle with school—not because he lacks intelligence but at least partly because educational institutions (public schools, Sunday school, and church youth groups) have expected him and others like him to fit a certain mold. When they don't, the fault is attributed to them instead of to educational processes that refuse to recognize different kinds of intelligence and different styles of learning. How many children have failed irreparably at school or been lost to the church because, as Brown says, our institutions are "simply incapable of dealing with diversity"?

Communicate to the average persons

Finally, if scholars are to have an impact on the church, especially on the thinking of the average layperson, their contributions must be accessible and understandable. By this I mean that scholars must talk and write in lay terms when they want to communicate with laypeople and nonscholars, resisting the urge to use the jargon of their profession or discipline.

This doesn't mean that there isn't an appropriate place for the language of a specific discipline. However, terms and concepts that are useful in the scholarly or academic arena, perhaps because they have become a sort of shorthand for ideas that everyone in that arena understands, often are gobbledygook to the average person. When scholars insist on using esoteric rather than common words, they risk confusing and frustrating their listeners and readers. For the most part, the scholars in this book write in language that is accessible, and for that I am grateful.

Scholarship as an Uneasy Calling

David Weaver-Zercher opens the book with the claim that scholarship is a spiritual calling, comparable to evangelism. My sense is that while people in the church wouldn't want to demean the life choices of the contributors to this volume, many would not put scholarship on par with evangelism as a spiritual gift. However, if they were to read the essays in this book, they might change their minds. I was moved by the ways in which the authors repeatedly referred to following the call of Christ in pursuing their intellectual gifts and in their desire to serve the church with those gifts. Might we not all benefit from seeing scholarship as one specific expression of the spiritual gifts of preaching, teaching, and prophesying?

I was also moved by the unease that many of these scholars feel in the church—whether they feel misunderstood, generally ignored, or practically condemned by their fellow church members. Indeed, in the course of this volume we heard laments about disenfranchisement, regrets over the lack of interest in academic issues, and frustrations about intellectual laziness and biblical illiteracy. The onus is therefore not simply on scholars to be accessible and down-to-earth, but also on the rest of us to actively solicit their input regarding the major issues we face in our churches. The shape of our Christian education programs, the styles of our worship services, the modes of cultural engagement, the roles we assume in our workplaces and communities, and the methods we use to meet the needs of people around us—all these issues and more can be illumined by good and careful thinking, something that the scholars among us have been well trained to do.

As I noted earlier, my Sunday school class is one place where this sort of interchange happens regularly. I think the scholars appreciate having a place in the church where they can participate without leaving their intellects at the door—a place, in fact, where their insights are warmly welcomed and appreciated. As a nonscholar but a lay leader seeking to make sense of my faith, I am grateful for all that expertise so readily at hand. It is one of the blessings that my congregation probably takes for granted far too often.

At the same time, we constantly have to resist the tendency to spend so much time analyzing an issue that we never get to the point of how this will affect the way we live our lives. We enjoy the intellectual debate—perhaps so much at that we avoid obeying what God is calling us to do right now.

In this as in many other things, balance is required. During the study on prayer to which I referred at the beginning of this chapter, I appreciated the times when class members described how they had prayed and what the outcome had been. More than providing great case studies for additional discussion, their stories challenged all of us to continue to pray even when we weren't sure how prayer worked or what we should be praying for. In prayer and other aspects of Christian faith and practice, we don't need to understand everything to act on what we do know and understand.

Finally, I am reminded of Paul's words in Ephesians, which he offers after reminding his readers of their spiritual gifts: "We must no longer be children, tossed to and fro and blown about by every wind of doctrine, by people's trickery, by their craftiness in deceitful scheming" (Eph. 4:14). While I do not want to underestimate the challenges of being a first-century Christian, the world is certainly not becoming less complex, and there is likewise no current shortage of trickery, deceitfulness, and scheming. Perhaps, then, the ideal role for the Anabaptist scholar wanting to "mind the church" is to use his or her particular spiritual gift to help guide us through the storms of ideas that presently confront us, and thereby bring us to the point where "the whole body, joined and knit together by every ligament with which it is equipped, . . . promotes the body's growth in building itself up in love" (Eph. 4:16).

In this task, I hope that all of us—scholars and nonscholars alike—will have the humility to acknowledge our human frailties and our need for God and each other. I want to be able to laugh and cry with everyone in my church community about our joys and sorrows, to share the common ground of Christian fellowship, and to learn from each other. I want to know and feel that we are all traveling on the same journey of faith, and that we are all learners as well as teachers.

NOTES

1. Terrance Tiessen, *Providence and Prayer: How Does God Work in the World?* (Downers Grove, Ill.: InterVarsity Press, 2000).

2. Donald B. Kraybill, *The Upside-Down Kingdom* (Scottdale, Pa.: Herald Press, 1978, 1990).

3. It is interesting to note that, like Kraybill, two other social scientists in this volume exhibit a distinct wariness of modern individualism. Psychologist Alvin Dueck recognizes the ongoing individualistic biases in psychology but notes that "the inner life is a representation of the many people who have shaped our lives." And economist James Harder juxtaposes the largely individualistic marketplace values against Anabaptist ethics of mutual accountability and mutual aid.

16: Response

Contours of the Christian Mind, Anabaptist and Reformed

David A. Hoekema

*I*N THE FIRST PLACE, TRUTH IS ALWAYS LOCAL AND PARTICULAR. We learn about ourselves, the world, and God from our experiences and through sustained, disciplined, and critical inquiry. Truth comes to us as embodied individuals, at particular moments, mediated through the communities to which we belong. If this must be said of truth with a lower-case *t*, it applies all the more to Truth in a theological sense, with a capital letter. We come to a saving knowledge of the one who described himself as the Way, the Truth, and the Life only as individuals in particular communities who open themselves to God's presence and self-revelation.

Yet truth, in the second place, is also universal. Nothing is "true for me" but not for you, however popular this meaningless phrase may have become. Truth is truth, regardless of who you are or where you stand, and its claim is universal.

This too applies with equal force to the Christian understanding that Christ embodies Truth. As Christians we affirm that Christ is the world's true light, not a lamp that lights our way but leaves everyone else in the darkness. In whatever way we may affirm the Christian doctrine of election—a doctrine that is openly avowed by Calvinists and also affirmed, even if only in whispers, by nearly all other Christians as well—it must never be interpreted to imply that Christ came to seek and to save only some of those who are lost. On the contrary, he came that the world through him might be saved (John 3:17). The Truth of salvation in Christ is for everyone, not just for some.

The tension between these two affirmations affects every Christian witness to the world. On the one hand, we proclaim God's self-revelation in history to a particular people at a particular time; on the other, we affirm its validity for all people at all times. To affirm one of these and deny the other is to forsake an important biblical teaching. We must affirm both: truth is particular, and it is also universal. This statement is not a contradiction but simply a consequence of the complexity that lies within the very notion of truth.

(Universal) Christianity and (Particular) Traditions

A similar tension between the universal and particular arises among Christians from diverse confessional traditions when they dispute matters practical or doctrinal. For every Christian is also something else—Mennonite or Reformed, Lutheran or Catholic. Our construal of basic Christian teachings is deeply shaped by our particular confessional and theological tradition (and denominations that insist that they acknowledge "no creed but Christ" are, ironically, sometimes the most sectarian of all).

Christian faith unites us across all denominational and ethnic boundaries, for we know that there is "one Lord, one faith, one baptism, one God and Father of all, who is above all and through all and in all" (Eph. 4:5-6). We recite the same historic creeds. We sing many of the same hymns; I have, for example, sung Luther's hymns in Catholic churches, and praise bands in gospel churches make use of eucharistic hymns from the Catholic charismatic movement. Yet we articulate our common Christian faith in ways that owe a great deal—more than we may realize—to the particular communities that have nurtured us and to their histories.

In reading the essays written for this collection I was reminded continually of both poles of this opposition. Much of what has been written here about Christian scholarship in the Anabaptist tradition applies with equal relevance to the work of scholars grounded in one of the other strands of Protestantism. Nearly all of the problems cited by several writers—mistrust of biblical scholars, for example, and impatience with critical inquiry—are frequent topics of conversation around the lunch table at my college, affiliated with the Christian Reformed Church. I have heard the same concerns expressed at campuses where I have taught or visited whose historic identity is Lutheran, Baptist, or Jesuit. The opportunities that several writers discern for a more forthright Christian witness in the context of contemporary scholarship are open to members of any Christian denomination, not just those who trace their roots to the radical Reformation.

Yet the characteristic emphases of the radical Reformation and its heirs—the gospel of forgiveness and reconciliation, the importance of purity in the church and in daily conduct, and a profound mistrust of secular authority—are much in evidence here. Both in their theology and in their practical proposals, the contributors to this collection stand unambiguously within the Anabaptist tradition.

Significantly, though, there are many similarities between the present situation of the Mennonite and Brethren churches and that of the Reformed churches which constitute my theological home. No one whose early church education took place in an Anabaptist church, I suspect, will need to be reminded of how cruelly the leaders of the Reformation, many of them Calvinists, treated the first Anabaptists, betraying their own ideals of liberty of faith and practice. Nevertheless, the two traditions today have arrived at remarkably parallel situations.

Anabaptists, like Calvinists, occupy a place on the conservative side of the theological spectrum of North American churches, upholding a high view of scriptural inspiration and high expectations for Christian conduct. Both represent small slices in the Protestant pie, in North America and abroad, yet both have gained visibility and influence out of proportion to their numbers. Their influence is seen in different areas: Reformed theological and philosophical writings, on the one hand, and Anabaptist ministries of reconciliation and society-building, on the other, provide a model other branches of the church strive to emulate.

Perhaps more fundamentally, the Anabaptist and the Reformed communities share the conviction that the church should uphold and proclaim its vision of Truth, particular as it is, in a way that touches and ultimately may transform society. The means by which this is to be done differ in important ways. Calvinists are more willing to shoulder the burdens of secular authority, for example, and Anabaptists more disposed to stand in oppositional witness. Yet the goal is much the same.

Encountering the Anabaptist Tradition

Since the focus on this collection has been on the personal as well as the scholarly, perhaps it is appropriate to say a word about my own encounter with the radical Reformation. I was raised in a household thoroughly steeped in the Reformed world view. My late father, Anthony Hoekema, having moved from the parish to the seminary faculty, wrote a series of theology texts that continue to be widely used in evangelical seminaries.[1] My mother, Ruth Hoekema, herself a pastor's daughter, wrote no textbooks, but her lifelong work as a teacher, pastor's spouse, and lay church leader has borne eloquent testimony to the Calvinist vision of the gospel's transformative power. In my college years, however, I became particularly interested in traditions with which I was unfamiliar, and my reading encompassed Jewish and Buddhist writers as well as those from diverse branches of the Christian church.

The moment when the Anabaptist voice first riveted my attention was at the height of the domestic conflict over the Vietnam War, in my third and fourth years of attending Calvin College. In the writings of Arthur Gish and John Howard Yoder, I recall, I found a spirit of bold and uncompromising prophetic witness that stood in sharp contrast to the compromises that Reformed churches were willing to make with the political authorities.[2]

I have a vivid mental picture of long afternoon sessions, sitting out on the campus lawn, when my friends and I would take turns reading aloud to each other from Anabaptist writers, seeking validation for our deep conviction that war must no longer be regarded as an acceptable instrument in the pursuit of national interest. Looking back today, it is clear that the Anabaptist churches were as deeply divided as the Reformed churches over Vietnam, and the willingness of many pastors and church leaders to mute the traditional pacifism of the radical Reformation mirrored inconsistencies in concrete application of the just war tradition by other Protestants. At the time, nevertheless, I was profoundly influenced by the forthright call that I found in Anabaptist writers to work for peace, whatever the cost, rather than wage war.

After leaving the Reformed haven of western Michigan for the challenges of graduate study at Princeton University and a first teaching appointment at St. Olaf College, I found a church home first among Episcopalians and later among Lutherans, even while continuing to see the gospel through Reformed lenses. Several friends and colleagues, and continued reading, have maintained my awareness of the Mennonites and Brethren and the ways in which their vision of church and society has been adapted to address the challenges of an increasingly pluralistic society.

There have been perhaps no more than a dozen occasions in my life when have I joined Anabaptist Christians at worship on Sunday morning, yet I have continued to feel a strong kinship with many elements of that tradition. For that reason I welcomed the invitation to read and respond to a collection of essays extending the Anabaptist vision of the Christian life to the calling of the teacher and scholar.

I read these essays, then, as a Reformed Christian aware that I owe a great debt to Anabaptist writers and friends who have helped me to understand the meaning of the gospel. Although the emphases sometimes fall in unexpected places, and the metaphors and historical allusions used by the writers reflect a tradition different from my own, I have no hesitation in affirming the principal recommendation that emerges from the entire collection: that Christians should be more broadly, more systematically, and more fruitfully engaged in the world of contemporary scholarship.

In other words, although I do not always know the words (I think I would recognize zwieback if it was served to me, but I'm not sure I could define *Gelassenheit*), the tune is familiar. It is being sung with minor variations on nearly every church college campus in the nation today, and by Christians who carry on their work at state universities and community colleges as well.

ANABAPTISTS AND CALVINISTS IN THE HUMANITIES

In the opening section of the collection, dealing with the disciplines of the humanities, the distinctive emphases and teachings of the Anabaptist tradition are perhaps most clearly articulated. Indeed, my philosophical colleague Caleb Miller seems to be laying down a gauntlet in the opening of his essay, where he draws a sharp contrast between Reformed and Anabaptist visions of the Christian life. In college and in seminary, exposed for the first time to the Reformed tradition that "dominated" parachurch organizations and evangelical theology, Miller writes:

I came to see that my Anabaptist differences with fellow Christians were more important (at least more important to me) than I had expected. Although I expected to encounter differences over such issues as pacifism, believers baptism, and free will, I was unprepared for the degree to which concessions to personal weakness and practical "necessity" figured in assessments of what could be expected of Christians.

While attracted to the intellectual rigors of Calvinism, Miller was disappointed to observe that his peers and instructors seemed to be willing to make almost any compromise with culture that purported to advance its transformation, willing to pronounce any vocation a Christian calling no matter how profoundly it might be compromised by sin. Miller describes vividly his own early rejection of distinctively Anabaptist doctrines concerning church and society and the ways in which he eventually arrived at a critical reaffirmation of the church tradition into which he was born.

Miller's portrayal of the failures of Reformed social thought, sharply worded as it is, deserves to be taken seriously by Calvinists, even if he overstates his case. (I, for one, know of no Reformed theologian who would recognize running a protection racket or a child pornography ring as a Christian calling, no matter how assiduously one sought to follow Christian principles and work for society's transformation in doing so.) Indeed, the rebuke Miller voices is one that Anabaptists may justly level against many of their fellow Christians, Calvinists included. Too often we have trimmed down the stringent demands of the gospel to fit our personal comfort zones. The witness of Mennonites working tirelessly for peace and reconciliation around the globe, no less than that of Amish farmers laboring patiently in their fields, speaks volumes about what it means to leave all behind and follow Christ. Anabaptists can teach the rest of the church a great deal about what it means to devote oneself wholly and without reservation to faithful kingdom service—in the world of the academy no less than in agriculture or relief work.

In describing his own development as a teacher and scholar, Miller exemplifies a spirit of openness that could serve as a valuable model for scholars in any discipline. At times, however, he draws the lines somewhat too sharply between the spirit of humility that is characteristic of Anabaptist life and thought and the triumphalism of other traditions. On the question of justifiable violence, for example, there is a sharp disagreement on the surface between the Anabaptist tradition of nonresistance to evil and the dominant Catholic and Protestant teaching that war is sometimes justified. Miller identifies this as an important contribution of the former tradition, and in historical terms he is justified in doing so. Yet in the modern era, when war's destructive effects have been multiplied beyond anything that the theologians of an earlier era would have dared to imagine, the practical implications of the two positions are scarcely distinguishable. Indeed, one might argue that "the just war" today has become a theoretical construct, as fictional as the economists' "perfectly competitive market."

On the Anabaptist side, interrelationships between economic, political, and military forces have been cited as justification for certain forms of forcible humanitarian intervention, as is described—and in part critiqued—in Mark Charlton's contribution to this volume. The sharp dichotomy between "peace churches" and "just war churches," then, has become considerably more blurred than it once was.[3]

Miller's goal, he writes, is to identify in the Anabaptist tradition a middle way between the Enlightenment's vain quest for certainty and the contemporary anti-realists' rejection of the very notion of truth. In his essay on what it means to be both a poet and a literary scholar, Jeff Gundy similarly seeks a middle way, affirming the importance both of the scholar's uncompromising search for knowledge and of the artist's rootedness in experience. He also offers a metaphor particularly rich in its implications for the life of Anabaptist scholars in the academy today: they have returned, he suggests, from a half-century's exile in the country, and today they are back in the city. Given the numbers of young people who have left the farm, this image rings true both literally and metaphorically, in the diminishing sense of separateness or isolation.

While living in small and homogeneous rural communities, it was not such a difficult task to uphold the Anabaptist distinctives, which Gundy identifies as the traditional trio of "discipleship, nonresistance, and the believers church." Separation helped nurture a sense of distinctive identity, and those whose lives revolved around the farm, the feedstore, and the church were not often asked to defend their beliefs or their values.

Today, working side by side with other Christians and nonbelievers in the office or the supermarket, Anabaptists find it more difficult to maintain a strong sense of identity. The same can be said—indeed, it is vividly demonstrated by many of the essays in this collection—of the situation of Mennonites and Brethren working in higher education. Gundy notes, too, that it is much easier to discern a distinctive identity when one looks to the past, whether the history of a particular denomination or a particular family history such as his, than to divine what this identity may mean in the future.

A common pattern emerges in the contributions of several contributors to this collection for whom affiliation with Anabaptism came about only after a lengthy personal journey of inquiry. Personal history, no less than family tradition and church history, figures prominently, for example, in Perry Bush's essay.

In his youth, writes Bush, he learned from his parents and others that biblical faith and social justice are inextricably linked. Bush recounts how he went from one sort of religious and social community to another in search of others of like mind, eventually finding his spiritual home in Anabaptism. It was not the theology of Menno Simons but the example of Mennonite youth, volunteering their time at Clarence Jordan's Koinonia Farm, that initially won his admiration and interest, even as he, a long-haired stranger from California, attracted their curiosity. What drew him in more deeply was the growing conviction, on the basis of scholarly research, that the Anabaptist tradition and its distinctive vision of the Christian's membership in two kingdoms best captured the heart of the Christian witness to society.

Several other essays in the volume recount a similar journey, sometimes instigated by an Anabaptist spouse or an influential teacher. Susan Biesecker-Mast, for example, describes the ways in which her childhood in a nominally Christian home prepared her first to welcome, then to reject, then once more to accept the gospel message as she encountered it during adolescence and early adulthood.

On one level her story is a familiar one: it is not unusual for the less religiously observant partner in a marriage to embrace the spouse's religious worldview. On another level, her account offers an unusually insightful narrative of how a mind and heart open to God's presence may come to know the truth through the patient and quiet witness of the Christian community. This story and its more subtle parallel in David Mosley's essay highlight the ways in which the churches of the radical Reformation appeal to religious seekers amid the noise and hucksterism of the contemporary religious world.

Perry Bush offers a concise summary of the difficult task that faces scholars working within this tradition today: it is "to help create a usable past for the health and maintenance of the church." This is first of all the work of historians and theologians, but it is also a calling that falls in some measure on every Christian. Exploration of the epistemology of religious faith, or the use of theological images in Latin American poetry, may appear on the surface to have little to do with the recovery of a particular theological inheritance. But in fact the relationship between any scholarly work in the humanities disciplines and the theological background is a close one, as each of the essays in this section reminds us. For we need to know ourselves before we can know the objects of our inquiry, and to know ourselves aright is to understand how we are formed and directed by our personal and communal histories.

Faithfulness and Objectivity in the Social Sciences

Moving from the humanities to what the Germans call the "human sciences," in the middle section of this collection, we find each of the contributors reflecting in some way on a central issue that faces the members of any historically sectarian church who take up the scientific study of society. To what extent, each writer asks, is the social scientist's view from a distance, with the neutral theoretical framework that this demands, compatible with continued membership in a closely knit religious community?

Al Dueck describes the sense of a divided self that resulted from his graduate study of linguistics and psychology—disciplines that were incomprehensible to his more traditional Mennonite mother. Dueck like other contributors was motivated by his sense of dislocation to look more deeply into the beliefs and stories that sustain a community and explain their power to shape individuals. He began to see that the quantitative observations of social scientists cannot capture what is most important about a community, and eventually, "after years of immersion in scientific rationalism," came to wonder whether "stories were not as significant for understanding human nature as science claimed to be."

Like Dueck, Donald Kraybill observes that his background in a distinctive church community fostered his interest in sociologically oriented questions. "What is the relation between the church and the larger society, between the culture of the church and mass culture, and between subgroups and the dominant society?" asks Kraybill. "How do groups create symbolic boundaries and manage them to deter assimilation?" According to Kraybill, "this focus on intergroup relations and cultural subgroups within mass society likely reflects my formative experience growing up in a Mennonite subculture that was undergoing rapid social change," indicating that for him, as for other social scientists, the life of the scholar and that of the church member exist in a delicate but potentially creative tension.

Unlike the other writers in this section, Polly Ann Brown was not raised in an Anabaptist subculture. Still, her moving personal account reveals a similar tension that blossomed during her years as an educator in a mostly Mennonite environment—and brought profound changes to her approach to educational theory. Having sought throughout her career to combat the pervasive tendency of educational systems to label and prejudge children, she found herself confronted at a key moment by her own tendency to categorize and judge. Brown's candid reflections on her experiences exemplify the spirit of humility and openness that—at best—characterizes both the practice of social science and the traditions of Anabaptist life.

Political science and economics are heavily committed to quantitative methods and institutional perspectives, and for that reason they pose unique problems for scholars in the Anabaptist tradition. Principled opposition to participation in government has discouraged serious study of the nature and structure of political authority, and a similar mistrust has spilled over to the study of economic structures.

Where Mennonites working in fields such as biblical studies and history can cite a long line of distinguished forebears, those attempting to bring an Anabaptist perspective to the study of political and economic realities feel as if they are breaking a trail for others to follow. Both James Harder and Mark Charlton offer helpful suggestions about what Christian scholarship in the Mennonite tradition might look like in these fields. It might begin, suggests Charlton, with a renunciation of the dominant paradigm of wholly autonomous individual choice as the driving force of all social structures, offering in its place a more communal vision of human life.

It is evident that Christian scholarship in the social sciences must overcome unique obstacles. Empirical methods and the ideal of neutrality dominate the social sciences no less pervasively than the natural sciences, and the relevance of the fundamental intellectual and religious orientation of the inquirer is only beginning to be widely acknowledged. At the same time, there is greater openness than ever before to the very values that might be expected to characterize Anabaptist contributions to the social sciences, such as the commitment to the community as well as the individual, openness to stories as well as facts, and a search for meanings that lie deeper than mere behavior. Social scientists rooted in the radical Reformation may feel isolated and misunderstood, but there are many reasons to anticipate that their work will be recognized as a valuable contribution to disciplines that are undergoing profound change.

Overcoming Mistrust of Biblical Scholarship

In the closing section of the anthology, four writers address areas of scholarship that lie close to the heart of the church's life and therefore are particularly prone to controversy: the disciplines related to theology and the study of the Bible. Each describes a life spent on the border regions between the church's use of Scripture and its academic study, between theology as it is preached from the pulpit and theology as it is refined and critiqued in the graduate seminar room.

That there can be Christian scholarship in the fields of theology and biblical studies is beyond dispute. What is very much open for argument, however, is whether the scholarly work of Christians, and of Anabaptist Christians in particular, should be different from that of colleagues who bring another faith perspective, or a secular outlook, to bear on their study of the same texts and doctrines.

From the beginning, Anabaptist church leaders have expressed a distaste for theology, instead upholding God's Word as the sole and sufficient guide to Christian faith and life. Early leaders believed they were following the Reformation's ideals more faithfully than did the Lutherans or Calvinists. And yet, like other Protestants, they were selective in their reliance on Scripture, and the "plain meaning" they found in the Bible often proved remarkably well fitted to their theological assumptions. The sharp words of Terry Brensinger's Jewish teacher could stand as a perpetual rebuke to the church: "I don't care what you Christians do with Leviticus, but do *something* with it!" To be truly faithful to Scripture would require Lutherans to "do something" with the book of James, ascetics to "do something" with the Song of Songs, and radical separatists in the Anabaptist tradition to "do something" with Romans 13.

What lay behind the Anabaptist suspicion of theology, several writers suggest, was a certain anti-intellectualism that persists to this day in Mennonite and Brethren circles. Mary Schertz observes, for example:

> Whereas . . . the enfranchisement of all believers as interpreters sounds wonderfully and nobly egalitarian, it has had some ill effects on the hermeneutic community. One is the disenfranchisement of biblical scholars. Many of us must overcome a kind of suspicion if we are to be heard in the church at all. But there has been a much more serious consequence. . . . [Namely] that very little serious reading of the Bible actually happens among all these interpreters in the church.

Similarly, Lydia Neufeld Harder finds evidence of "an underlying fear [in the Anabaptist tradition] that scholarly activity will rely solely on human knowledge and that it will thereby lead to false teachings, pride, and the wrong use of power." Jay McDermond recounts the warning he received from his bishop about a particular seminary's dangerous "openness to scholarship," all too characteristic an example of church leaders' fear of the sort of lively and critical theological discussion that keeps a church healthy and alive.

This attitude no doubt owes something to the history of relations between the radical Reformation and the rest of the church. "After all," Neufeld Harder notes, "it was the educated theologians and preachers who persecuted early Anabaptists." All the same, it is discouraging to note the frequency with which the writers of these essays have encountered explicit or implicit discouragement from pastors and teachers who do not regard biblical or theological scholarship as a legitimate Christian calling.

The responsibility for this situation lies not only with fearful or uninformed church leaders but also with the spirit of skepticism that has dominated so much of the realm of scholarship. In the field of biblical studies in particular, many leading scholars have proceeded on the false assumption that before they enter the library or the classroom they must leave their faith in the cloakroom, securely locked away until the end of the day or the weekend.

The small band of biblical scholars associated with Robert Funk's Jesus Seminar have reinforced this impression powerfully in the public mind. Rigorous and critical study of the Bible, they have told the nation's television viewers and newsweekly readers, means setting aside all notions of inspiration and authority and putting the text under a historical and literary microscope. Such purportedly "neutral" methods are of course no less deeply influenced by the scholars' guiding assumptions than are those of more traditional biblical theology, yet they are widely accepted as objective and scientific. In the churches, unfortunately, such distortions have provoked an equal and opposite reaction of suspicion and mistrust toward every kind of critical study of the Bible.

A solution to this impasse can be found in a concept put forward by John Howard Yoder and cited by several contributors to this collection: we must think of the church as a whole, and of each distinct theological community within the larger church, as a *hermeneutic community*. The responsibility for interpreting Scripture does not fall on biblical scholars alone, but rather on a community in which close analysis is carried out as a service to other believers. Biblical scholars should see themselves not as scientists performing experiments on texts, as if they were lifeless objects of study, but rather as participants in a shared quest to discern all that God has revealed in Scripture. Such an attitude rules out none of the historical or literary tools of the academy, but it denies them any authority greater than that of Scripture itself.

It is in this spirit that David Weaver-Zercher, in his introduction to this collection, echoes a recent paper by Douglas and Rhonda Jacobsen in calling on his colleagues to affirm a "scholarly faith." To separate the Bible's use in worship and daily life from its meaning for scholars introduces a false dichotomy. Faith itself must always be critical and open-minded, and scholarship must be undertaken in a spirit of faithful obedience.

Many Christians—not just Anabaptists—might find it difficult to think of scholarship as comparable to evangelism "in spiritual significance," as Weaver-Zercher urges. But an adequate understanding of what it means in the contemporary world to go out and preach the gospel will welcome, not reject, the contributions of scholars who press for a deeper understanding—not just in the theological disciplines but in other areas of inquiry as well. What else can it mean to serve God with our whole hearts and our whole minds?

In describing her early career in a Mennonite high school, Polly Ann Brown observes that the community in which she worked tended to divide people into two groups: some are *workers* and others are *thinkers*. She eventually realized that she needed to persuade them that thinkers can be workers, and that workers who learn to be thinkers become better, not worse, at their work. A Mennonite scholar interviewed by Richard Hughes (and cited by Mark Charlton in his essay) observes that the Anabaptist tradition is dissatisfied with the emphasis in other Protestant traditions on "transform[ing] living by thinking" and has sought instead an educational approach that "transforms thinking by living and by one's commitment to a radically Christocentric lifestyle."[4] This emphasis need not imply a denigration of the scholar's calling but can instead provide the basis for a persuasive vision of what it means to pursue the vocation of the scholar in a community committed to daily imitation of Christ.

Conclusion: Tensions That Remain

Unlike many of the contributors to this volume, I have not had the privilege of being a student or colleague of Professor E. Morris Sider, whose retirement is the occasion on the writing of these essays. Thanks to the personal reminiscences that several contributors have set down here, however, I have a vivid impression of his work as a teacher and as a scholar. It is evident from the accounts of his colleagues and students that he has exemplified the spirit of engagement with both the academy and the church that "scholarly faith" requires. I am happy to join with others in congratulating Professor Sider on the completion of a distinguished career and his college, Messiah College, for having provided the environment in which he has worked.

As I look back on the rich variety of personal stories and intellectual challenges posed by the contributors to this volume, I find myself still uncertain whether there is, or should be, a distinctively Anabaptist mode of scholarship. Without question the particular social and theological teachings of the radical Reformation have exercised a profound effect on the formation and work of the contributors whose essays are collected here. Yet the results of their scholarship seldom bear clear identifying marks of these influences. Perhaps the Anabaptist character that can be found in the work of these scholars, and of others whom they cite, is to be found less in any specific content than in the spirit in which they undertake their intellectual work, a spirit that is characterized at its best by a unique synthesis of forthright witness and theological humility.

What is abundantly clear, in any case, is that scholars who stand within the community of Anabaptist churches are already making, and will continue to make, important contributions to the cause of Christian scholarship in North America today. In the past, it might be argued, the Reformed churches have taken the lead in theoretical reflection about the integration of faith and learning, in parallel with the long tradition of Thomism and its competitors in the Catholic intellectual tradition. In the present, we may look to the churches of the radical Reformation to help all Christians to join head and hand and heart together, uniting careful theorizing with uncompromising obedience. In this way we may all be better able to translate scholarly faith into faithful practice.

Notes

1. Among them are Anthony A. Hoekema, *The Bible and the Future* (Grand Rapids, Mich.: Eerdmans, 1979); *Tongues and Spirit-Baptism: A Biblical and Theological Evaluation* (Grand Rapids, Mich.: Baker Book House, 1981); *Created in God's Image* (Grand Rapids, Mich.: Eerdmans, 1986); and *Saved By Grace* (Grand Rapids, Mich.: Eerdmans, 1989).

2. Especially influential were John Howard Yoder, *The Politics of Jesus* (Grand Rapids, Mich.: Eerdmans, 1972) and Arthur G. Gish, *The New Left and Christian Radicalism* (Grand Rapids, Mich.: Eerdmans, 1970). Yoder's book, reprinted most recently in 1994, continues to exercise a broad influence, while Gish's now seems curiously dated.

3. This is a theme that I have explored elsewhere, e.g., in "The Just War Tradition and the Nuclear Debate," *Peace and Change: A Journal of Peace Research* 10, no. 3-4 (Fall/Winter 1984): 145-54; "Protestant Statements on Nuclear Disarmament," *Religious Studies Review* 10 (1984): 97-102; "Reformed Pacifism," *Bulletin of the Peace Studies Institute* 14 (1984): 23-30; "Evangelicals Confront the Arms Race," *The Reformed Journal* 33, no. 8 (August 1983): 10-13; "Intentions, Threats, and Nuclear Deterrence," *Bowling Green Studies in Applied Philosophy* 5 (1983): 111-25; and "Nuclear Politics and Christian Ethics," *Christian Scholar's Review* 12 (1983): 217-25.

4. Richard T. Hughes and William B. Adrian, *Models for Christian Higher Education: Strategies for Success in the Twenty-First Century* (Grand Rapids, Mich.: Eerdmans, 1997), 6. In his introduction to the volume, Hughes attributes the remark to an unnamed member of the Goshen College faculty.

17: Response

Conclusion: The Life of the Mind as a Life of Service

Shirley Hershey Showalter

I TRIED NOT TO WRITE THIS ESSAY. I tried to pass this invitation on to someone else—someone with indisputable credentials for the task.

By the definition used most widely in the academy today I am not a true "scholar." The research university has defined this word to mean the publication of numerous books or "seminal" monographs in a specialized area. Even though a minority of professors in higher education, including those at research universities, have actually achieved this level of impact, standards for advancement within the ranks (the military metaphor is not coincidental) have tightened substantially since the 1960s, and the term itself has constricted accordingly.[1]

The typical scholar today writes as a specialist for other specialists and hopes to write at least one book, frequently two, before tenure. Occasionally editors, even those at the top of the scholarly establishment, decry these facts.

In an recent essay titled "Rescue Tenure from the Tyranny of the Monograph," Lindsay Waters, executive editor for the humanities at Harvard University Press, says standards for excellence are being eroded by too much specializing too early in a career: "Our publications need to be more like those of Swift and Voltaire—proper humanistic emanations that offer persuasive accounts of the world, no matter how much they flaunt their improprieties, rather than empty exercises of scientific competence designed to please two men in New Haven and no one else in this world."[2]

My major professors in graduate school were trained in New Haven and Cambridge (i.e., Yale and Harvard), and they expected me to publish. Predictably, they had less respect for teaching institutions than for those classified by the Carnegie Foundation as "Research I" institutions. My dissertation advisor, Robert M. Crunden, made up a name for institutions that lacked the tenure requirement of significant published research. "East Jesus Tech," he called them. To him, any college name that included a compass point, a religious affiliation, or vocational training in its name was automatically suspect.

When I first darkened the doorway to his office in Garrison Hall, his words to me were, "Eastern WHAT College?" The answer, "Mennonite," was one he heard a lot during the four years I worked with him.

Six years later he included Goshen College on his summer itinerary so that he could see firsthand why I behaved so strangely. I enjoyed talking with Bob about my life choices, testing my ideals about the life of the mind (grounded in community, including family and church) against his agnostic dismissal of them. His resistance dramatized the rigidity of academic politics that a subtler mentor would not have taught. As a newcomer to the academy, I, at first, quaked inwardly at these diatribes, but eventually I saw his blatant prejudices as helpful.

I grew more comfortable with my choices over time, partly through defending them to Bob. I tried to embrace simultaneously scholarship, teaching, service, friendship, motherhood, administration, and the inner life; not surprisingly, there have been rough places along the way, splinters on the wooden staircase I call my life. Bob's sudden death in 1999, at the age of fifty-eight, was a sad occasion for me. I miss his ferocity, his grudging affection, and his surprisingly strong support—but I never envied his life.

My Life and My Work

My own life has been full of binary oppositions. Edith Wharton once described herself as "too fashionable for Boston and too intellectual for Philadelphia." I have been, successively, too intellectual for Lititz and too Mennonite for Austin, too busy for the PTA and too attached to my children to rely exclusively on childcare, too feminist to feel at home in the Rotary and sometimes not feminist enough for friends and colleagues, too interested in "the big picture" to be a specialist and too interested in the particular to be a grand theorist, and, finally, too much a faculty member to be an administrator and too much an administrator to be a faculty member. Like Whitman, I contain multitudes, and I celebrate the rough and the smooth.

One consequence of my multiple and competing commitments is that, so far, I have not published a book. That is not to say I haven't "published," both orally and in writing. I have written essays for peer-reviewed journals and many other church and journalistic publications; I have delivered papers at numerous conferences; and my dissertation was enthusiastically endorsed by my doctoral committee as well as several leading scholars in my field. Nevertheless, after the birth of my second child—and in concert with focusing my intellectual energies on the needs of Goshen College—I withdrew from the process of revising my dissertation for publication by Indiana University Press.

One of my colleagues, anthropologist Ron Stutzman, told me that faculty in our kind of college often view scholarship as "an object of longing." I know what he meant. As I was working on this paper, I returned to some of the texts of my dissertation and discovered again the sheer joy of reading Willa Cather in her own words. The words that spoke loudest to me this time were these: "A book is made with one's own flesh and blood of years. It is cremated youth. It is all yours—no one gave it to you."[3]

I hope I will write at least one book some day. If I do, it will contain a lot of cremated youth, and it will be my own. Yet, I have never been as severe in my life as Cather was in hers, pruning away everything else so that her art could grow. To the contrary, my own work has come, and will continue to come, in the form of conversations with many communities.

For now, at least, my scholarship comes in the form of speeches, academic papers, and essays I write in connection with being president of Goshen College. So many of these—scores, if not hundreds, each year—are written in the "back burner" of my brain. Often they are ephemeral, a few words on the back of an envelope, wisps of meaning that may or may not alight in either my mind or my audience's. Occasionally, I actually take a week to write something, as I did this essay, but even that much time comes in blocks of two or three hours. The kind of sustained attention to one idea, needed by more traditional scholars, I do not have.

Nevertheless, I find that sometimes in the late nights or early mornings, when I carve out time to write an essay or a speech, I reach a place of self-forgetting, a place where I am no longer aware of all the effort I am expending to seek coherence. At those times coherence finds me. Then everything I am and have known deeply, either by study or experience, seems instantly available to me, ordered through the lens of one idea. What is peripheral finally and suddenly falls away, and what is left appears as though it were an object, a thing of beauty. I fill up with song. I then know inside my own body what Willa Cather described in Thea Kronborg: "She had begun to understand that—with her, at least—voice was, first of all, vitality; a lightness in the body and a driving power in the blood. When she had that, she could sing."[4]

Of course, Cather could only write these words after she "hit the home pasture" and stopped imitating Henry James.[5] I can write them only after coming back to favorite passages of the books I have read many times, and that are now reading me. In moments when I need them, they come to me. And sometimes, as I gaze into the faces of the members of my own community, the same kind of transformation occurs in my speaking. What I'm saying comes out "like silk off a spool," as Emily says in *Our Town*.[6]

As often as possible, then, I reject the kind of dualistic thinking that forces me to choose one life over another. Instead, I look for multiple realities and multiple ways to do scholarship, reconciling those elements in myself and in my work that might otherwise be enemies. Above all, I seek to know the shape of my own mind and my own spirit so that I can help others know theirs. My professional colleagues, professors and editors alike, have endorsed my work with enough frequency and fervor to give me external confidence in my ability to do research and to connect with many audiences. But external validation can never make up for a lack of internal confidence. The journey toward my own form of scholarship has taken fifty-two years—and is still in progress.

Finding an Authentic Voice

The ultimate goal, of course, is to find one's authentic self and one's true voice, each of which emerges in and from community. When I joined the Lititz (Pennsylvania) Mennonite Church at the age of twelve, I was taught that the two distinguishing doctrines of Anabaptists from the sixteenth century to the present were "nonresistance" and "nonconformity." I first tried to understand these ideas through stories, the most dramatic of which was the *Martyr's Mirror* engraving of Dirk Willems saving his captor from certain drowning. When I discovered that these stories (and my identity as a Mennonite) could actually contribute to my intellectual as well as my spiritual life, I hit the "home pasture."

Other writers in this collection have hit their own versions of the "home pasture," writing to the church as well as to other scholars. The home pasture is not always a pastoral, verdant place. It can be experienced as a desert, in fact. But it is nonetheless a place of identity formation, which theologian Miroslav Volf reminds us is the essential work of our time.[7]

I was impressed by the recurring theme within these *Minding the Church* essays of searching for an authentic voice that speaks to the academic world *and* to the church from a place that is grounded in *both* traditions. I have found sustenance for my own identity by reading these chapters, and I believe Anabaptist colleges and churches will continue their own identity formation by sharing this book widely and pondering these stories of faith and learning as they alternately collide, intersect, and reverberate.

How do we keep multiple, contending, sometimes contradictory, scholarly and churchly voices together within and outside ourselves? My Goshen College colleague, historian John D. Roth, encourages his students to "live in tension" between commitment to Truth and openness to new truth. In a similar vein, former Goshen president J. Lawrence Burkholder has argued for more than forty years that Mennonites must realize "that their attempts to be obedient to Christ and 'be' the true church must take into consideration the 'ambiguities' of their actual situation."[8]

Of course, living with tension and ambiguity is not a new thing for intellectuals. And for that reason, reclaiming some of our old ideas—and perhaps even some of our traditional language about the faith—may prove beneficial. Indeed, this age-old Anabaptist language, reappropriated from the perspective of "the life of the mind," might help us locate a space in which to serve each other and the truth that sets us free.

Nonconformity and the Anabaptist Scholar

The term *nonconformity* is not much in vogue these days at Anabaptist-related colleges, a casualty of our less sectarian attitudes toward the world. Many of us can remember the word's former prominence and recall its sometimes oppressive connotations. Perhaps more than anything it meant a strict division between the church and the world, and it ruled out certain sorts of activities, certain styles of dress, and certain fields of professional pursuit. Some advocates of nonconformity would no doubt have frowned on scholarship, and especially so if they thought the purpose of that scholarly work was to advance the scholar's standing in the world.

In some ways I can sympathize with those who wish to abandon the term. Still, in our haste to flee from it, we Anabaptists may be neglecting our greatest intellectual inheritance.

Simply put, all good scholarship is nonconformed to something. In his oft-cited text, *The Structure of Scientific Revolutions*, Thomas Kuhn underscores the "defiance" needed by scholars to escape standard intellectual paradigms and advance new revolutions in thought.[9] Similarly, scholarship that is committed to an "upside-down kingdom" will be rigorously defiant, asking questions about ideas and systems that the comfortable and powerful may not think of (or conveniently ignore).

In that regard, Anabaptist scholars are likely to be lurkers on the periphery rather than upholders of the dominant consensus. Indeed, if we were to list the dissertation titles of the faculty teaching in our institutions, we would no doubt see the influence of an Anabaptist education even when the subject has nothing to do with Anabaptist theology or church history. Similarly, with respect to our former students (e.g., recent Goshen College grads), I could list a number of scholarly projects that show a distinct bent toward nonconformity—research critiquing the U.S. legal system, the Silicon Valley computer industry, and Western imperialism in many parts of the world.

In this volume, too, many writers have revealed a defiant willingness to critique their disciplines or disciplinary colleagues in light of biblical imperatives. In some instances, this willingness to offer an Anabaptist-informed critique has distanced them from the mainstreams of their disciplines, and perhaps disadvantaged them professionally.

Economist Jim Harder, for example, notes that his critique of "runaway economism" runs precisely counter to most economic theory, and he further notes that "a budding economist who expresses interest in a 'values-oriented' course of [economic] study" will face an uphill battle. In a similar fashion, historian Perry Bush has begun to ask questions about economic justice that most professional U.S. historians—even prominent Christian historians—have failed to address. For her part, Lydia Neufeld Harder found it necessary to carve out new territory in both university and church to name herself a theologian. She imagines herself on a "wall" between the two worlds, witnessing to the God she has come to know and critiquing both institutions when they fail to remember each other.

Why do we do research? Why do we write? Nonconformed Anabaptist scholars write for more than "two men in New Haven." The authors in this book write to serve and to know. They write to understand their deepest questions and in hopes that their communities will benefit. They write to unmask, to defamiliarize, and to challenge, even as they seek the "implicate order" or "hidden wholeness" underneath.[10]

If this work sounds paradoxical, rest assured it is. As poet and Bluffton professor Jeff Gundy says, "I have come to believe that the only way I can truly serve my community is to be as fiercely individual as I can manage." Service to others comes from knowing the contours of one's own mind and spirit and honoring them. Conformity to the publish-or-perish system as it is practiced elsewhere ought not to be our aim. Yet silence is not the answer either. Once again, we need a "third way," a way of active nonconformity that encourages and names many different kinds of scholarship and values all of them: radical dissent, integration, and affirmation.

David Weaver-Zercher has set a high alternative standard in this volume for what a scholar does and who the scholar is. By his definition, scholarship is "the discovery, development, and transmission of original or creative ideas to scholarly and/or lay audiences." This definition is much broader than most. It does not require printed text as the vehicle, and it takes lay audiences seriously. It could apply to a business person, it could apply to a pastor, it could even apply to a college administrator. I doubt that all academics, even those in Anabaptist-related colleges, would feel comfortable with so much breadth. However, I am one who does.

Weaver-Zercher's definition of scholarship is not only broad, it is also very high. The audience may be one million Mennonites world-wide, for example, or twenty thousand readers of a magazine, instead of two men in New Haven. But the scholar must offer something new.

Herein lies yet another paradox. Bill Stott, one of my professors at the University of Texas at Austin, liked to remind me, quoting Ecclesiastes, that there is nothing new under the sun. But there are, he said, new ways to interpret, new slants to take on "all the truth." Bill expected me to be precise, to weigh up every word, to exercise the hermeneutics of suspicion upon myself. Later, after he had broken free in his own scholarship, he urged me to be passionate, to break the rules, and to write from the heart.

One of the most radical redefinitions of scholarship, nonconformed to the dominant model, is that of the late Ernest L. Boyer, a 1948 graduate of Messiah Bible College who later served as president of the Carnegie Foundation for the Advancement of Teaching. I don't know whether Boyer would have agreed with me or not, but I have often viewed his work as unnamed Anabaptism extended to the higher education community.

In his 1990 book *Scholarship Reconsidered*, Boyer identified four different functions of scholarly activity: discovery, integration, application, and teaching.[11] Boyer admitted that the "scholarship of discovery," which emphasizes specialized research in view of securing new knowledge, constituted the dominant university paradigm for research. But without dismissing its importance, he sought to broaden the academy's perspective by awarding greater value to the three less celebrated forms of scholarship: the "scholarship of integration," which places isolated facts into a larger perspective and connects them to each other; the "scholarship of application," which engages the world and makes knowledge useful; and the "scholarship of teaching," which begins (but does not end) when teachers share what they know with their students.

Rather than seeing teaching as research's frumpish cousin, Boyer described teaching as a "dynamic endeavor involving all the analogies, metaphors, and images that build bridges between the teacher's understanding and the student's learning." What's more, wrote Boyer, such an endeavor does more than *transmit* knowledge; it actually *transforms* and *extends* it. Boyer concluded, "What we urgently need today is a more inclusive view of what it means to be a scholar—a recognition that knowledge is acquired through research, through synthesis, through practice, and through teaching."[12]

While Boyer's ideas were viewed as radical in many quarters, his emphasis on synthetic, practical knowledge underscored what many Anabaptist institutions had been doing for years. Due to our insistence on putting both education and the gospel into practice, we Anabaptists have a rich heritage of experience-based learning. While such programs (e.g., service-learning and study-abroad programs) are commonplace today, we were nonconformed to the dominant system in developing them, placing them into our curricula long before they became popular.

That Anabaptists would be leaders in these sorts of educational endeavors should not be surprising, for our heritage informs us that such practices are powerful shapers of beliefs. Perhaps, however, we have not taken them seriously enough as *knowledge*. Recognizing our own epistemology is just as important as delineating our own theology. And ongoing research about how and why experience changes cognitive thought is essential to this process.

Two writers who may help us in this search are Donald A. Schön and Parker Palmer, both of whom are active nonconformists in an academic world dominated by what Schön calls "technical rationality" and Palmer calls "objectivism."[13] In an article entitled "The New Scholarship Requires a New Epistemology," Schön calls for "building up communities of inquiry capable of criticizing [a less objectivist form of research] and fostering its development."[14] For his part, Palmer talks about the need for educational communities to foster "good talk about good teaching."[15]

The epistemology Palmer espouses, that of knowing as loving, could readily be extended to include "good talk about good research." Similarly, Jane Tompkins has been writing and speaking about her quest for community since 1992, and her description of a "culture of conversation" should resonate with every vital faith-and-learning community.[16]

When I read Boyer, Palmer, Tompkins, and Schön—all of whom call for community-based knowing, an ethic of love, applying what we know to the needs of the world, and committing ourselves to the high calling of teaching and learning—I get excited about the future of Anabaptist scholarship. In fact, I think we may be at the dawn of a new age of spiritually based intellectual inquiry, conversation, and publication.

Humility and the Anabaptist Scholar

Nonresistance, the complement of nonconformity as a traditional Anabaptist distinctive, is another word that has fallen out of favor. In fact, with respect to many Anabaptist scholars, *resistance* has assumed a more positive connotation, for nonresistance seems too passive, too supportive of the status quo. Yet if nonresistance is redefined to be dialectical rather than absolute, it too might help us. Indeed, a recovered nonresistance might be an answer to the "how" question of scholarship: by what practices might we do scholarship that would allow ourselves and others to recognize it as Anabaptist?

The writers in this volume speak of humility as one of these ways. Their awareness of the incomplete nature of all knowledge (and their openness to the possibility that they could be wrong) lead them repeatedly to spiritual and intellectual insights. For instance, learning theorist Polly Ann Brown's account of revising her learning theory indicates that, applied to intellectual work, the *non* in nonresistance can improve our scholarship. Brown describes a painful awareness of having resisted the truth in herself and finally admitting she had to stop resisting:

> I began to see the contradictions between the principles I had outlined and the way I related to others. The model advocated dialogue; I often presented my ideas through monologue. The model stressed the need for transformation; yet I was maintaining the status quo by retreating from potential conflict.

Philosopher Caleb Miller likewise underscores the central place of humility in his work—namely, the importance of admitting "that virtually everything we take ourselves to know remains susceptible to error."

In sum, if nonconformity allows us to challenge received wisdom and the status quo, nonresistance allows us to challenge our own instinct to fight when we are challenged. Such nonresistance is essential for producing good scholarship, for if we fail to resist certainty in ourselves, we will more likely produce dogma than knowledge.

In addition to helping scholars to recognize their limitations, humility fosters a tradition of "oral scholarship" that the mainstream academy does not much value. Oral scholarship starts with hospitality in the classroom, the office, and one's own home. It includes a living acquaintance with the subject, a willingness to face doubts directly, and the embrace of mystery. (I would guess that many students of Anabaptist scholars have witnessed true reverence in the classroom and in long conversations outside the classroom.)

Oral scholarship means giving away ideas instead of hoarding all of them for private research. It sets high standards for thinking—one's own and one's students'—sustaining students in difficulty but not allowing them to give less than their best. It crosses boundaries between fields and expects to connect people and ideas and practices. Amid conflict it seeks peace. It may mean putting the church or the college ahead of one's own career. It asserts truth while remaining open to new truth and listens for other voices even as it speaks.

At the risk of glorifying the past, we should nonetheless acknowledge that our scholarly Anabaptist forebears knew the value of this type of scholarship, perhaps better than we know it today. In the last hundred years, some of what might have become published work was instead shared with students, colleagues, and church members. There was often joy in this way because whatever sacrifices were made were freely chosen, and there was honor simply in being known as "an excellent professor." To be a college professor was to profess faith and learning as inextricably intertwined realities. One prayed for the grace to live what one knew. What was gained—thoughtful talk, service projects, going abroad to study—these were also shared. Sometimes they became lectures and discussions. Occasionally they became books and articles.

In this rich environment of oral scholarship, the relative lack of "seminal monographs" did not correlate with a lack of intellectual activity. Indeed, when I arrived at Goshen College in 1976, the senior faculty included not only President J. Lawrence Burkholder, who left an endowed chair at Harvard Divinity School to become president, but Carl Kreider, Mary Oyer, Mary Eleanor Bender, Frank Bishop, Atlee Beechy, and John Oyer. These people, whose names were known to almost every educated Mennonite at the time, trained students who today are teaching in some of the best research universities in the world. I have heard these graduates testify that they searched the world over and never found character as deep nor minds more subtle and original as those of the faculty who shaped their early adulthood. (Jeff Gundy's tributes in this volume to Nick Lindsay and Jack Dueck are cases in point.)

I am sure that every Anabaptist college has its own venerated generations, not least Messiah College, where E. Morris Sider (to whom this book is dedicated) taught for many years. From what I know of Professor Sider, he was the kind of scholar who touched the lives of students outside the classroom, always willing to share the best of his oral scholarship with them. Now, as the scholarship of Anabaptist historians moves beyond denominational history (Professor Sider's forte), I can only hope that the generosity that existed among the first generation of scholars will continue into the second and third and beyond.

We need to be honest with ourselves, of course. Not all our former professors stayed vital through the community-based practice of oral scholarship. Even in places where oral scholarship was rigorously practiced, learning sometimes lagged and minds became lazy. However, it is also true that not all professors in prestigious research universities continue as star researchers after they achieve tenure. Moreover, the individualistic and even selfish approach to scholarship that is frequently fostered by the university model can quickly undo the kind of community life we Anabaptists claim to value.

It should not be surprising, then, that I have chosen (rather unconsciously until now) the Goshen scholars as my models over my graduate advisor, Bob Crunden. Correspondingly, I see a challenge to those of us now in our fifties and sixties. We need to articulate our own understanding of scholarship and define the epistemology on which it is based. We need to counterbalance the voice of the graduate advisor each new Ph.D. hears so clearly, no matter how many miles separate him or her from graduate school. We cannot allow scholarship as "object of longing" to be our only theme, no matter how understandable it is. That way leads to bitterness and diminution of intellectual and spiritual force.

The Future of Anabaptist Scholarship

In his 1837 essay, "The American Scholar," Ralph Waldo Emerson wrote that "our long apprenticeship . . . draws to a close."[17] The same can be said for Anabaptist scholars today. If we are true to our Anabaptist heritage, we will pioneer a new scholarship that is nonconformed and nonresistant. In the course of doing so, we will challenge the dominant publish-or-perish paradigm, even while publishing more and more creatively than we have ever done before. While most of us will remain teacher-scholars, some of us will become scholar-teachers. But none of us will become bitter by longing for a different model of scholarship than the one we ourselves can authentically create.

The strength of our future scholarship rests on many factors, but none more crucial than our ability to forge links between past and present. Some Anabaptist scholars are already doing that work. For instance, during her time on the Goshen College campus during the 1999-2000 school year, Stanford undergraduate Katherine Lemons spent numerous hours with Mary Eleanor Bender, Goshen's professor emerita of French.

Scholars of different types but with similar interests (Lemons works in comparative literature and Bender taught a course for years called "Literature in Twentieth-Century Thought"), these women visited in the Bender living room, talking about Goshen in the 1950s and about art in relation to ethics. In the course of one conversation, Bender commented to her younger colleague that "no one would have the heart to feed the hungry, never having been witness to beauty for its own sake."[18]

Later, Lemons wrote about how those very words had teased her mind and spirit. She recognized the originality (nonconformity) in Bender's thought, and, in a subsequent letter to Bender, described why she viewed Mary as a true scholar:

> Your statement . . . stems from an instinct which is as rare as it is important and as clear as it is risky—risky to the way that society functions and to the way that people treat the economy of their deeds within it. The construction of the thoughts you articulated also reflect a way of thinking, literally and philosophically, which has fueled me in my questions and explorations throughout the duration of our meetings.[19]

According to Lemons, Bender's unusual mind is not only nonconformed to the world, it is also nonresistant to the evil of dogma. It is "simultaneously youthful and yet contains wisdom available only to those who have lived substantially in the world of contradictions and paradox." Lemons has requested permission to return to Goshen, so that she might meet with Bender on a regular basis. She wants to discover, she told Bender, "not so much about you as about your thought and its development, about what has brought you to the place in which you find yourself intellectually and philosophically, about your relationship to your own ways of thinking."[20]

What does a Stanford undergraduate find in a retired Goshen College faculty member that she cannot find in one of the world's greatest universities? She has found a true scholar—though one who has never published an article in a scholarly journal, let alone a book. She has found a great mind at home with a great spirit and in love with learning. She has found also a muse for her own writing:

> [W]ords are the instruments of reason for me and for passion: they are the slippery grade that I scramble over as I make sense of myself and as I become my thoughts and become familiar with my thoughts. . . .[I]t would be both a deep pleasure and a profound honor . . . to articulate what happens when we talk together in your living room, the traffic outside punctuating in its ebbs and flows, . . . the continual fluctuation of the light from red to green to red to green, our words as they dance and dip, almost visible as they rise from our lips.[21]

Scholarship in the Anabaptist tradition does not get better than this. The young woman is wise enough to tell the older that she wants to find out "not so much about you as about your thought and its development," knowing perhaps that Mary's humility would be a barrier to a focus on her life and knowing also that Mary herself is curious about minds, including her own. The descriptive passage about the almost-visible dancing words is a coded message from one admirer of Virginia Woolf's work to another. The patterns, rhythms, and embodiment in this passage speak to a poetic, tacit form of knowledge. The young woman is coming with only her questions. The older woman promises no answers. In fact, she insists that the arrangement will work only if Katherine claims the ideas that arise from this process as her own.

Whatever we do as Anabaptist scholars in the future, I hope we will not fail to recognize the contributions of both the young and the retired scholars among us. Mary Eleanor Bender is fond of quoting her father—historian, dean, and church leader Harold S. Bender—as saying, "You can do a lot of good in the world if you don't care who gets the credit." Such *Gelassenheit* (yieldedness) is not an annihilation of self but enlargement of the meaning of the work—from mine to ours, and from ours to God's.

What, then, is the future of Anabaptist scholarship? Just as the first hundred years of our apprenticeship produced a variety of Anabaptist scholars—those who published usable histories of Mennonite and Amish life, those who wrote for church periodicals and popular journals, and those whose oral scholarship left remarkable legacies in their students and their classrooms—so too will the next stage in our individual and collective development contain many paths. I hope to see much more engagement with the larger academic world in the next decade. I also hope to see challenges to that world, such as the corrective this book offers to the monolithic use of the research university model as applied to church-related colleges. I hope that we will be able to create centers for scholarship of many different kinds and that we will become known as leaders in pedagogy and service as well as leaders in our disciplines. Finally, I hope that we will demonstrate increasing leadership in developing a "peaceable curriculum" and then find ways to increase that curriculum's potency.

What we aspire for has a name. Her name is wisdom, Sophia. Since she was there at the beginning of creation (Prov. 8:22), we can count on her presence to guide us through ambiguity, paradox, and dialectic into a place that endures, even after time shall be no more. It is this faith, and the faith of the unity of creation in Christ, that is the first foundation, not only of the church, but of scholars within the church.

NOTES

This chapter is presented with thanks to Adam Derstine and Alicia Miller, my students this semester, and to the faculty at Goshen College, past and present, who have been my mentors in scholarship.

1. Because of an emphasis on teaching and community life and a course load of seven or eight courses per year, most professors at Anabaptist colleges have not published a book; of those who have, only a small percentage have published with well-known university or trade presses. The best-selling book by a Mennonite author continues to be Doris Janzen Longacre's *More-With-Less Cookbook* (Scottdale, Pa.: Herald Press, 1976, 2001). Two other influential books are Donald B. Kraybill's *The Upside-Down Kingdom* (Scottdale, Pa: Herald Press, 1978, 1990) and John A. Hostetler's *Amish Life* (Scottdale, Pa.: Herald Press, 1952), both of which have reached popular and academic audiences in many disciplines. John Howard Yoder's *The Politics of Jesus* (Grand Rapids, Mich.: Eerdmans, 1972) will continue to influence the field of theology for a long time.

2. Lindsay Waters, "Rescue Tenure from the Tyranny of the Monograph," *The Chronicle of Higher Education*, April 20, 2001, B9.

3. Willa Cather, as quoted in James Woodress, *Willa Cather: Her Life and Art* (Lincoln, Neb.: University of Nebraska Press, 1970), 167.

4. Willa Cather, *The Song of the Lark* (New York: Houghton Mifflin, 1915, 1943), 381.

5. "This was the first time I walked off on my own feet—everything before was half real and half an imitation of writers whom I admired. In this one I hit the home

pasture." Willa Cather, writing about her book *O Pioneers!* (1913), quoted in Woodress, *Willa Cather: Her Life and Art*, 156.

6. Thornton Wilder, *Three Plays: Our Town, The Skin of Our Teeth, The Matchmaker* (New York: HarperPerennial, 1985), 30.

7. Writes Volf, "It may not be too much to claim that the future of our world will depend on how we deal with identity and difference." Miroslav Volf, *Exclusion and Embrace: A Theological Exploration of Identity, Otherness, and Reconciliation* (Nashville, Tenn.: Abingdon Press, 1996), 20.

8. J. Lawrence Burkholder, *The Problem of Social Responsibility From the Perspective of the Mennonite Church* (Elkhart, Ind.: Institute of Mennonite Studies, 1989), 223.

9. See Thomas S. Kuhn, *The Structure of Scientific Revolutions* (Chicago: University of Chicago Press, 1962, 1970), 158.

10. These phrases are from David Bohm ("implicate order") and Thomas Merton ("hidden wholeness"), and are quoted by Parker J. Palmer, *The Courage to Teach: Exploring the Inner Landscape of a Teacher's Life* (San Francisco: Jossey-Bass Publishers, 1998), 61, 97.

11. Ernest L. Boyer, *Scholarship Reconsidered: Priorities of the Professoriate* (Princeton, N.J.: Carnegie Foundation for the Advancement of Teaching, 1990), 15-25.

12. Ibid., 23 ("dynamic endeavor"), 24 ("urgently need").

13. Donald A. Schön, "The New Scholarship Requires a New Epistemology," *Change* 27, no. 6 (November/December 1995): 34. In *The Courage to Teach*, Palmer writes that objectivism, the mode of knowing that dominates contemporary education, "portrays truth as something we can achieve only by disconnecting ourselves, physically and emotionally, from the thing we want to know" (51).

14. Schön, "The New Scholarship," 34.

15. Palmer, *The Courage to Teach*, 144.

16. Jane Tompkins, "The Way We Live Now," *Change* 24, no. 6 (November/December 1992): 12.

17. Ralph Waldo Emerson, "The American Scholar," in *American Literature, American Culture*, ed. Gordon Hutner (New York: Oxford University Press, 1999), 48.

18. Katherine Lemons recalled that comment in a letter to Mary Eleanor Bender, January 29, 2001.

19. Ibid.

20. Ibid.

21. Ibid.

In Honor of
E. Morris Sider

*T*HIS FESTSCHRIFT IS PUBLISHED IN HONOR OF E. MORRIS SIDER, professor emeritus of history and English literature at Messiah College in Grantham, Pennsylvania.

Professor Sider's teaching career has spanned five decades in a variety of educational settings. In the late 1940s, he taught elementary school in Ontario; in the 1950s, he served as principal of Niagara Christian College; and in 1963, he joined the history faculty at Messiah College. Although now officially retired from the Messiah College faculty, he continues to contribute to campus life by teaching his now legendary course on Brethren in Christ life and thought.

Morris Sider completed his Ph.D. at the University of Buffalo in 1966 and has rarely rested his pen since. Most of his published work, which includes more than twenty books and countless journal articles, has focused on Brethren in Christ history. In *Nine Portraits: Brethren in Christ Biographical Sketches* (1978), Professor Sider began a long and productive career as a historical biographer, a career that included biographies of Messiah College president and Mennonite Central Committee executive C. N. Hostetter Jr. (*Messenger of Grace*) and Brethren in Christ Church leaders Henry Ginder and Charlie Byers (*Leaders Among Brethren*). He is currently writing a biography of the Canadian Brethren in Christ churchman E. J. Swalm and is co-editing (with Dorcas Steckbeck and Rebecca Ebersole) a book of biographical sketches of Brethren in Christ women leaders.

Professor Sider has also written a number of institutional histories, including histories of Messiah College, Upland College, Roxbury Holiness Camp, and the Brethren in Christ Church in Canada. In all of these works, he has demonstrated thoroughgoing research skills, a deep compassion for his subjects, and a desire to write clearly and accessibly.

More than merely writing for his academic colleagues, Professor Sider has sought through his writing to serve the larger Brethren in Christ Church, helping lay people understand their church's history and the people who made it. Professor Sider's current writing projects, which include a two-volume history of Brethren in Christ missions and a multi-volume Brethren in Christ encyclopedia (of which he is general editor), reflect those same concerns.

In addition to his research and writing, Professor Sider has served the Brethren in Christ denomination in numerous other ways. He has been archivist of Messiah College and the Brethren in Christ Church, executive director of the Brethren in Christ Historical Society, and since 1978 editor of *Brethren in Christ History and Life*. He has served on various denominational boards and committees, including the Board of Administration and the Board for Ministry and Doctrine.

Professor Sider was the assistant moderator for the Brethren in Christ General Conference during the 1986-88 biennium and, more recently, was the assistant moderator for the denomination's Susquehanna Conference. In 1994, he founded the Brethren in Christ Studies Center at Messiah College, which was recently renamed the E. Morris and Leone Sider Institute for Anabaptist, Pietist and Wesleyan Studies.

Morris and his wife, Leone Dearing Sider, were married in 1951. They are members of the Grantham (Pa.) Brethren in Christ Church, the parents of two daughters, Karen and Donna, and the grandparents of two grandsons, Jonathan and Benjamin.

Index

A

academic freedom, 105-106
   limits of, 25, 37, 40, 134
acculturation. *See* Mennonites, acculturation of
Africa, 127-128, 144-149, 153, 214-215, 224-225
ambiguity, intellectual, 44, 227, 254, 259, 264
American Philosophical Association, 48-49
Amish, 23, 35, 43, 56, 79
   scholarship about, 66-67, 102, 106-108, 226, 263
Anabaptism, 9-12, 23
   sixteenth-century, 10-11, 33, 113, 169-170, 188, 194, 196
   persecution of, 9, 113, 115, 123, 196, 237, 246, 254
   theology of, 170, 172, 188
anti-intellectualism. *See* learning, fear of
anti-realism
   moral, 52-53
   philosophical, 55-56, 241
Aristotle, 59, 65
arts, the, 37, 224, 262. *See also* music; poetry
Associated Mennonite Biblical Seminary, 181-189, 210-212
Association of Mennonite Economists, 133-134
atheism, 48
   methodological, 22, 26n.7

B

baptism, believers, 47, 64, 69, 107, 113, 240
Baptists, 182, 216, 237
Beachy Amish, 46-47, 53, 224
believers baptism. *See* baptism, believers
Bellah, Robert N., 105

Bender, Harold S., 36-37, 72, 80, 263
Bender, Mary Eleanor, 260, 262-263
Berger, Peter L., 22, 26n.7, 102-105, 109
Bethel (Kan.) College, 72, 81, 127
Bible
   interpretation of, 103-104, 134-135, 168, 172-178, 186-191, 197-198, 227-230
   reading of, 75, 172-173, 182-183, 189-90, 227, 230
   study of, 51, 119-120, 141-142, 164, 168, 170-195, 199-205, 210-213, 217-218, 226-227, 245-247
biblical studies. *See* Bible, study of
Blake, William, 33
Bluffton College, 19, 40-42, 72, 82
Boyer, Ernest L., 27n.13, 257-258
Brethren in Christ Church, 15-16, 72, 79, 142-144, 171, 179, 210-211, 216-217, 228, 266-267
Brethren in Christ Historical Society, 16, 267
Brueggemann, Walter, 198
Buddhism, 238
Bultmann, Rudolf, 212
Burkholder, J. Lawrence, 36-37, 254, 260

C

Calvin College, 26, 238
capitalism, 131
   criticism of, 135
   praise of, 134-135
Carnegie Foundation for the Advancement of Teaching, 27n.13, 257
Carter, Jimmy, 75
Cather, Willa, 252-253
Catholicism. *See* Roman Catholicism
certainty, intellectual, 53-55, 241, 259

charismatic Christianity. *See* Pentecostalism
Charles, Howard H., 211-212
Christian ministries (academic discipline), 208-221
church, 63-64, 104-105, 114, 120, 194-195, 198. *See also* community
   criticism of, 43, 176-178, 189-190, 194, 200-201, 209, 246
   and opposition to learning, 32, 58n.1, 176-177, 211-212, 246-247
   purpose of, 19, 23, 68-70, 76, 80, 117, 141, 188-189
   tensions with scholars, 25, 42, 177-178, 186-187, 193-199, 206-207, 211, 217-219, 224, 226, 233, 236, 246-247
   theology of the, 10-11, 68-70, 114, 141, 169, 179, 209. *See also* two-kingdom theology
Church of the Brethren, 23
Churches of Christ, 10-11
Civil Rights Movement, 74, 76, 82, 99
Civilian Public Service, 35, 79, 100
Cobb, John B. Jr., 126
Cold War, 99-100
colleges. *See* universities
community, 104-105, 107, 118-119, 170, 181, 226, 251
   experience of, 64, 68-69, 97, 124, 152-153, 234, 259-260
   importance of, 14, 114, 136-137, 258
   intentional, 75, 77-78, 117, 119
   oppressiveness of, 44, 161
Complex Humanitarian Emergencies, 146-149
conflict resolution. *See* peacemaking
Conrad Grebel University College, 42, 72
conscientious objection, 35, 38, 40, 142-143. *See also* pacifism
consumerism, 138, 139n.14

D

Dante, 33, 92
Darwin, Charles, 48
Day, Dorothy, 77, 219
deconstruction, 91-94, 97n.2
Denck, Hans, 194
Derrida, Jacques, 63, 91-93, 97n.2
Descartes, Rene, 48, 54
discipleship, 11, 14, 20, 33, 36, 97, 114-115, 141, 170, 189, 194, 241, 248
discipline, church, 47, 97
disobedience, civil, 77
diversity, 20, 156, 163, 202-203, 232
   cultural, 20, 52
   religious, 205-206, 216
doubt, 208-209, 259. *See also* ambiguity, intellectual
dress, plain, 76-77, 100-101, 142, 255
dualism, theological. *See* two-kingdom theology
Dueck, Jack, 36-39, 260

E

Eastern Mennonite University, 72, 101-102
Eco, Umberto, 91
economic forces, 127-131, 136
economic sanctions, 149, 225
economics, 83, 126-139, 224-226, 231, 234n.3, 244, 255-256
   Anabaptists' suspicion of, 129-132, 226
   interest in, 126-129, 131, 138, 145
economism, 126-127, 136, 138, 255
ecumenism, 15-16, 47, 181-182, 236
education (academic discipline), 152-167, 231-231, 244. *See also* learning; teaching
Einstein, Albert, 26n.3
Elizabethtown College, 139n.3
Emerson, Ralph Waldo, 261
environmentalism, 150, 164
epistemology, 50, 55-56, 58n.9, 122, 243
   incarnational, 14, 138, 150-153, 156, 248, 258
ethics, 167n.24, 186, 189, 201-202, 262
   discipline of, 51-53, 56, 116-117
ethnicity. *See* diversity, cultural; Mennonites, ethnic

evaluations, student. *See* grading; testing
evangelicalism, 16, 47, 61-63, 73-75, 79, 83, 213
    criticism of, 67-69, 75, 79, 85n.7
evangelism, 19, 62-63, 69, 73, 112, 177-178, 229, 232, 247
evil, problem of, 50, 56-57

F
faith, scholarly, 22-23, 214-220, 220n.3, 247-248. *See also* scholarship, faith-informed
feminism, 66, 114, 251-252. *See also* women, roles of
Fitzgerald, F. Scott, 44
Freire, Paulo, 157
Fresno Pacific University, 72, 114, 116
Freud, Sigmund, 63, 114
Fuller, Millard, 76
Fuller Theological Seminary, 73-74, 85n.4, 119
fundamentalism, 188

G
Geertz, Clifford, 123
Gelassenheit, 33, 53-56, 239, 263
gender. *See* feminism; women, roles of
Girard, René, 123-124
globalization, 129, 136-137, 231
Goshen College, 19, 26, 33, 36-38, 42, 52, 72, 88, 94-95, 132, 251-255, 260-262
Goulet, Denis, 128
grading, 32, 160-161
graduate school, 10, 38-39, 63, 65, 78-81, 90, 102-103, 112-113, 128, 145, 153-154, 196-200, 212-213, 238, 251
Graham, Billy, 73
Greek mythology, 95-96

H
Habitat for Humanity, 76-77, 242
Hauerwas, Stanley, 116
heresy, 31, 33, 58n.1
hermeneutic community, 177, 186-191, 197-198, 227-230, 246-247

Hershberger, Guy F., 36, 72, 80-81
Hesston College, 40
history, 26n.4, 72-86, 102, 114, 127, 129, 141-142, 169-173, 208, 242, 256, 266
    of United States, 23-24, 27n.11, 78-79, 82-83
    as usable past, 72-73, 79, 82-85, 243, 263
holiness, 174, 210. *See also* purity
homosexuality, 150, 229
Hopes, David Brendan, 32-33
Hostetler, John A., 102
Hughes, Richard T., 9-12, 150, 151n.12, 248, 249n.4
humanities, the, 20, 24, 31-98, 239-243
humility, intellectual, 53-56, 108-109, 197, 228, 234, 240, 244, 249, 259-260, 263
    false, 187-188
    lack of, 54-55, 228, 255
hunger, 145-146, 150

I
individualism, 31, 33, 43, 60-61, 104-105, 188, 209, 226, 256
    critique of, 107, 116-117, 178, 234n.3
interfaith dialogue, 205-206, 225
interiority, 118-119
interpretation, biblical. *See* Bible, interpretation of
InterVarsity Christian Fellowship, 47, 75
Islam, 205, 225

J
Jesus Christ, 62-64, 69-70, 85, 88-89, 218, 264
    following, 11-12, 121, 204, 213, 219, 240, 254
    life of, 67, 103, 106, 119, 144, 158, 225
    and Old Testament, 171
    as Savior, 73, 208, 216, 235-236
    suffering of, 116, 119
    teachings of, 11, 67, 76, 79, 103, 156, 171, 201

as Word of God, 97, 113, 201
Jesus Seminar, 247
Jordan, Clarence, 242
Judaism, 168, 238
Juhnke, James C., 23-24, 81, 83
Jung, Carl, 114, 122
justice
    Anabaptists and, 76-77, 81, 152, 182
    concerns for, 74-78, 127-128, 145, 223
    scholarship and, 82-85, 135-138, 148-150, 155-158, 175, 224-225
just war tradition, 143, 147-149, 238, 240-241

K

Kant, Immanuel, 52-53
King, Martin Luther Jr., 35, 74, 82-83
Koinonia Farm. *See* Habitat for Humanity
Kuhn, Thomas, 255

L

labeling, 153-154, 159-160, 232, 244. *See also* testing
    criticism of, 154-156
Lancaster Mennonite High School, 101
language, 89-97, 111-113, 119-124, 164, 197-205, 243
    philosophy of, 50, 91-93, 121
language(s)
    biblical, 170-173, 183-184
    love of, 33, 76, 170, 183
learning, 155, 162-164
    and family dynamics, 73-74, 154, 156, 160-163
    fear of, 100, 111, 159, 187-188, 201, 209, 227, 233, 246
    joy of, 84, 108, 159-161, 169-171, 183, 188, 210-215, 224, 263
    theories of, 155-157, 164, 231-232, 259
Lewis, C. S., 73
liberation theology, 156, 190, 202
Lind, Millard, 184
Lindsey, Nick, 33, 36-37, 39, 260

Lindsey, Vachel, 37
linguistics. *See* language
literacy, 97, 153-154, 159, 162
literary criticism, 91-92, 97n.2
literature, 31-45, 90, 173, 183, 208, 241, 262-263, 266
liturgy, 10, 89, 177-178, 181, 216-217, 229
Locke, John, 54
logic, 46, 56-57
Luther, Martin, 219, 236
Lutheranism, 35, 216, 219, 236-237, 245-246

M

Marsden, George M., 20-21, 26n.7, 83, 85n.4
martyrdom. *See* Anabaptism, sixteenth-century, persecution of
Marx, Karl, 63, 76, 102, 114
materialism, 126-127, 135, 178
Mennonite Board of Education, 40
Mennonite Brethren Bible College, 112
Mennonite Brethren Biblical Seminary, 119
Mennonite Brethren Church, 23, 79, 111, 114
Mennonite Central Committee, 127-128, 144-147, 205, 223-225, 266
Mennonite Economic Development Associates, 133, 139n.2
Mennonites
    acculturation of, 33, 84, 100-101, 104
    ethnic, 27n.14, 59-60, 70, 76-77, 111, 113, 117, 121, 124, 165, 182, 185, 243
    nonethnic, 27n.14, 59-60, 70n.1, 76-77, 88, 153
    sectarianism of, 10, 53, 100-101, 112, 119, 142-143, 241-244, 255
Mennonite World Conference, 203
Merton, Thomas, 77, 213, 219, 265n.10
Messiah College, 13, 15, 19, 72, 143, 151n.1, 168-170, 210, 214-215, 228, 248, 257, 260, 266-267
Methodism, 35, 60, 168, 219
moral theory. *See* ethics

272 • INDEX

music, 87-98, 129, 181
   performance of, 87-89, 95-97

N

New Testament studies, 103-104, 181-192, 211-213. *See also* Bible
Nietzsche, Friedrich, 63, 93
nonconformity, 254
   scholarship and, 11-12, 255-258, 261-262
non-foundationalism, 122-123. *See also* postmodernism.
nonresistance. *See* pacifism
nonviolence. *See* pacifism
nuclear war/weapons, 75, 77, 99, 106, 167n.24

O

objectivity, 31-32, 133, 265n.13
   defined, 20
   myth of, 73, 84, 99, 104, 120, 123, 201, 247
Old Testament studies, 73, 168-180, 229. *See also* Bible
Ong, Walter J., 97
oppression
   political, 135, 144-145, 202
   of women. *See* women, oppression of
originality, 17-18, 252-253, 257, 262

P

pacifism, 74-75. *See also* peacemaking
   in Anabaptist tradition, 35-36, 63, 77, 79-84, 141-144, 153, 169-171, 182, 202-203, 238
   arguments for, 51
   and scholarship, 23-24, 79-84, 147-149, 173-174, 240-241
Palmer, Parker J., 258, 265n.13
peacemaking. *See also* pacifism
   and Anabaptism, 14, 100, 141, 202, 205, 237, 240-241
   and scholarship, 123-124, 146-150, 164-165, 173-174
   as way of life, 67, 158
pedagogy. *See* teaching
Peirce, Charles Sanders, 91

Pentecostalism, 16, 88-89, 94, 219
perspectivalism, 20-24, 26nn.3-4
philosophy, 46-58, 90, 93-96, 129, 200, 224, 237
   and Christianity, 46, 48-50, 56-57, 58nn.1, 5
   history of, 48, 52-54
physics, 20, 26n.3
piety, Christian, 73, 80, 113, 145, 171
Plantinga, Alvin, 49-50, 56-57
Plato, 87, 91
poetry, 32-33, 37-41, 87, 90, 164, 243
   Mennonite, 38-39, 42-43
political science, 76, 140-151, 224-226, 231, 241, 244
   and Anabaptists, 130, 140-142
   and Reformed tradition, 140-141
poor, the. *See* poverty
post-Christendom, 215-219
postmodernism, 84, 86n.18, 104, 112, 122-123. *See also* non-foundationalism
poverty, 79, 127-128, 135, 137, 145, 214, 225
prayer, 96, 222, 233
preaching, 171-172, 179, 191, 217-218
Presbyterianism, 75, 153
professional associations. *See* scholars, professional associations of
psychology, 111-125, 218, 234n.3, 243
   American orientation of, 117-118
purity, 10, 194-195, 237

Q

Quakers, 74

R

racism, 74, 82-83, 85n.5, 161, 164
reading, 35, 159-160, 210. *See also* Bible, reading of
Reagan, Ronald, 78, 85n.7, 128
realism, philosophical, 55-56
reason, 46, 56-57, 95
reconciliation. *See* peacemaking
Reformed tradition, 16, 47-48, 140-141, 235-240, 245

contributions of, 20, 49-50, 150, 237, 249
views of the state, 141, 237
Regehr, Ernie, 150
relativism, moral, 52-53. *See also* ethics
restorationism, 10-11
rhetoric, 59-71, 229
   definition of, 65-66, 70n.5
   reputation of, 65, 70n.4
Rogers, Carl R., 117
Roman Catholicism, 16, 35, 60, 128, 181-182, 197, 219, 236-237, 241, 249
Roten, Gertrude, 210
rural life, 34-35, 100-101, 154, 160, 224
   decline of, 33, 100-101, 241

S

sabbaticals, 18, 185
Saussure, Ferdinand, 91
Schaeffer, Francis, 46, 49
scholars
   criticism of, 197, 211, 222, 228, 232, 250-251
   elitism of, 163, 197, 228-232, 251
   marginalization of, 42, 177, 189-190, 203, 217, 226, 233, 244-246
   productivity of, 13-14, 18, 184-185, 250, 252, 264n.1
   professional associations of, 24, 48-49, 132-134, 176, 179
   as prophetic voices, 9, 106-107, 115, 177-178, 186, 217, 220, 255-256
   as threatening to establishment, 9, 25, 42, 200, 217, 255-256
scholarship
   authenticity of, 253-254
   Christian, 13-14, 19-23, 50, 56-57, 119-120, 237, 239, 249
   distinctiveness of, 14, 20-23, 53
   as Christian calling, 19-20, 50, 196-197, 217, 232-234
   definitions of, 18, 24, 27n.13, 250, 256-257

faith-informed, 22
interdisciplinary, 88, 90, 130, 200, 260
motivations for, 18, 22, 101, 163, 185, 206
oral, 259-264
resources for, 14, 185, 206
rewards for, 18, 26n.2, 108, 185
in service to church, 23-25, 56-57, 81-85, 95, 106, 124, 128-138, 149-151, 171-179, 186-191, 195, 205-207, 212-220, 224-233, 266-267
in service to world, 24, 26n.9, 95, 136-138, 145-149, 198-199, 224-225, 258, 264
and teaching, 17-18, 83, 94
Schrag, Martin H., 169-170
sectarianism. *See* Mennonites, sectarianism of
semiotics, 91, 94
service learning, 258
sexual abuse, 118, 202
Sider, E. Morris, 13, 16, 72, 169-170, 248, 260-261, 266-267
Sider, Ronald J., 74, 145
Simons, Menno, 33, 114, 196, 242
sin, 54, 135, 148, 195
Smith, C. Henry, 72
social sciences, the, 20, 24, 99-167, 231-232, 243-245
Society of Christian Philosophers, 48
sociology, 99-110, 114, 129-131, 200, 226, 234n.3, 243-244
Socrates, 93
Sophists, 66
Soros, George, 139n.14
spiritual formation, 217-219
Stafford, William, 31, 38, 40
starvation. *See* hunger
Stassen, Glen H., 148-149
state, the, 80-81
   views of the, 141-143, 146-148, 237
Steinem, Gloria, 66
structuralism, 90, 94
suffering, 114-117

T

Tabor College, 114, 116
teachers, inspiring, 37, 164, 169-171, 210, 260-261, 266-267
teaching, 11-12, 17-19, 94-95, 152, 164, 185, 264
    methods, 93, 152, 155-156
    and scholarship, 17-19, 257, 260-261
Tertullian, 58n.1, 112
testing, 153-154
    criticism of, 154-155, 161
theism, 50-51, 58n.9, 208
    arguments for, 49-50, 57
theology
    Anabaptists' distrust of, 196, 245-246
    disciplinary dominance of, 121-122, 129-130
    discipline of, 51, 101-103, 193-207, 218, 226, 245-246, 256
    teaching of, 19, 169-170
therapy, 114-115
    and peacemaking, 114, 123-124
Tillich, Paul, 165n.2
truth, 31-32, 198-205, 209, 235-237, 257, 260, 265n.13
    search for, 19-21, 44, 56-57, 193, 241, 247
    versus Truth, 31, 158, 204, 235, 254
two-kingdom theology, 51-53, 77, 80-81, 141-142, 147-148, 169, 209, 242

U

United Nations, 145-146
universities
    research, 18, 250-251
    teaching, 13, 18-19, 251
urbanization, 33-34, 100

V

Victim Offender Reconciliation Program, 150
Vietnam War, 35, 37, 40, 74, 99, 143-145, 238
violence, 23-24, 67, 114, 123-124, 146-149. *See also* war
Volf, Miroslav, 254, 265n.7
voluntary service, 76-77, 102

W

war, 24, 27n.11, 83, 146-149, 225, 238. *See also* Vietnam War; World War I; World War II
    in the Bible, 171-174
    just. *See* just war tradition
wealth, 79, 85, 126, 131-132, 135-137
Weber, Max, 102, 104, 109
Wenger, John C., 210
Wharton, Edith, 251
Wiebe, Rudy, 38
Willimon, William H., 209
Wink, Walter, 148-149, 163
wisdom, 18, 87, 93-96, 262-264
Wittgenstein, Ludwig, 121
Wittlinger, Carlton O., 169
women
    oppression of, 160-161, 183, 186, 196, 202
    roles of, 160-161, 196, 230
Woolf, Virginia, 263
World War I, 35, 142
World War II, 40, 79-80, 100, 169
worship. *See* liturgy
writing, Mennonite, 38, 41-43, 45n.7
Wuthnow, Robert, 105

Y

Yoder, John Howard, 27n.9, 31, 67, 79-80, 83, 103, 116, 197-198, 210, 238, 247

Contributors

Susan Biesecker-Mast is associate professor of communication at Bluffton College in Bluffton, Ohio, where she teaches in the areas of classical rhetoric, media studies, and argumentation. Over the last several years, her published essays have focused on how twenty-first century Anabaptists witness to their contemporary world. She co-edited *Anabaptists and Postmodernity* (Pandora Press U.S., 2000) with Gerald Biesecker-Mast and is currently writing a book on tourism in the Holmes County, Ohio, Amish settlement. In the latter work, she is exploring how middle American identity is reinforced by tourism in Holmes County yet challenged by an Amish witness. She is a member of First Mennonite Church in Bluffton and is mother to Anna Lynn Biesecker-Mast.

Harriet Sider Bicksler is a publications specialist for a training institute that provides continuing education opportunities for children's mental health professionals in the public sector. Since 1981, she has edited *Shalom!*, a Brethren in Christ publication on peace and social concerns. In addition to being active in the Grantham (Pa.) Brethren in Christ Church, she has served in a variety of denominational capacities and is the current board chair of Mennonite Central Committee U.S. Harriet is the author or editor of several books and numerous articles and essays. She and her husband, Dale Bicksler, have two young adult children, a son-in-law, a dog, and a cat.

Terry L. Brensinger received a B.A. from Messiah College, an M.Div. from Asbury Theological Seminary, an M.A. in Near Eastern Archaeology from Drew University, and an M.Phil. and Ph.D. in Old Testament, also from Drew. From 1985-2001, he taught Old Testament at Messiah College, where he also served as chair of the Department of Biblical Studies, Religion and Philosophy from 1997-2001. Among his many publications are a commentary on Judges in the Believers Church Bible Commentary series and *Within the Perfection of Christ: Essays on Peace and the Nature of the Church* (Evangel Press, 1990) which he co-edited with E. Morris Sider. In August 2001, he became lead pastor of the Grantham (Pa.) Brethren in Christ Church. Terry and his wife, Deb, are parents of two sons and a daughter.

Polly Ann Brown graduated with a B.A. in English literature from Eastern College (now University) in St. Davids, Pennsylvania. She subsequently received an M.S. degree and a Ph.D. in education from the University of Pennsylvania, where she was awarded the Phi Delta Kappa doctoral dissertation award. She has since taught at the University of Pennsylvania, Chestnut Hill College, and Eastern Mennonite University's Lancaster, Pennsylvania, campus. She presently serves on the Eastern University board. Although now semi-retired, Polly Ann continues to observe in and write about both public and private schools. She and her husband, Kenneth, are members of the Norristown (Pa.) New Life Mennonite Church. They have four adult children and three grandchildren.

Perry Bush is professor of history at Bluffton College. He received his Ph.D. in history from Carnegie Mellon University in 1990 and has taught at Bluffton since 1994. He is the author of two books, *Two Kingdoms, Two Loyalties: Mennonite Pacifism in Modern America* (Johns Hopkins, 1998) and *Dancing with the Kobzar: Bluffton College and Mennonite Higher Education, 1899-1999* (Pandora Press U.S., 2000), as well as a number of articles on U.S. peace and religious history. He and his spouse, Elysia, are the parents of Kerry, Jackson, and Cassidy Bush, and are members of First Mennonite Church in Bluffton.

Mark W. Charlton graduated with a B.A. in history from Messiah College in 1970. He subsequently received an M.A. degree in political science from the University of Western Ontario and a Ph.D. from Laval University. He is currently professor of political science and international studies at Trinity Western University in Langley, British Columbia, where he lives with his wife, Lucille, and sons Christopher, Daniel, and David. Professor Charlton is the author of *The Making of Canadian Food Aid Policy* (McGill-Queen's University Press, 1990) and editor of *Crosscurrents: Contemporary Political Issues* and *Crosscurrents: International Relations in the Post-Cold War Era*, both published by Nelson Canada.

Alvin C. Dueck is the Evelyn and Frank Freed Professor of Integration of Psychology and Theology at Fuller Theological Seminary in Pasadena, California. Before assuming that role, he directed the Marriage and Family Counseling program at the Mennonite Brethren Biblical Seminary in Fresno, California, and before that he taught psychology at Tabor (Kan.) College and Fresno Pacific University. He received his Ph.D. in psychology from Stanford University, and has done postdoctoral work in social theory (University of Notre Dame), theology (Associated Mennonite Biblical Seminary), psychology of religion (Yale University), and family therapy (Heidelberg University). His lectures on Christianity and therapy, presented at Fuller Theological Seminary in 1986, have since been published as *Between Jerusalem and Athens: Ethical Perspectives on Culture, Religion, and Psychotherapy* (Baker Books, 1995).

Jeff Gundy has published three books of poems: *Rhapsody with Dark Matter*, *Flatlands*, and *Inquiries*, as well as *A Community of Memory: My Days with George and Clara* (University of Illinois Press, 1996), a book of creative nonfiction. Raised in central Illinois, he studied at Goshen College and Indiana University. Since 1984 he has taught English, writing, and general education at Bluffton College in Ohio, where he is now professor of English and chair of the English/Language Department. He has received two C. Henry Smith Peace Lectureships and four Ohio Arts Council fellowships in poetry. He and his wife, Marlyce, have three sons.

James M. Harder received his Ph.D. in economics from the University of Notre Dame in 1990. Before that, he served with Mennonite Central Committee in Kenya and Mennonite Economic Development Associates in Tanzania. From 1990-2001 Harder chaired the Economics and Business Department of his alma mater, Bethel College, in Kansas. He has authored book chapters relating economics to issues of war and to environmental stewardship, as well as numerous articles and book reviews. In addition to his academic work, Harder currently serves on the executive board of Mennonite Church USA. In 2001, he joined the faculty of Bluffton College in Ohio, where he is special assistant to the President and professor of economics and business. He and his wife, Karen Klassen Harder, have two children.

Lydia Neufeld Harder earned her B.Th. from Canadian Mennonite Bible College, a B.A. from Goshen College, an M.Th. from Newman

College, and a Th.D. from Emmanuel College at the Toronto School of Theology (1993). She directed the Toronto Mennonite Theological Center from 1994-1999 and is presently an adjunct faculty member at Conrad Grebel University College in Waterloo, Ontario. The author of *Obedience, Suspicion and the Gospel of Mark* (Wilfrid Laurier Press, 1998), Neufeld Harder has published articles in the *Conrad Grebel Review* and the *Mennonite Quarterly Review*, and has contributed chapters to a variety of books. She currently serves on the editorial council of the Believers Church Bible Commentary series and the Mennonite Central Committee Peace Committee. She is married to Gary Harder, pastor of the Toronto United Mennonite Church. They have three children and six grandchildren.

David A. Hoekema, professor of philosophy at Calvin College in Grand Rapids, Michigan, served previously as academic dean and as interim vice president for student life at Calvin. Before 1992 he was executive director of the American Philosophical Association and associate professor of philosophy at the University of Delaware. He is the author of *Campus Life and Moral Community* (Rowman and Littlefield, 1994) and *Rights and Wrongs: Coercion, Punishment, and the State* (Susquehanna University Press, 1986). He has edited a collection of essays on *Christianity and Culture in the Crossfire* with Bobby Fong, president of Butler University, and is presently working on a collection of essays on religion and politics in Russia with Alexei Bodrov, rector of St. Andrew's Biblical-Theological Institute in Moscow. Hoekema currently serves as president of the Society for Values in Higher Education. He is a member of the Christian Reformed Church. David and his wife, Susan, who has worked as a history teacher and is now engaged in the practice of law, maintain a nest now empty of two children.

Donald B. Kraybill has authored, coauthored, and edited more than fifteen books, including *The Upside-Down Kingdom* (Herald Press, 1978, 1990), which received the National Religious Book Award; *The Riddle of Amish Culture* (Johns Hopkins, 1989, 2001), a standard reference for understanding the Amish; and (with Carl Bowman) *On the Backroad to Heaven: Old Order Hutterites, Mennonites, Amish, and Brethren* (Johns Hopkins, 2001). His most recent book (with C. Nelson Hostetter) is *Anabaptist World USA* (Herald Press, 2001). Kraybill holds a Ph.D. in sociology and serves as professor of sociology and Anabaptist Studies at Messiah College in Pennsylvania, where he previously served as provost. Before that he directed the Young Center for Anabaptist and Pietist Studies at Elizabethtown College in Pennsylvania and has served in various leadership roles in the Mennonite Church and the Church of the Brethren.

J. E. McDermond, associate professor of Christian ministries and spirituality, has taught in England and Kenya as well as at Messiah College since 1987. He is an ordained Brethren in Christ minister, has pastored in Indiana, and has served as an interim preacher for various congregations. He is a self-confessed Anglophile whose current favorite authors are British novelists Catherine Fox and Joanna Trollope. He is married to Wanda Thuma-McDermond, who grew up as an "MK" (missionary kid). They have two sons, Malcolm and Duncan.

Caleb Miller is associate professor of philosophy and chair of the Department of Philosophy at Messiah College. He earned a B.A. in philosophy and history from Drake University in 1980, an M.A.T.S. in theology from Gordon-Conwell Theological Seminary in 1983, and a Ph.D. in philosophy from the University of Notre Dame in 1991. Before teaching at Messiah, he was assistant professor of philosophy at Goshen College from 1987-1993. His primary research interests are moral theory, applied ethics, epistemology, and philosophy of religion. He has been active in the leadership of the Society of Christian Philosophers. He is a member of the Slate Hill Mennonite Church in Camp Hill, Pennsylvania.

David L. Mosley is professor of music and humanities at Goshen College in Goshen, Indiana. During his fifteen years on the faculty he has taught courses in the areas of musicology, literature, and philosophy. He is presently the conductor of the college's orchestra and wind ensemble. A frequent presenter at both national and international conferences, Mosley's publications have appeared in numerous journals, including the *Journal for Aesthetics and Art Criticism*, the *Journal of the International Horn Society*, and the *Yearbook of Interdisciplinary Studies in the Fine Arts*. He is also secretary of the International Association for Word and Music Studies. At his chapter's writing Mosley was a member of the College Mennonite Church in Goshen, Indiana. He is presently an oblate of St. Meinrad Archabbey, a Benedictine monastery in St. Meinrad, Indiana.

Mary H. Schertz is professor of New Testament at the Associated Mennonite Biblical Seminary in Elkhart, Indiana. She received her

Ph.D. from Vanderbilt University and has been happily occupied teaching Greek and New Testament for the past fourteen years. She is also the director of the Institute of Mennonite Studies and has recently published *Seeing the Text: Exegesis for Students of Greek and Hebrew* (Abingdon, 2001) with coauthor Perry B. Yoder. During a recent sabbatical at the Institute for Ecumenical and Cultural Research at St. John's University in Minnesota, she worked on the Luke volume of the Believers Church Bible Commentary series.

Shirley Hershey Showalter became president of Goshen College in 1997. Since arriving at at the college in 1976 with her husband, Stuart, former professor of communication who now directs career services, she has taught English and history, becoming full professor and chair of the English Department. In 1990, she won the Sears Roebuck Foundation "Teaching Excellence and Campus Leadership Award"; ten years later, she received a Knight Presidential Leadership Award of $150,000 to use at her discretion to strengthen the college. Born in Lancaster, Pennsylvania, Showalter earned a bachelor's degree in English from Eastern Mennonite College and received her master's and doctoral degrees from the University of Texas at Austin. Shirley and Stuart are the parents of two children, Anthony and Kate.

David L. Weaver-Zercher received his Ph.D. in American religious history from the University of North Carolina at Chapel Hill in 1997 and has since been a member of the faculty at his alma mater, Messiah College. In addition to teaching in Messiah's religion and history departments, he is director of the college's Sider Institute for Anabaptist, Pietist and Wesleyan Studies and acting chair of the Department of Biblical and Religious Studies. His book, *The Amish in the American Imagination* (Johns Hopkins, 2001), examines the functions of "the Amish" in the imaginations of those who buy, sell, and consume Amish-themed products. Dave and his wife, Valerie, live in Harrisburg, Pennsylvania, with their one-year-old son, Samuel.

www.ingramcontent.com/pod-product-compliance
Lightning Source LLC
Chambersburg PA
CBHW070544160426
43199CB00014B/2360